First World War

and Army of Occupation

War Diary

France, Belgium and Germany

46 DIVISION
139 Infantry Brigade
Sherwood Foresters
(Nottinghamshire and Derbyshire Regiment)
1/6th Battalion
4 February 1915 - 29 June 1919

WO95/2694/1

The Naval & Military Press Ltd
www.nmarchive.com
Published in association with The National Archives

Published by

The Naval & Military Press Ltd

Unit 10 Ridgewood Industrial Park,

Uckfield, East Sussex,

TN22 5QE England

Tel: +44 (0) 1825 749494

www.naval-military-press.com

www.nmarchive.com

This diary has been reprinted in facsimile from the original. Any imperfections are inevitably reproduced and the quality may fall short of modern type and cartographic standards.

Contents

Document type	Place/Title	Date From	Date To
Heading	WO95/2694/1		
Miscellaneous	6th. Battalion, Sherwood Foresters, Notts & Derby Infantry Brigade, North Midland Division	07/10/1914	07/10/1914
Miscellaneous	Reorganization of T.F. into Home and Imperial Service Units.	07/10/1914	07/10/1914
Miscellaneous	6th Battalion The Sherwood Foresters. Notts and Derby Infantry Brigade. North Midland Division.	09/11/1914	09/11/1914
Miscellaneous	6th Battalion The Sherwood Foresters. Notts and Derby Infantry Brigade. North Midland Division.	01/11/1914	01/11/1914
Heading	139th Inf. Bde. 46th Div. Battn. disembarked Havre from England 26.2.15. 6th Battn. The Sherwood Foresters (Nottinghamshire And Derbyshire Regiment). February 1915		
War Diary	Braintree	04/02/1915	25/02/1915
War Diary	Southampton	25/02/1915	25/02/1915
War Diary	Harvre	26/02/1915	27/02/1915
War Diary	Terdeghen	28/02/1915	28/02/1915
Heading	O.C. 6th Batt Sherwood Foresters.		
Heading	139th Inf. Bde. 46th Div. 6th Battn. The Sherwood Foresters (Nottinghamshire And Derbyshire Regiment). March 1915		
War Diary	Terdeghen	03/03/1915	04/03/1915
War Diary	Ploegsteert	05/03/1915	08/03/1915
War Diary	Outtersteene	09/03/1915	09/03/1915
War Diary	Bac St. Maur	11/03/1915	12/03/1915
War Diary	Neuf Berquin	13/03/1915	30/03/1915
Miscellaneous	A Form Messages And Signals		
Heading	139th Inf. Bde. 46th Div. 6th Battn. The Sherwood Foresters (Nottinghamshire And Derbyshire Regiment). April 1915		
War Diary	Outersteene	02/04/1915	02/04/1915
War Diary	Bailleul	03/04/1915	04/04/1915
War Diary	Locre	05/04/1915	05/04/1915
War Diary	Kemmel	07/04/1915	07/04/1915
War Diary	Locre	12/04/1915	12/04/1915
War Diary	Kemmel	15/04/1915	15/04/1915
War Diary	Locre	16/04/1915	20/04/1915
War Diary	Kemmel	24/04/1915	24/04/1915
War Diary	Locre	29/04/1915	29/04/1915
War Diary	Kemmel	27/04/1915	27/04/1915
Heading	139th Inf. Bde. 46th Div. 6th Battn. The Sherwood Foresters (Nottinghamshire And Derbyshire Regiment). May 1915		
War Diary	Kemmel	02/05/1915	02/05/1915
War Diary	Locre	04/05/1915	04/05/1915
War Diary	Kemmel	09/05/1915	30/05/1915
Heading	Appendices I & II		
Miscellaneous	Appendix I	07/05/1915	07/05/1915
Miscellaneous	Music On The March.	10/05/1915	10/05/1915

Heading	139th Inf. Bde. 46th Div. 6th Battn. The Sherwood Foresters (Nottinghamshire And Derbyshire Regiment). June 1915		
War Diary	Kemmel	03/06/1915	21/06/1915
War Diary	Zillebeke	23/06/1915	29/06/1915
Heading	139th Inf. Bde. 46th Div. 6th Battn. The Sherwood Foresters (Nottinghamshire And Derbyshire Regiment). July 1915		
War Diary	Bivouac	29/06/1915	03/07/1915
War Diary	Ypres	04/07/1915	04/07/1915
War Diary	Maplecopse	11/07/1915	22/07/1915
War Diary	Sanctuary Wood	23/07/1915	27/07/1915
War Diary	Bivouac G. 18 O. 2.8	29/07/1915	29/07/1915
Heading	139th Inf. Bde. 46th Div. 6th Battn. The Sherwood Foresters (Nottinghamshire And Derbyshire Regiment). August 1915		
War Diary	Maple Copse	03/08/1915	03/08/1915
War Diary	Sanctuary Wood	05/08/1915	19/08/1915
War Diary	G. 22. B. 8.5	20/08/1915	20/08/1915
War Diary	Canal I.33 34.c	23/08/1915	29/08/1915
War Diary	G.22. B. 8.5	30/08/1915	30/08/1915
Heading	139th Inf. Bde. 46th Div. 6th Battn. The Sherwood Foresters (Nottinghamshire And Derbyshire Regiment). September 1915		
War Diary	Busseboom	02/09/1915	02/09/1915
War Diary	Ouderdom	04/09/1915	04/09/1915
War Diary	Canal I 33	04/09/1915	30/09/1915
Heading	139th Inf. Bde. 46th Div. 6th Battn. The Sherwood Foresters (Nottinghamshire And Derbyshire Regiment). October 1915		
War Diary	Abeele	01/10/1915	01/10/1915
War Diary	Fouquereuil	01/10/1915	03/10/1915
War Diary	Hinges	04/10/1915	05/10/1915
War Diary	Mazingarbe	06/10/1915	06/10/1915
War Diary	Fouquereuil	08/10/1915	15/10/1915
War Diary	Verquin	16/10/1915	19/10/1915
War Diary	Lapugnoy	21/10/1915	26/10/1915
War Diary	Bethune	28/10/1915	30/10/1915
Heading	139th Inf. Bde. 46th Div. 6th Battn. The Sherwood Foresters (Nottinghamshire And Derbyshire Regiment). November 1915		
War Diary	Bethune	01/11/1915	04/11/1915
War Diary	Pacaut	05/11/1915	06/11/1915
War Diary	L.A. Couture	09/11/1915	27/11/1915
War Diary	Vielle Chapelle	28/11/1915	30/11/1915
Heading	Appendix I		
Miscellaneous	Report on Bombing Enterprise. Appendix 117	27/11/1915	27/11/1915
Heading	139th Inf. Bde. 46th Div. 6th Battn. The Sherwood Foresters (Nottinghamshire And Derbyshire Regiment). December 1915		
War Diary	Lacouture	03/12/1915	03/12/1915
War Diary	Trenches	03/12/1915	03/12/1915
War Diary	Richebourg & Lacouture	04/12/1915	04/12/1915
War Diary	Robecq	06/12/1915	23/12/1915
War Diary	Boeseghem	24/12/1915	26/12/1915
War Diary	Isbergues	27/12/1915	02/01/1916

War Diary	Promotions	04/01/1916	04/01/1916
War Diary	Isbergues	06/01/1916	07/01/1916
War Diary	Marseilles	09/01/1916	09/01/1916
War Diary	London. Gazette	06/01/1916	07/01/1916
War Diary	Isbergues	10/01/1916	10/01/1916
War Diary	London Gazette	13/01/1916	14/01/1916
War Diary	Marseilles	25/01/1916	25/01/1916
War Diary	Pont Remy	28/01/1916	28/01/1916
War Diary	Coulonvillers	03/02/1916	10/02/1916
War Diary	Beaumetz	10/02/1916	19/02/1916
War Diary	Puchevillers	20/02/1916	28/02/1916
War Diary	Puchevillers	25/02/1916	29/02/1916
Heading	Appendices 10 War Diary of 6th Sherwood Foresters for March 1916 A Division for attack		
War Diary	Beauval	06/03/1916	06/03/1916
War Diary	Ivergny	06/03/1916	08/03/1916
War Diary	Maizieres	09/03/1916	09/03/1916
War Diary	Mont St Eloy	10/03/1916	20/03/1916
War Diary	Trenches	22/03/1916	22/03/1916
War Diary	Acq	25/03/1916	25/03/1916
War Diary	Trenches	26/03/1916	26/03/1916
War Diary	Acq	27/03/1916	27/03/1916
War Diary	Fermont Cappel	31/03/1916	31/03/1916
Miscellaneous	C Form (Duplicate). Messages And Signals		
Miscellaneous	Instructions issued verbally to Lieut-Colonel G.D. Goodman, 6th Battalion Sherwood Foresters, and other Officers concerned.		
Miscellaneous	Orders by Lieut Col. G.D. Goodman for Attack On Crater Opposite Birkin C.T.	25/03/1916	25/03/1916
War Diary	Cappel Fermont	02/04/1916	02/04/1916
War Diary	Trenches	03/04/1916	03/04/1916
War Diary	Acq	05/04/1916	09/04/1916
War Diary	Cappel Fermont	16/04/1916	17/04/1916
War Diary	Divl School	17/04/1916	17/04/1916
War Diary	Trenches	17/04/1916	18/04/1916
War Diary	Acq	19/04/1916	19/04/1916
War Diary	(Inclusive)	19/04/1916	29/04/1916
War Diary	Anzin	23/04/1916	23/04/1916
War Diary	Maroeuil	24/04/1916	29/04/1916
War Diary	Anzin & Roclincourt	29/04/1916	29/04/1916
Operation(al) Order(s)	Operation Order No. 53. by Brig General. C.T. Shipley. C.B. Commanding 139th Inf Brigade.	16/04/1916	16/04/1916
Miscellaneous	O.C. 6th Bn Sherwood Foresters	16/04/1916	16/04/1916
Operation(al) Order(s)	Operation Order No 7 by Lt. Col G.D. Goodman Commanding 6th Bn Sherwood Foresters		
Miscellaneous	A Form Messages And Signals		
Miscellaneous	From:- O.C. 66 Sherwood Foresters to:- Hd Qrs 139th Bde.	17/04/1916	17/04/1916

War Diary	Penin	02/05/1916	06/05/1916
War Diary	Ivergny	06/05/1916	07/05/1916
War Diary	Humbercamps	09/05/1916	18/05/1916
War Diary	Fonquevillers	19/05/1916	19/05/1916
War Diary	Humbercamps	19/05/1916	20/05/1916
War Diary	Fonquevillers	27/05/1916	30/05/1916
Miscellaneous	3 Army Ref School		
Miscellaneous	A Form Messages And Signals		

War Diary		03/06/1916	03/06/1916
War Diary	Fonquevillers	04/06/1916	06/06/1916
War Diary	Humbercamps	06/06/1916	06/06/1916
War Diary	Sus St Leger	07/06/1916	17/06/1916
War Diary	Trenches	22/06/1916	24/06/1916
War Diary	Gaudiempre	23/06/1916	28/06/1916
War Diary	Fonquevillers	28/06/1916	30/06/1916
Miscellaneous	6th Battn Sherwood Foresters. Detail of Working Parties 22/23rd June 1916	22/06/1916	22/06/1916
Miscellaneous	6th Battn Sherwood Foresters. Detail of Working Parties 23/24th June 1916	23/06/1916	23/06/1916
Miscellaneous	Point Of Birkin	02/04/1916	02/04/1916
Miscellaneous	B Form. Messages And Signals.		
Miscellaneous	Right Sector Action To Be Taken In Case Of An Enemy Mine Explosion.		
War Diary	Foncquevillers	01/07/1916	02/07/1916
War Diary	Warlincourt	03/07/1916	03/07/1916
War Diary	Bailleulmont	04/07/1916	04/07/1916
War Diary	Saulty	05/07/1916	05/07/1916
War Diary	Bailleulmont	03/07/1916	15/07/1916
War Diary	Bellacourt	16/07/1916	24/07/1916
War Diary	G.D Goodman	27/07/1916	27/07/1916
War Diary	By 6/Sherwood Foresters	28/07/1916	31/07/1916
Operation(al) Order(s)	Operation Order No 2 By Lieut Colonel G.D. Goodman C.M.G. Commanding 6th Battalion Sherwood Foresters.	30/06/1916	30/06/1916
Miscellaneous	To Headquarters, 139th Infantry Brigade,	03/07/1916	03/07/1916
Miscellaneous	Extract from 46th Divisional Routine Orders dated 17th July 1916	17/07/1916	17/07/1916
Miscellaneous	Instructions to Raiding Party.	28/07/1916	28/07/1916
Diagram etc	Plan (Not To Scale.) IV		
Miscellaneous	From:- Officer Commanding, 6th Battalion Sherwood Foresters	29/07/1916	29/07/1916
Miscellaneous	139th Infantry Brigade.	30/07/1916	30/07/1916
War Diary	Bailleulval	02/08/1916	07/08/1916
War Diary	Bellacourt	06/08/1916	08/08/1916
War Diary	Trenches	10/08/1916	10/08/1916
War Diary	Bellacourt	11/08/1916	18/08/1916
War Diary	Trenches	16/08/1916	16/08/1916
War Diary	Bellacourt	19/08/1916	19/08/1916
War Diary	Trenches	22/08/1916	22/08/1916
War Diary	Bailleulval	26/08/1916	26/08/1916
War Diary	Trenches	28/08/1916	28/08/1916
War Diary	Bellacourt	28/08/1916	31/08/1916
Miscellaneous	Instructions to Raiding Party.	31/08/1916	31/08/1916
Diagram etc	Plan Not To Scale		
War Diary	Trenches	01/09/1916	03/09/1916
War Diary	London Gazette	07/09/1916	07/09/1916
War Diary	Bellacourt	07/09/1916	07/09/1916
War Diary	Trenches	07/09/1916	15/09/1916
War Diary	Bailleulval	16/09/1916	18/09/1916
War Diary	Trenches	17/09/1916	20/09/1916
War Diary	London Gazette	22/09/1916	22/09/1916
War Diary	Trenches	26/09/1916	26/09/1916
War Diary	Bellacourt	27/09/1916	30/09/1916
War Diary	Trenches	01/10/1916	03/10/1916

War Diary	Bellacourt	05/10/1916	05/10/1916
War Diary	Basseux	05/10/1916	05/10/1916
War Diary	Trenches	07/10/1916	07/10/1916
War Diary	Bailleulval	11/10/1916	11/10/1916
War Diary	Basseux	11/10/1916	11/10/1916
War Diary	London Gazette	12/10/1916	12/10/1916
War Diary	Trenches	13/10/1916	13/10/1916
War Diary	Bellacourt	15/10/1916	15/10/1916
War Diary	Trenches	16/10/1916	19/10/1916
War Diary	Bellacourt	22/10/1916	26/10/1916
War Diary	Trenches	30/10/1916	30/10/1916
War Diary	Sus St Leger	01/11/1916	01/11/1916
War Diary	Barly	03/11/1916	03/11/1916
War Diary	Coulonvillers	05/11/1916	11/11/1916
War Diary	Gapennes	13/11/1916	20/11/1916
War Diary	London Gazette	21/11/1916	21/11/1916
War Diary		05/11/1916	21/11/1916
War Diary	Gapennes	22/11/1916	22/11/1916
War Diary	Agenville	22/11/1916	23/11/1916
War Diary	Barly	25/11/1916	25/11/1916
War Diary	Sus St Leger	26/11/1916	06/12/1916
War Diary	Souastre	09/12/1916	12/12/1916
War Diary	Trenches	13/12/1916	18/12/1916
War Diary	Souastre	22/12/1916	22/12/1916
War Diary	Trenches	24/12/1916	24/12/1916
War Diary	Souastre	26/12/1916	30/12/1916
War Diary	Souastre	28/12/1916	30/12/1916
War Diary	Trenches	31/12/1916	31/12/1916
War Diary		01/01/1917	12/01/1917
War Diary	Souastre	13/01/1917	31/01/1917
War Diary	Trenches	04/02/1917	04/02/1917
War Diary	Souastre	06/02/1917	06/02/1917
War Diary	Halloy	07/02/1917	07/02/1917
War Diary	C. in C.s list Fa 121	13/02/1917	13/02/1917
War Diary	Halloy	18/02/1917	18/02/1917
War Diary	Beaudricourt	19/02/1917	26/02/1917
War Diary	Simencourt	27/02/1917	27/02/1917
War Diary	Achicourt	28/02/1917	28/02/1917
War Diary	Fosseux	01/03/1917	01/03/1917
War Diary	Halloy	02/03/1917	02/03/1917
War Diary	Souastre	03/03/1917	04/03/1917
War Diary	Fonquevillers	05/03/1917	10/03/1917
War Diary	C in C's list	13/03/1917	18/03/1917
War Diary	St Amand	19/03/1917	20/03/1917
War Diary	Bayencourt	21/03/1917	21/03/1917
War Diary	Courcelles	23/03/1917	23/03/1917
War Diary	Warloy-Baillon	24/03/1917	24/03/1917
War Diary	Villers Bocage	25/03/1917	25/03/1917
War Diary	Bacouel	27/03/1917	28/03/1917
War Diary	Berguette	28/03/1917	28/03/1917
War Diary	Ligny Lez Aire	03/04/1917	13/04/1917
War Diary	Oblinghem	14/04/1917	14/04/1917
War Diary	Noeux Les Mines	15/04/1917	19/04/1917
War Diary	Angres	19/04/1917	19/04/1917
War Diary	Lievin	20/04/1917	20/04/1917
War Diary	Petit Sains	22/04/1917	22/04/1917

War Diary	Lievin	23/04/1917	25/04/1917
War Diary	Marquepples Ferme	25/04/1917	29/04/1917
War Diary	Angres	30/04/1917	30/04/1917
Miscellaneous	List of Officers, Warrant Officers & Sergeant Present at the Division held on 3rd April 1917	03/04/1917	03/04/1917
Miscellaneous	O.C. A Coy B Coy D Coy to C Coy for information O.C.S Appendix II	20/04/1917	20/04/1917
Operation(al) Order(s)	Operation Order No. 1. By Major C.B. Infantry Commanding Appendix IV	22/04/1917	22/04/1917
Miscellaneous	Report By O.C. 1/6th Sherwood Foresters on the attack on Fosse 3 De Lievin on 23rd April 1917 Appendix V	23/04/1917	23/04/1917
Miscellaneous	A Form Messages And Signals		
Miscellaneous	Report By O.C. A Coy. 6th Sheet For Operation night 21/22 April 1917 Appendix 3	21/04/1917	21/04/1917
War Diary	Petit Sains	06/05/1917	06/05/1917
War Diary	Extract from C. in C's. List No. 133	06/05/1917	06/05/1917
War Diary	Trenches	08/05/1917	19/05/1917
War Diary	Petit Sains	21/05/1917	25/05/1917
War Diary	Trenches	26/05/1917	31/05/1917
War Diary	Trenches	30/05/1917	30/05/1917
War Diary	Marqueffles Farm	30/05/1917	30/05/1917
War Diary	Trenches	31/05/1917	02/06/1917
War Diary	Lievin Sector	03/06/1917	07/06/1917
War Diary	Fosse. 10 (Sains En Gohelle)	07/06/1917	09/06/1917
War Diary	Fosse 10	10/06/1917	10/06/1917
War Diary	Marqueffles Farm	11/06/1917	16/06/1917
War Diary	Fosse 10	18/06/1917	22/06/1917
War Diary	Bde Support	24/06/1917	30/06/1917
War Diary	Trenches	01/07/1917	01/07/1917
War Diary	Fosse 10, Sains en Gohelle	02/07/1917	02/07/1917
War Diary	Trenches	03/07/1917	03/07/1917
War Diary	Night	03/07/1917	04/07/1917
War Diary	Frevillers	04/07/1917	23/07/1917
War Diary	Drouvin	24/07/1917	24/07/1917
War Diary	La Bourse	26/07/1917	26/07/1917
War Diary	I Corps Schools	28/07/1917	28/07/1917
War Diary	La Bourse	29/07/1917	30/07/1917
War Diary	Trenches	30/07/1917	31/07/1917
Miscellaneous	From:- Officer Commanding, 6th Sherwood Foresters.	05/07/1917	05/07/1917
Heading	Operations Etc. 139th Infy Brigade 6th Sherwood Foresters Notts & Derby 139th Infy Brigade		
War Diary		05/08/1917	05/08/1917
War Diary	St. Elie Sector	05/08/1917	13/08/1917
War Diary	Philosophe	17/08/1917	25/08/1917
War Diary	Cambrin Sector	26/08/1917	28/08/1917
Miscellaneous	I Corps No. 37 (G.O.) 46th Division G. 742/83 Appendix 3	15/08/1917	15/08/1917
Miscellaneous	139th Bde 411/25/G. Appendix 2	15/08/1917	15/08/1917
Miscellaneous	I Corps No. 77 (G.O) 46th Division No. G. 742/90	16/08/1917	16/08/1917
War Diary	Cambrin Sector	01/09/1917	01/09/1917
War Diary	Fouquieres	02/09/1917	07/09/1917
War Diary	Cambrin Sector	09/09/1917	13/09/1917
War Diary	Annequin	14/09/1917	20/09/1917
War Diary	Les Brebis	21/09/1917	21/09/1917
War Diary	Hill 70 Right.	22/09/1917	29/09/1917
Miscellaneous	G. 742/196		

Operation(al) Order(s)	46th Division Order No. 254	24/10/1917	24/10/1917
Operation(al) Order(s)	46th Division Order No. 258	29/10/1917	29/10/1917
Miscellaneous	Headquarters, 11th Division.	24/10/1917	24/10/1917
Operation(al) Order(s)	46th. Division Order No. 254	24/10/1917	24/10/1917
Miscellaneous	Headquarters, 11th. Division.	24/10/1917	24/10/1917
Operation(al) Order(s)	46th. Divisional Artillery Order No. 235	25/10/1917	25/10/1917
Miscellaneous	139th Inf. Bde D.M.G.O.	25/10/1917	25/10/1917
Miscellaneous	11th. Division No. G.S. 242	25/10/1917	25/10/1917
Miscellaneous	G. 742/217		
Miscellaneous	Headquarters, I Corps R.A.	25/10/1917	25/10/1917
Miscellaneous	O.C. Loos Group. Headquarters, 46th Division	27/10/1917	27/10/1917
Miscellaneous	O.C. Loos Group. Hulluch Group.	31/10/1917	31/10/1917
Operation(al) Order(s)	139th Infantry Brigade Order No. 148	31/10/1917	31/10/1917
Map	Cite St Auguste (3)		
Map	Les Tilleuls		
War Diary	Hill 70	04/10/1917	31/10/1917
Heading	Cover for Documents. Raids 6th Sherwood Fors 4/5 11 17		
War Diary	Hill 70	03/11/1917	15/11/1917
War Diary	Support	16/11/1917	16/11/1917
War Diary	Noyelles	17/11/1917	17/11/1917
War Diary	Fouquieres	20/11/1917	22/11/1917
War Diary	St Elie Sector	28/11/1917	29/11/1917
Operation(al) Order(s)	Operation Order No. 13. Lieut. Colonel M.S.K Toller D.S.O. Commanding The Robin Hoods In the Field Appendix D	02/11/1917	02/11/1917
Miscellaneous	Lieut King O.O. No 13		
Miscellaneous	Headquarters 46th Division	03/11/1917	03/11/1917
Miscellaneous	Headquarters, 46th Division.	03/11/1917	03/11/1917
Operation(al) Order(s)	I. Corps Counter-Battery Order No 51	04/11/1917	04/11/1917
Miscellaneous	G. 742/228		
Miscellaneous	G. 742/227	29/10/1917	29/10/1917
Miscellaneous	46 Division	04/11/1917	04/11/1917
Miscellaneous	Report On Raid Carried Out By 1/6th Battalion Sherwood Foresters on Night November 4th 1917	04/11/1917	04/11/1917
Miscellaneous	Report on Artillery Arrangements For Raid Of 139th. Infantry Brigade On 4th November, 1917	04/11/1917	04/11/1917
Miscellaneous	Headquarters, 46th Division	07/11/1917	07/11/1917
Operation(al) Order(s)	Operation Order No. 14 by Lieut. Col. W.S.N. Foller D.S.O. Commanding The Robin Hoods In the Field	08/11/1917	08/11/1917
Heading	A B C D		
Heading	I.O.		
Miscellaneous	46th Division. No. 153 (G.O). 10th November, 1917	10/11/1917	10/11/1917
Operation(al) Order(s)	Operation Order No. 16. by Lieut-Col. W.S.N. Toller, D.S.O. Commanding. The Robin Hoods. In the Field.	15/11/1917	15/11/1917
Operation(al) Order(s)	Operation Order No. 17. by Lieut-Col. W.S.N. Toller, D.S.O. Commanding. The Robin Hoods. In the Field.	21/11/1917	21/11/1917
Operation(al) Order(s)	Operation Order No. 18. by Lieut-Col. W.S.N. Toller, D.S.O. Commanding. The Robin Hoods. In the Field.	24/11/1917	24/11/1917
Heading	Intelligence Officer (2 Copies O.O. 18. for War Diary) Appendix E		
Operation(al) Order(s)	Operation Order No. 19 by Lieut-Col. W.S.N. Toller, D.S.O., Commanding, The Robin Hoods, In the field	27/11/1917	27/11/1917
Miscellaneous	Report On Raid Carried Out By 1/6th Battalion Sherwood Foresters, On Night November 4th, 1917	04/11/1917	04/11/1917

Miscellaneous	Report on Artillery Arrangements For Raid Of 139th Infantry Brigade On 4th November, 1917	04/11/1917	04/11/1917
War Diary	Philosophe	03/12/1917	03/12/1917
War Diary	St Elie Right	04/12/1917	10/12/1917
War Diary	Verquin	11/12/1917	17/12/1917
War Diary	St Elie Right	17/12/1917	22/12/1917
War Diary	Bde Reserve	28/12/1917	28/12/1917
Miscellaneous	To Headquarters 139th Infantry Bde	01/12/1917	01/12/1917
Miscellaneous	O.C. "A" Coy.	08/12/1917	08/12/1917
Miscellaneous	Relief Orders By. Major. V.O. Robinson. M.G. Comdg. 1/6th Bn. Sherwood Foresters	15/12/1917	15/12/1917
Miscellaneous	Lewis gun N.W.		
Miscellaneous	O.C. 'A' 'B' & 'D' Coys.	17/12/1917	17/12/1917
Miscellaneous	To O.C. Companies. Battn Intelligence Officer	15/01/1918	15/01/1918
Miscellaneous	To be handid over on relief.	17/12/1917	17/12/1917
Miscellaneous	To O.S.C. Companies	20/12/1917	20/12/1917
Miscellaneous	Relief Orders by Lt. Colonel. B.W. Vann M.g. Comdg. 1/6th Bn. the Sherwood Foresters	21/12/1917	21/12/1917
Miscellaneous	Relief Orders by Lieut. Colonel. B.W. Vann M.G. Comdg. 1/6th Bn. the Sherwood Foresters	24/12/1917	24/12/1917
Miscellaneous	Report on Patrol Carried Out by 2/Lt. C.F. Barhal and 2/Lt. A. Lake of 6th Sherwood Foresters on 22nd December, 1917	22/12/1917	22/12/1917
Miscellaneous	I Corps Monthly Record of Patrol work of exceptional merit December 1917	21/12/1917	21/12/1917
War Diary	St Elie Sector	02/01/1918	03/01/1918
War Diary	Honours Awards	01/01/1918	30/01/1918
Miscellaneous	Headquarters, 46th Division.	03/01/1918	03/01/1918
Miscellaneous	Relief Orders by Lieut Colonel B.W. Vann. M.G., Comdg. 1/6th Bn Sherwood Foresters	02/01/1918	02/01/1918
Miscellaneous	Relief Orders by Lieut Colonel B.W. Vann. M.G., Comdg. 1/6th Bn Sherwood Foresters	08/01/1918	08/01/1918
Operation(al) Order(s)	Warning Order No. 1 by Lieut-Col. W.S.N. Toller, D.S.O., Commanding, The Robin Hoods In the field,	14/01/1918	14/01/1918
Miscellaneous	Battalion Warning Order By Lieut Colonel. B.W. Vann. M.C., Comdg. 1/6th Bn. Sherwood Foresters	15/01/1918	15/01/1918
Miscellaneous	Relief Orders By Lieut Colonel B.W. Vann. M.G., Comdg. 1/6th Bn. Sherwood Foresters.	16/01/1918	16/01/1918
Miscellaneous	Relief Orders By Lieut Colonel B.W. Vann. M.G., Comdg. 1/6th Bn. Sherwood Foresters.	18/01/1918	18/01/1918
Miscellaneous	Relief Orders By Lieut Col B.W. Vann. M.G., Comdg. 1/6th Bn. Sherwood Foresters.	19/01/1918	19/01/1918
Miscellaneous	Reference O.O./A/9. Para. 2		
Miscellaneous			
Operation(al) Order(s)	Operation Order No. 20. by Lieut. Col. B.W. Vann. M.G., Cmdg. 1/6th Bn. Sherwood Foresters.	30/01/1918	30/01/1918
Miscellaneous	Report on Enemy Raid on Appendix I	18/01/1918	18/01/1918
Miscellaneous	Appendix II War Diary.		
Miscellaneous	First Army to G.S. 969 I corps no. 596. (G.b) 46th Division G. 727/500	07/01/1918	07/01/1918
War Diary		05/02/1918	05/02/1918
War Diary	Lapugnoy	06/02/1918	07/02/1918
War Diary	Burbure	09/02/1918	09/02/1918
War Diary	Laires	10/02/1918	28/02/1918
War Diary	Laires	23/02/1918	23/02/1918
Heading	1/6 War Diary March 1918		

Heading	20th Division 12th K.R.R.C. Vol. 3 Sept 15		
War Diary	Laires	01/03/1918	06/03/1918
War Diary	Beuvry	11/03/1918	19/03/1918
War Diary	London Gazette	19/03/1918	19/03/1918
War Diary	Beuvry	20/03/1918	20/03/1918
War Diary	Annequin	22/03/1918	24/03/1918
War Diary	Cambrin Sector	27/03/1918	27/03/1918
War Diary	Sailly La Bourse	28/03/1918	28/03/1918
War Diary	Brigade Support Cite St Pierre	31/03/1918	31/03/1918
Operation(al) Order(s)	Operation Order No. 22 By Lieut Col B.W. Vann M.C., Commanding 1/6th Sherwood Foresters	09/03/1918	09/03/1918
Operation(al) Order(s)	Operation Order No. 23 By Lieut Colonel B.W. Vann M.C., Commanding 1/6th Sherwood Foresters	19/03/1918	19/03/1918
Operation(al) Order(s)	Operation Order No. 24 By Major V.Q. Robinson, M.C., Commanding 1/6th Battalion Sherwood Foresters	19/03/1918	19/03/1918
Operation(al) Order(s)	Operation Order No. 5. Major V.O. Robinson. M.C. Cmdg. 1/6th Sherwood Foresters	23/03/1918	23/03/1918
Miscellaneous	Relief Orders by Major V.O. Robinson M.G. Cmdg 6th Sherwood Foresters	27/03/1918	27/03/1918
Miscellaneous	Relief Orders by Major V.O. Robinson M.G. Cmdg 6th Sherwood Foresters	30/03/1918	30/03/1918
Miscellaneous	To O.'s. C "A" "B" "C" "D" "HQ" Companies Battn. Intelligence Officer. Medical Officer.	31/03/1918	31/03/1918
Heading	139th Brigade. 46th Division. 1/6th Battalion Sherwood Foresters April 1918		
War Diary		03/04/1918	03/04/1918
War Diary	Cite St Pierre Sector	05/04/1918	05/04/1918
War Diary	St Emile Sector	09/04/1918	11/04/1918
War Diary	Petit Sains	12/04/1918	12/04/1918
War Diary	Houchin	18/04/1918	18/04/1918
War Diary	Vaudricourt	20/04/1918	20/04/1918
War Diary	Houchin	23/04/1918	23/04/1918
War Diary	Fouquieres	23/04/1918	28/04/1918
War Diary	Verquin	30/04/1918	30/04/1918
Operation(al) Order(s)	Operation Order No 26 By Lieut Col. B.W. Vann. M.G. Cmdg. 1/6th Bn. Sherwood Foresters	09/04/1918	09/04/1918
Operation(al) Order(s)	Operation Order No 27 by Lieut Col. B.W. Vann. M.G. Cmdg. 1/6th Bn. Sherwood Foresters	11/04/1918	11/04/1918
Operation(al) Order(s)	Operation Order No 28 by Lieut Col B.N. Vann M.G. Commanding 1/6th Bn Sherwood Foresters	12/04/1918	12/04/1918
Operation(al) Order(s)	Operation Order No. 31 By Lieut Col B.W. Vann, M.G. Commanding 1/6th Bn. Sherwood Foresters	24/04/1918	24/04/1918
War Diary	Verquin	02/05/1918	02/05/1918
War Diary	Gorre	04/05/1918	04/05/1918
War Diary	Le Quesnoy	06/05/1918	06/05/1918
War Diary	Gorre	08/05/1918	10/05/1918
War Diary	Vaudricourt	14/05/1918	14/05/1918
War Diary	Essars	16/05/1918	20/05/1918
War Diary	Bruay	23/05/1918	23/05/1918
War Diary	Essars	25/05/1918	25/05/1918
War Diary	Vaudricourt	27/05/1918	27/05/1918
War Diary	Vaudricourt Wood	28/05/1918	30/05/1918
Operation(al) Order(s)	Operation Order No. 33. by Lt. Col. B.W. Vann. M.G. Commanding 1/6th Sherwood Foresters	04/05/1918	04/05/1918
Operation(al) Order(s)	Operation Order No. 35. by Lieut. Colonel. B.W. Vann. M.G. Cmdg 1/6th Sherwood Foresters	06/05/1918	06/05/1918

Operation(al) Order(s)	Operation Order No. 21. by Lieut. Col. B.W. Vann. M.G. Cmdg 1/6th Sherwood Foresters	08/05/1918	08/05/1918
Operation(al) Order(s)	Operation Order No. 36. by Lt. Col. B.W. Vann. M.G. Commanding 1/6th Battalion Sherwood Foresters	10/05/1918	10/05/1918
Operation(al) Order(s)	Operation Order No 37. by Lieut. Col. B.W. Vann. M.G. Cmdg 1/6th Bn Sherwood Foresters	14/05/1918	14/05/1918
Operation(al) Order(s)	Operation Order No 38. by Lt. Col. B.W. Vann. M.G. Commanding 1/6th Battn Sherwood Foresters	15/05/1918	15/05/1918
Operation(al) Order(s)	Operation Order No 48. by Lieut. Col. B.W. Vann. M.G. Cmdg 1/6th Sherwood Foresters	19/05/1918	19/05/1918
Operation(al) Order(s)	Operation Order No. 39. by Lieut. Col. B.W. Vann. M.G. Commanding. 1/6th Battalion Sherwood Foresters	19/05/1918	19/05/1918
Operation(al) Order(s)	Operation Order No. 41 By Major. V.O. Robinson, M.C Commanding 1/6th Battalion Sherwood Foresters	25/05/1918	25/05/1918
Operation(al) Order(s)	Operation Order No. 42. by Major V.O. Robinson M.G., Cmdg. 1/6th Battn. Sherwood Foresters	30/05/1918	30/05/1918
Heading	Cover for Documents. Nature of Enclosures. 70. Raid 6th Sherwoods 7th June 18		
War Diary	London Gazette	03/06/1918	03/06/1918
War Diary	Left Subsector Night Gorre Sector	06/06/1918	08/06/1918
War Diary	Verquin	10/06/1918	11/06/1918
War Diary	London Gazette	14/06/1918	14/06/1918
War Diary	Essars	15/06/1918	18/06/1918
War Diary	Trenches	19/06/1918	19/06/1918
War Diary	Vaudricourt	23/06/1918	26/06/1918
War Diary	Trenches	27/06/1918	28/06/1918
Operation(al) Order(s)	Operation Order No 43, by Major V.O. Robinson M.G. Commanding 1/6th Battalion Sherwood Foresters.	02/06/1918	02/06/1918
Operation(al) Order(s)	Operation Order No 44 by Major V.O. Robinson M.G. Commanding 1/6th Sherwood Foresters.	04/06/1918	04/06/1918
Operation(al) Order(s)	Operation Order No 44 by Major V.O. Robinson M.G. Commanding 1/6th Battn. Sherwood Foresters	06/06/1918	06/06/1918
Miscellaneous	I Corps No. 287 (G.O) 46th Division G. 70/5. 46th Division.	10/06/1918	10/06/1918
Miscellaneous	46th. Division. No. 70/4		
Miscellaneous	Headquarters, 46th Division.	07/06/1918	07/06/1918
Miscellaneous	46th Division. No. 287 (G.O.) 10th June, 1918	10/06/1918	10/06/1918
Miscellaneous	A Form Messages And Signals		
Miscellaneous	46th Division No 70/2		
Operation(al) Order(s)	I Corps Counter-Battery Order No 79	06/06/1918	06/06/1918
Miscellaneous	46th Division No. G. 1510/1	06/06/1918	06/06/1918
Miscellaneous	46th Division		
Miscellaneous	46th Division No. G. 1510	06/06/1918	06/06/1918
Operation(al) Order(s)	Operation Order No. 47. by Lieut. Colonel. B.W. Vann. M.G. Cmdg. 1/6th Bn. Sherwood Foresters	14/06/1918	14/06/1918
Miscellaneous			
War Diary	Le Quesnoy	01/07/1918	01/07/1918
War Diary	Vaudricourt Park	02/07/1918	05/07/1918
War Diary	Trenches	05/07/1918	15/07/1918
War Diary	Verquin	16/07/1918	21/07/1918
War Diary	Trenches	24/07/1918	27/07/1918
War Diary	Essars	02/08/1918	02/08/1918
War Diary	Vaudricourt Park	04/08/1918	06/08/1918
War Diary	Gorre	09/08/1918	14/08/1918
War Diary	Essars	16/08/1918	16/08/1918
War Diary	Fouquieres	20/08/1918	20/08/1918

War Diary	Essars	20/08/1918	20/08/1918
War Diary	Vaudricourt Park	21/08/1918	30/08/1918
War Diary	Gorre Sector	31/08/1918	31/08/1918
Miscellaneous	Report on Operations 29th September 18 at 3rd-30 the Battalion was in its appointed assembly Position. Appendix A	29/09/1918	29/09/1918
Miscellaneous	46th Division. G. 114/23. 29th September, 1918	29/09/1918	29/09/1918
Miscellaneous	Special Order of The Day By Lieut. General Sir Walter Braithwaite, K.C.B., Commanding IX Corps.	30/09/1918	30/09/1918
War Diary	Levergies	10/10/1918	10/10/1918
War Diary	Mericourt	12/10/1918	14/10/1918
War Diary	Fresnoy	16/10/1918	30/10/1918
Miscellaneous	Special Order of The Day by Major-General G.F. Boyd, C.M.G. D.S.O. D.C.M. Commanding 46th Division. Appendix I	03/10/1918	03/10/1918
Miscellaneous		04/10/1918	04/10/1918
Miscellaneous	Translation of an Article in "Le Journal" dated 4/10/1918. Prodic'ous Exploit By The Heroes Of The 46th Division	04/10/1918	04/10/1918
Miscellaneous	Special Order of The Day By Lieutenant General Sir Walter Braithwaite, M.C.B. Commanding IX Corps.	05/10/1918	05/10/1918
Miscellaneous	Special Order of The Day by Major-General G.F. Boyd, C.M.G. D.S.O. D.C.M. Commanding 46th Division.	05/10/1918	05/10/1918
Miscellaneous	Special Order of The Day by Major-General G.F. Boyd, C.M.G. D.S.O. D.C.M. Commanding 46th Division.	13/10/1918	13/10/1918
Miscellaneous	Special Order of The Day by Major-General G.F. Boyd, C.M.G. D.S.O. D.C.M. Commanding 46th Division.	15/10/1918	15/10/1918
Miscellaneous	Special Order of the Day by Brigadier General J. Harington. D.S.O. Commanding, 139th Infantry Brigade.	15/10/1918	15/10/1918
Miscellaneous	Special Order of The Day by Major General G.F. Boyd, C.M.G., D.S.O., D.C.M, Commanding 46th Division.	17/10/1918	17/10/1918
War Diary	Bohain	02/11/1918	04/11/1918
War Diary	Catillon	05/11/1918	06/11/1918
War Diary	Prisches	09/11/1918	09/11/1918
War Diary	Boulogne	11/11/1918	14/11/1918
War Diary	Landrecies	14/11/1918	30/11/1918
War Diary	Landrecies	23/11/1918	30/11/1918
Operation(al) Order(s)	Operation Order No 80 by Lieut Colonel G.S. Clayton., D.S.O. Commanding 1/6th Battalion The Sherwood Foresters. Appendix I	05/11/1918	05/11/1918
Miscellaneous	Au Divin Messee Appendix 2		
Miscellaneous	Special Order of The Day by Major General G.F., Boyd, C.M.G., D.S.O., D.C.M. Commanding 46th. Division. Appendix 3	13/10/1918	13/10/1918
Miscellaneous	1/6th Battalion The Sherwood Foresters. Battalion Inter Company League Table Up To 30th November 1918 Appendix 4	30/11/1918	30/11/1918
Miscellaneous	Special Order Of The Day by Major General G.F. Boyd., C.M.G., D.S.O., D.C.M. Commanding 46th Division. Appendix 5	29/11/1918	29/11/1918
War Diary	Landrecies	01/12/1918	10/12/1918
War Diary	Chesterfield	11/12/1918	11/12/1918
War Diary	Landrecies	11/12/1918	11/01/1919
War Diary	Cartignies	13/01/1919	20/02/1919
War Diary	Bethencourt	27/02/1919	29/06/1919

WO95/2694 (1)

1

STATEMENT accompanying War Diary.

5th.August to 30th.September,1914.

6th.Battalion, Sherwood Foresters,

Notts & Derby Infantry Brigade,

North Midland Division

Mobilization centre - Chesterfield.

Temporary War Station - Derby.

Subsequent Stations occupied - Luton, Harpenden.

1. MOBILIZATION :- On the whole mobilization worked smoothly. Before the men left training Camp at Hunmanby they were warned of the probability of mobilization with the result that all who had been in Camp reported themselves at their Company Headquarters early on the morning of the 5th.August. Of the remainder 11 were absent on mobilization of which 5 have subsequently rejoined with a satisfactory explanation. The billeting arrangements at Chesterfield, Ripley (on march to duty) and Derby had been previously arranged with care and worked satisfactorily.

2. TRAINING :- A certain number of the N.C.O's were too old for their position and should not have been allowed to re-engage, others were obviously unfitted and had been promoted for other reasons than military efficiency. These have either been transferred to the Home Service Battalion or have been allowed to remain on reverting. But until this could be done, the training was hampered. Classes for instruction have been held since mobilization under the Permanent Staff with beneficial results.

6th NOD
Feb '15
June 19

3. ADMINISTRATION :-
(1) Quartermaster's Department.

I think it is very desirable that whenever possible either the Quartermaster or Quartermaster Sergeant should be promoted from the permanent Staff.

(2) PAY LISTS :-

The Pay Lists present a great difficulty to Territorial Sergeants though they are gradually improving. It would be of great advantage if Sergeant Instructors could be absorbed and promoted Colour Sergeants of Companies as was the case with the Volunteer service Companies in the South African War. Besides the benefit to the Battalion these N.C.O's are prejudiced by losing their promotions which would now come to them in their line Battalions.

(3) ORDNANCE :- Difficulties have naturally been experienced in obtaining boots, equipment & clothing, but with the assistance of the County Association these are gradually being overcome.

(4) BILLETING :- Some confusion has arisen as to the payments for billeting in private houses. It was understood from the Divisional Circular memo: of 15th.September,1914 that 6d should be paid in certain cases but it now appears that 9d. and 3/- must be paid in all cases. The first payments gave rise to some dissatisfaction in certain cases.

(5) CORRESPONDENCE :- Much extra work is caused in the Orderly Room by the duplication of returns particularly as regards clothing and Unit Kits.

(6) TRANSPORT and REMOUNTS :- The horses obtained on moblization were generally good, particularly the Pit ponies for pack transport. The carts and waggons

however required considerable adaption and the first watercarts obtained (from Chesterfield Corporation) were too heavy and had to be returned.

Major,

Commanding 6th.Sherwood Foresters.

HARPENDEN.

7th.October,1914.

REORGANIZATION of T.F. into Home and Imperial Service Units.

It is difficult to say at this moment whether the Force could be successfully organised in peace time on two bases. This Battalion has for some years had from 60 to 80 per cent of Imperial Service men - some hesitated to join in peace from the fear that Imperial Service Units would be employed on purely garrison duties as the Militia at St.Helena in the South African War. The prospects of volunteering in the future for Imperial Service would be killed if any Units of the New Army were to be employed in the field before Territorial Force Units who have been preparing themselves (however feebly) for war while the others shirked their duty.

PREPARATION of Units for Imperial Service.

Musketry training and particularly field firing is very desirable. I have already submitted an application to take my Battalion to Edale for a few days - where unique opportunities would be afforded for field firing at comparatively little expense.

G. D. Goodman Major,
Commanding 6th.Sherwood Foresters.

HARPENDEN

7th.Octr;1914.

Copy

Statement to accompany War Diary for October, 1914.

6TH BATTALION THE SHERWOOD FORESTERS.

Notts and Derby Infantry Brigade.

North Midland Division.

Peace Station:- CHESTERFIELD.

War Station:- HARPENDEN.

TRAINING: The training of the Battalion has continued on Progressive lines, with the result that Officers and N.C.O's have acquired more confidence and there is less hesitation when they are called upon for initiative. The operations at SUNDON from 7th to 9th October when the Division occupied and entrenched a position were the first of the kind undertaken by the troops and the work with pick and shovel came naturally to most of the men of this Battalion.

ADMINISTRATION: Considerable delay arose in delivery of the clothing ordered by the Derbyshire County Association but by the end of the month practically every man had received a new suit of service dress and was in possession of a good pair of boots. Half the greatcoats had been renewed.

In response to an appeal by the Commanding Officer loans of Field Glasses have been made to the Battalion BY the Hon.Colonel, Col J.C.Cavendish.A.D.C., The National Service league and residents of the County.

G. D. Goodman

LIEUT. COLONEL

COMMANDING 6th Bn THE SHERWOOD FORESTERS

(NOTTINGHAMS...

Harpenden.

9th Novr 1914.

Copy.

Statement to accompany War Diary

1st to 30 November 1914.

6th Battalion Sherwood Foresters

Notts & Derby Infantry Brigade

North Midland Division

Mobilization centre:- Chesterfield.

Temporary War Station:- Derby.

Subsequent stations occupied:- Luton, Harpenden, Braintree.

1. TRAINING:-Prior to the move from HARPENDEN the training became more advanced, in the Brigade Battalions operated against each other and in the Division, Brigades with Artillery attached did the same. As the forces engaged were not too large useful experience was gained by Senior Officers and the interest of all ranks was maintained. In the work of the Battalion the need for careful inter-communication between detachments and the weakness of relying on verbal messages was perhaps the point most clearly demonstrated.

2. DISCIPLINE:- A few cases have arisen of hesitation in obeying or noncompliance with an order but punishment by forfeit-ure of pay seems to have a good effect and there is a distinct advantage in avoiding short sentences of detention. The N.C.O's are learning to rely more on themselves and are much more ready to bring men up for breaches of discipline than they were on mobilisation.

3. ADMINISTRATION:- Orders for the move into Essex came on a Sunday evening prior to a whole holiday & therefore the Battalion was at a disadvantage. Certain Companies moved away without their full kit owing to careless performance of duties, but this is not likely to occur again, otherwise adminstration has much improved and complaints as to supplies

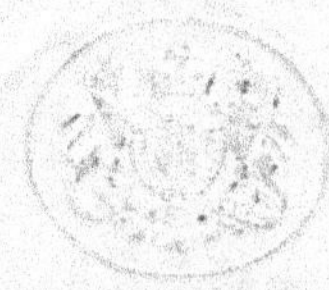

and rations are very rare. Billeting duties on the march were very well performed by the advance parties.

4. ORGANISATION:- The 1st reinforcements joined the Battalion at HARPENDEN. Unfortunately they were mostly untrained and N.C.O's had to be detailed for their training & preliminary musketry. In view of the necessity for drafts the training of the Reserve Battalion, especially in musketry, assumes great importance and some supervision should be exercised. A marked distinction should be made in the training and privileges of those men of the Reserve Battalion who undertake Imperial Service.

Braintree. G. D. Goodman Lieut Colonel.

5th December 1914. Commanding 6th Batta; The Sherwood Foresters.

139th Inf.Bde.
46th Div.

Battn. disembarked
Havre from England
26.2.15.

6th BATTN. THE SHERWOOD FORESTERS (NOTTINGHAMSHIRE AND DERBYSHIRE REGIMENT).

F E B R U A R Y

1 9 1 5

Instructions regarding War Diaries and Intelligence Summaries are contained in F. S. Regs., Part II. and the Staff Manual respectively. Title pages will be prepared in manuscript.

WAR DIARY
of 1/6th SHERWOOD FORESTERS
INTELLIGENCE SUMMARY.
(*Erase heading not required.*)

Army Form C. 2118.

Place	Date	Summary of Events and Information	Remarks and references to Appendices
BRAINTREE	4-2-15.	Musketry party under Capt. SAXBY, proceeded to LUTON. 8 officers 280 or	G.D.G.
		10 men transferred to depot, medically unfit.	
"	5-2-15	1 NCO & 1 man transferred Reserve battalion, medically unfit.	G.D.G.
"	8-2-15	18 NCOs & men transferred to Reserve battalion medically unfit	G.D.G.
"	15-2-15	11 NCO's & men transferred to Reserve battalion medically unfit.	G.D.G.
"	19-2-15.	The N M Division was inspected by "His Majesty the King" on the eve of its departure for the continent at HALLINGBURY PARK. His Majesty authorised the change of name of the brigade from "NOTTS & DERBY Infantry Brigade" to "The SHERWOOD FORESTERS BRIGADE".	G.D.G.
		First reinforcements (made up by 71 from Reserve Bn) left at BRAINTREE under 2nd Lt SYALANDS	G.D.G.
"	25-2-15	The Battalion left by 2 trains at 5 a.m. and 6.40 a.m. ~~for~~	
SOUTHAMPTON	"	" " embarked Headqrs. A & B Companies and Transport on "MAIDAN" C & D Companies under Major Hall on "King Edward"	G.D.G. G.D.G.
HARVRE	26-2-15	The men were fitted out with skin waistcoats and extra stores drawn	G.D.G.
"	27-2-15	The Battalion (less 15 & 16 platoons under Capt. Hills) entrained at GARE MARITIME in early morning	G.D.G.
TERDEGHEN	28-2-15	The Battalion detrained at CASSEL & marched to billets	G.D.G.

1/6th Batt
Sherwood Foresters.

139th Inf.Bde.
46th Div.

6th BATTN. THE SHERWOOD FORESTERS (NOTTINGHAMSHIRE AND DERBYSHIRE REGIMENT).

M A R C H

1 9 1 5

Attached:

Appendix I.

Instructions regarding War Diaries and Intelligence Summaries are contained in F. S. Regs., Part II. and the Staff Manual respectively. Title pages will be prepared in manuscript.

WAR DIARY of 1/6th Sherwood Foresters INTELLIGENCE SUMMARY.

(Erase heading not required.)

Army Form C. 2118.

Hour, Date, Place	Summary of Events and Information	Remarks and references to Appendices
TERDEGHEN 3-3-15	Telegram to Division from H. M. The King.	G.D.G. see Appendix I
TERDEGHEN 4-3-15	Battalion marched to S. SYLVESTRE where with 5th Battn. it was inspected by the Colonel – Gen. Sir H. L. SMITH-DORRIEN – A.D.C. GC.B. DSO. Then embussed for BAILLEUL (where Band left). Then marched to OOSTROOVE FARM near PLOEG STEERT and billeted there attached to 11th Brigade – Brig. Gen. HASLER.	G.D.G.
PLOEG STEERT 5th to 8th March.	The Battalion attached Head qrs A + C. Companies to SOMERSET L. I. + B + D Co to 1/RIFLE BRIGADE in trenches and working parties – L/Cpl. Redfern "C" Company killed on 8th with working party	G.D.G.
OUTTERSTEENE 9-3-15	Battalion with S.F. Brigade marched to billets, picking up Band at BAILLEUL	G.D.G.
BAC ST. MAUR 11-3-15	Battalion with SHERWOOD FORESTERS Brigade marched at an hours notice and billeted in factories – Remainder of N. MIDLAND Division about SAILLY. BAND to HAZEBROUCK where they played before Sir JOHN FRENCH and the Prince of WALES.	G.D.G.
do 12-3-15	SHERWOOD FORESTERS Brigade detached to II CAVALRY DIVISION under Major Gen. GOUGH.	G.D.G.
NEU'F BERQUIN 13-3-15	BRIGADE marched to billets adjoining II CAVALRY DIVISION.	G.D.G.
do 21-3-15	Lt Col. GOODMAN + Major HALL visited 1st Battalion at ROUGE CROIX where GEN. SMITH-DORRIEN addressed that Battalion	G.D.G.
do 23-3-15	Battalion moved to billets about 1½ miles further out	G.D.G.
do 24-3-15	1st Battalion commanded by MAJOR MORLEY took over our old billets. They were met by the C.O. + Band + drums + drums of 5th Battalion and the 6th Battalion lined the road + cheered	G.D.G.

(9 29 6) W 3332—1107 100,000 10/13 H W V Forms/C. 2118/10.

Army Form C. 2118.

WAR DIARY
or
INTELLIGENCE SUMMARY.
of 1/6th Sherwood Foresters

(*Erase heading not required.*)

Instructions regarding War Diaries and Intelligence Summaries are contained in F. S. Regs., Part II. and the Staff Manual respectively. Title pages will be prepared in manuscript.

Hour, Date, Place	Summary of Events and Information	Remarks and references to Appendices
NEUF BERQUIN. 25.3.15	1st Battalion marched to SAILLY	G.D.G.
30.3.15	Band to OUTTERSTEENE to play for Bde of LONDONS service	G.D.G.
	The following officers were gazetted and joined the Battalion during March as 2nd Lieutenants	
	Gazette 3rd March: Lt. G.S. RIVINGTON dated 26 Feb	
	" A.H. GOODALL	
	Gazette 12 March: " T.L. DARBYSHIRE from 18th Alberta Dragoons	
	Coy. Quartermaster Sgt. L.G. DICKENSON dated 13 March	
	Surgeon Capt. A.W. SHEA promoted Surgeon Major from 5 August 1914.	G.D.G.

"A" Form. Army Form C. 2121.

MESSAGES AND SIGNALS. No. of Message

Prefix Code m.	Words	Charge	This message is on a/c of:	Recd. at m.
Office of Origin and Service Instructions.	Sent			Date
I	At m.		Service.	From
	To			
	By		(Signature of "Franking Officer.")	By

TO — App

Sender's Number	Day of Month	In reply to Number	AAA

— Special Order. —

The following Copy of telegram has been received and is published for information of all ranks.

"Please convey to G.O.C. N. Mid: Divn the following message from H.M. The King, in bidding you all God-speed I offer my best wishes for the success of the North Midland Division George R.I. (Ends)

From
Place 3rd March 1915
Time

The above may be forwarded as now corrected. (Z) E. M. Morris Major

Censor. Signature of Addressor or person authorised to telegraph in his name

B Maj. N.M.D Bde

*This line should be erased if not required.

3602 M. & Co. Ltd. Wt. W929/549—100,000. 6/14. Forms C2121/10.

139th Inf.Bde.
46th Div.

6th BATTN. THE SHERWOOD FORESTERS (NOTTINGHAMSHIRE AND DERBYSHIRE REGIMENT).

A P R I L

1 9 1 5

Instructions regarding War Diaries and Intelligence Summaries are contained in F. S. Regs., Part II. and the Staff Manual respectively. Title pages will be prepared in manuscript.

WAR DIARY or ~~INTELLIGENCE SUMMARY.~~ 6th Sherwood Foresters

(*Erase heading not required.*)

Army Form C. 2118.

Hour, Date, Place	Summary of Events and Information	Remarks and references to Appendices
OUTERSTEENE. Good Friday 2/4/15	Church parade 8 a.m. The Battalion with 5th Battalion marched to billets here from NEUF BERQUIN (DOULLEU COMMUNE)	G.D.G.
BAILLEUL 3/4/15	The Battalion with 5th Battalion marched to billets here	G.D.G.
" Easter Day 4/4/15	Services + Church parade.	G.D.G.
LOCRE 5/4/15	The Battalion with 5th Battalion marched to billets	G.D.G.
KEMMEL 7/4/15	The Battalion took over G + H trenches from 8th Battalion the two Battalions working in pairs :- Remained in trenches four days.	G.D.G.
	Casualties 1 officer Lieut. J. Davies slightly wounded (at duty) 5 N.C.O's + men killed 8 wounded	G.D.G.
	4 being killed + 1 wounded by one H.E. Shell (C [illegible]) in one [illegible] [illegible] + 1 Sergt. + Sergt. Dakin + 12 men - Sergt. Dakin reported [illegible] for coolness	G.D.G.
LOCRE 12/4/15 a.m.	Relieved by 8th Bn + returned to our billets	G.D.G.
	Find working parties during rest	
	No 2366 Sergt. J. H. Hutchins Killed 13/4/15	G.D.G.
KEMMEL 15/4/15	Returned to trenches for [illegible] days. 8 N.C.O's + men killed 14 wounded (10 at duty)	G.D.G.

(9 29 6) W 3332—1107 100,000 10/13 H W V Forms/C. 2118/10.

6th Sherwood Foresters

Army Form C. 2118.

Instructions regarding War Diaries and Intelligence Summaries are contained in F. S. Regs., Part II. and the Staff Manual respectively. Title pages will be prepared in manuscript.

WAR DIARY
or
INTELLIGENCE SUMMARY.

(*Erase heading not required.*)

Hour, Date, Place		Summary of Events and Information	Remarks and references to Appendices
LOCRE	16/4/15.	London Gazette A/Sgt Maj. W. SEATON to be 2nd Lieut. April 1st 2nd Lieut. W. SEATON to be temp. Capt. April 1st	G.D.G.
do	20/4/15	Promotions 4506 Coy. Sgt. Major A. JACKMAN to be Acting Sgt. Major 456 Coy. Q.M. Sgt H. H. HOLLAND to be Coy Sgt. Maj. 'A' Coy 425 Coy Q.M. Sgt J. ATHERTON transferred to 'A' Coy 2410 Sgt. T. J. Henshall to be Coy Q.M. Sgt 'B' Coy 2377 L/Cpl. G. W. KNOWLES to be Corpl. for good service in trenches.	G.D.G.
do	do	Battalion dug at night 1200 yards of communicating trench from G4	G.D.G.
do	do	Battalion dug further lengths of communicating trench, while doing so it was withdrawn to KEMMEL and kept in Reserve until arrival of 7th Battn. when it returned to LOCRE.	G.D.G.
KEMMEL	24/4/15	Returned to trenches for 4 days Killed 2 other ranks Wounded Lt. J. TOLSON + 13 other ranks	G.D.G.
LOCRE	29/4/15 a.m.	Relieved by 8th Battalion & returned to rest billets Casualties in working parties and fatigues Other ranks Killed 1 wounded 6	G.D.G.
KEMMEL	27/4/15	Gallery dug and fired from G2 blowing in German gallery 2nd Lieut. H. F. SEVERN [illegible] gallantly rescued Lt. DANIELS [illegible]	G.D.G.

139th Inf.Bde.
46th Div.

6th BATTN. THE SHERWOOD FORESTERS (NOTTINGHAMSHIRE AND DERBYSHIRE REGIMENT).

M A Y

1 9 1 5

Attached:

Appendices I & II.

Instructions regarding War Diaries and Intelligence Summaries are contained in F. S. Regs., Part II. and the Staff Manual respectively. Title pages will be prepared in manuscript.

WAR DIARY or ~~INTELLIGENCE~~ SUMMARY.

(Erase heading not required.)

6th Sherwood Foresters

Army Form C. 2118.

Hour, Date, Place	Summary of Events and Information	Remarks and references to Appendices
KEMMEL 2/5/15	Returned to G & H trenches for four days Casualties 8 O.R. killed 15 O.R. wounded (1 subsequently died).	G.D.G
LOCRE night of 5/6th	Band played 7th Canadian Battalion & 2nd Canadian Inf Brigade on passing through LOCRE en route from YPRES TO BAILLEUL	Appendix I. Letter from Major ODLUM comdg 7th Canad to O.C. see also letter in DAILY TELEGRAPH: 18th May Appendix II G.D.G
KEMMEL 9/5/15	Returned to trenches after 3 days rest for four days and took over trenches J1 to L4 & 6 from 8th Infantry Brigade. 2nd ROYAL SCOTS 1st & 4th GORDONS and a portion from 2nd SUFFOLKS who closed to the left. Trenches not very good – communicating trenches bad. Hd.qrs. ROSSIGNOL ESTAMINET	G.D.G
" 10/5/15	2nd Lieut H.F. SEVERNE killed on getting into J2 trench. J1 J2 & J10 handed over to 7th Battalion Casualties – 1 officer killed. O.R. 1 killed 25 wounded	G.D.G G.D.G
" 14/5/15 a.m. 1 a.m.	N. Mid. Division becomes 46th Division & Brigade 139th Infantry Brigade Relieved by 5th Battalion 1 One Company to SIEGE FARM 2 in bivouac 1 in farms WEST of LITTLE KEMMEL on road to LOCRE.	G.D.G G.D.G
17/5/15	Returned to trenches for 4 days.	G.D.G
19/5/15	Handed over J3 Right & J3 Left trenches to 7th Battalion Casualties O.R. 3 killed, 7 wounded	G.D.G
21/5/15	Relieved by 5th Battalion & to Bivouac & SIEGE FARM	G.D.G
25/5/15	Returned to trenches for 5 days 2nd Lieut G. GLOSSOP wounded slightly	G.D.G
28/5/15	A Company 8th K.R.R. Rgt O.R. killed 4 wounded 22 Lieut SEYMOUR attached for instruction	G.D.G
30/5/15	Relieved by 5th Battalion – to Bivouac & SIEGE FARM	G.D.G

A P P E N D I C E S I & II.

May

Appendix I

May 7th. 1915.

Dear Colonel Goodman,

On the night of the 5th inst. at 1 a.m., when the 7th Canadian Battalion, leading the 2nd Canadian Infantry Brigade, was marching htrough LOCRE, I was very much surprised and just as much delighted, to see a band fall in and take up the march with the Battalion.

The music, at such a time and in such a place was quite a novelty; but it was just the thing wanted. Our men were nearly all in. The music backed them up at once.

I am afraid that if it had not been for the cheering effect of the band many would not have got through at all.

On inquiry, I found that the band belonged to your Regiment.

May I say, that I consider this the most striking instance of thoughtful kindness with which we have met since we set out on the campaign.

Yours very sincerely,
(Sgd) Victor W. Odlum. Major.
O.C.7th Battalion.

TO/

Lieut.Col. Goodman.
Commanding
8th Battalion Sherwood Foresters.
North Midland Division.

MUSIC ON THE MARCH.

PLAYING OUT YPRES HEROES.

To the Editor of "The Daily Telegraph."

Sir—It is perfectly certain that we can do with a lot more music. Listen to a minor incident which occurred a few nights ago. We were coming out from the Ypres salient. "Bloody Vipers" I believe they call it in the best circles. The regiment had been up on the Hill for six days, and we had left more behind us than we cared to contemplate. We had been in reserve trenches for seven days, playing at rabbits in the hedgerows while the Germans squirted shrapnel and high explosive at us. We were relieved and were marching out to rest billets. It was not a long march, about fourteen miles in all, but it was very hot, and the cobble stones were hard on the feet. After about ten miles of it we were not downhearted. No, but I think everyone was fed up, and I know I was infernally thirsty.

Suddenly, just past midnight, out of the darkness, came a burst of music. It was a good old brass band playing with all its stops out. The effect was instantaneous. The men who had been stumbling and crawling along in the dark bucked up at once. Behind us were the guns rumbling in the distance, above us the stars, below us the unending cobble stones, but all round us was the music.

"Hold your hand out, Naughty Boy." Naughty or not, it certainly made us hold our heads up.

"What the devil!" "Where is it?" "Shut up, you fool, can't you listen?" These were some of the remarks.

For about twenty minutes it played. Played us from a state of suspended animation into buoyant activity. Then it ceased as suddenly as it had begun—so suddenly that it was hard to believe that it had ever been. But that it had been was shown by its effects. Thirst-producing mouth-organs appeared, sore feet and heavy packs were forgotten, and the battalion sang down the cobble-stones into ——. Yes, and kept on singing until housed for the night.

The remnants of the medical detail behind me were singing, "Roaming in the Gloaming," and through the strains of the Bromilow idyll a remark reached my ear. "That damned noise means a hell of a lot." Not, perhaps, too complimentary to the musicians, but right in the meaning. The Canadians will remember how the band of the Sherwood Foresters played them through the darkness at midnight out of "Bloody Ypres."—Yours, &c.,

GEORGE GIBSON, Capt., C.A.M.C.,
7th Canadian Infantry (1st British Columbia Regt.), B.E.F.

May 10.

139th Inf.Bde.
46th Div.

6th BATTN. THE SHERWOOD FORESTERS (NOTTINGHAMSHIRE AND DERBYSHIRE REGIMENT).

J U N E

1 9 1 5

WAR DIARY 6th Sherwood Foresters Army Form C. 2118.

or

INTELLIGENCE SUMMARY.

(Erase heading not required.)

Instructions regarding War Diaries and Intelligence Summaries are contained in F. S. Regs., Part II. and the Staff Manual respectively. Title pages will be prepared in manuscript.

Hour, Date, Place		Summary of Events and Information	Remarks and references to Appendices
KEMMEL	3/6/15	Returned to trenches for 5 days. ~~1 officer~~ Killed 3 other ranks wounded 1 officer + 8 O.R. Head Quarters moved to HOWITZER FARM. Took over L2 + L3 & M1, M2 & VIERSTRAAT. 5 Shropshire L.I. attached	[illegible]
"	8/6/15	Relieved by 5th Battalion — to Bivouacs (all 4 companies)	[illegible]
	12/6/15	Returned to trenches for 4 days — 6th K.O.Y.L.I. (Major Rigg) attached for instruction. On 15th the enemy blew up J3 right and heavily bombarded the line. Chief casualties sustained by 8th Battalion & K.O.Y.L.I. — Killed 2 wounded 4 O.R.	[illegible]
	16/6/15	Relieved by 5th Battalion & returned to KEMMEL BIVOUACS	[illegible]
	19/6/15	Battalion addressed by Lt. Gen. SIR CHARLES FERGUSSON comdg 2nd Corps who praised the way the men had worked.	
	20/6/15	Left KEMMEL 9 pm having at 3 pm handed over bivouacs to 1st K.O.Y.L.I. (Major HEATHCOTE).	[illegible]
	21/6/15	In huts on OUDERDOM – VLAMERTINGHE Road.	
ZILLEBEKE	22/6/15	Took over trenches East of ZILLEBEKE from 4th YORKS. R. & 5th DURHAM L.I. Total casualties 1 officer (Lt JAMES) wounded. O.R. 1 killed 16 wounded	[illegible]
	29/6/15	Relieved by 5th LEICESTER REGT. Moved to farm between POPERINGHE & WESTOUTRE. Extracts from LONDON GAZETTE of 10 June 1915 Lieut V.O. ROBINSON – temp Capt	[illegible]
		" " " 14 " " C J WHEATCROFT " "	[illegible]

(9 29 6) W 3332– 1107 100,000 10/13 H W V Forms/C. 2118/10

139th Inf.Bde.
46th Div.

6th BATTN. THE SHERWOOD FORESTERS (NOTTINGHAMSHIRE AND DERBYSHIRE REGIMENT).

J U L Y

1 9 1 5

Instructions regarding War Diaries and Intelligence Summaries are contained in F.S. Regs., Part II. and the Staff Manual respectively. Title pages will be prepared in manuscript.

WAR DIARY or INTELLIGENCE SUMMARY.

(Erase heading not required.)

6/Sherwood Foresters

Army Form C. 2118.

Hour, Date, Place	Summary of Events and Information	Remarks and references to Appendices
29/6/15 BIVOUAC	LIEUT J.D.B. SYMONDS + 96 men joined from ENGLAND	
3/7/15. BIVOUAC	Lieut & Qmr. W.N. BROOMHEAD rejoined from ENGLAND.	F.B.S.
4/7/15 YPRÉS	Working party of 200 under Capt. E.H. HEATHCOTE shelled on return. 9 killed & died 21 wounded – 2 previously wounded.	F.B.S.
11/7/15 MAPLE COPSE	Battalion moved into Support (2 Cos.) & trenches A.6–9. East of ZILLEBEKE.	F.B.S.
18/7/15 do.	Handed over trenches and 2 companies (D & B) garrisoned R4 5 & 6 and remained in support SANCTUARY WOOD. – A & C in MAPLE COPSE.	F.B.S.
19/7/15 do.	HOOGE mine exploded – heavy bombardment.	F.B.S.
20/7/15 do.	Battalion stood to arms at night heavy bombardment.	F.B.S.
22/7/15 do.	CAPTS. F.M. DICK, E.B. JOHNSON and LIEUTS J.S. SAMPSON and G.L. PERCIVAL JOINED from England having joined bivouac day before. Casualties – wounded officers nil. O.R. killed 3 wounded 19.	F.B.S.
23/7/15 SANCTUARY WOOD	Took over A8–12 + B1 & B2 from 5th Battn.	F.B.S.
24/7/15 do.	10 West Yorks attached for instruction	F.B.S.
25/7/15 do.	German aeroplane shot down & observer fell in rear of our trenches	
27/7/15 do.	7 Border Regt attached for instruction	F.B.S.
29/7/15. BIVOUAC G.18 c 2.8	Moved to bivouac on relief by 5th Battn. O.R. 3 killed 12 wounded.	F.B.S.
	Early the next morning the enemy attacked at HOOGE and took trenches on left of our Brigade.	F.B.S.

(9 29 6) W 3332—1107 100,000 10/13 H W V Forms/C. 2118/10.

139th Inf.Bde.
46th Div.

6th BATTN. THE SHERWOOD FORESTERS (NOTTINGHAMSHIRE AND DERBYSHIRE REGIMENT).

A U G U S T

1 9 1 5

Instructions regarding War Diaries and Intelligence Summaries are contained in F. S. Regs., Part II. and the Staff Manual respectively. Title pages will be prepared in manuscript.

WAR DIARY
or
INTELLIGENCE SUMMARY.
(*Erase heading not required.*)

6th Sherwood Foresters

Army Form C. 2118.

Hour, Date, Place	Summary of Events and Information	Remarks and references to Appendices
3/8/15 MAPLE COPSE	Moved into support relieving 4/ Leicester Regt. Relieving in support of 8th Bttn in SANCTUARY WOOD very heavy bombardments on both sides.	[illegible]
5/8/15 SANCTUARY WOOD	Took over A8 – 12 & B1 B2 from 5th Bttn. Order of Companies ABCD [illegible] returned in MAPLE COPSE 1/2 2nd Bttn.	[illegible]
7/8/15 do.	Constructed [illegible] Bttn. Hd qrs. in field in rear of A12	[illegible]
8/8/15	[illegible] Lt K K MAUGHAN 2Lt BROWN 2Lt E V CREE joined	[illegible]
9/8/15 do.	Recapture of trenches at HOOGE. 2nd Battalion on right. 2nd Lieut W L BROWN joined.	[illegible]
19/8/15 do.	Relieved by [illegible] Royal Fusiliers Lt Col [illegible] (17th Brigade)	[illegible]
20/8/15 G 22 B. 8.2	Casualties 1 Lieut. [illegible] 2nd Lt W L BROWN wounded. O.R. Killed 8 Wounded 52 (died 2) Moved 1 AM into Bivouac G 22 B. 8.2. All Brigade out. Capt. C. R. Johnson took over Adjt. from Capt. E. J. [illegible] who had acted from 31/7/15 on Capt. Johnson going to hospital.	[illegible]
23/8/15 CANAL I. 33, 34 C	Took over 27. 28 29. BLUFF & 30 from 2/ SUFFOLK REGT (Major [illegible] TURNER) and 1/ GORDON HIGHrs (Lt W L BROWN) Hd qrs South of CANAL.	[illegible]
29/8/15	Relieved by 8th Bttn. Casualties O.R. Died of wounds 2 Much shelling during tour. Wounded 11	[illegible]
30/8/15 G 22 B. 8	Moved 1.45 AM into 2nd bivouac	[illegible]

(9 29 6) W 3332 1107 100,000 10/13 H W V Forms/C. 2118/10.

139th Inf.Bde.
46th Div.

6th BATTN. THE SHERWOOD FORESTERS (NOTTINGHAMSHIRE AND DERBYSHIRE REGIMENT).

S E P T E M B E R

1 9 1 5

Army Form C. 2118.

Instructions regarding War Diaries and Intelligence Summaries are contained in F. S. Regs., Part II. and the Staff Manual respectively. Title pages will be prepared in manuscript.

WAR DIARY of 6th Bn Sherwood Foresters. ~~INTELLIGENCE SUMMARY.~~

(*Erase heading not required.*)

Hour, Date, Place		Summary of Events and Information	Remarks and references to Appendices
2. 9. 15.	BUSSEBOOM.	Moved to Bivouac at OUDERDOM.	
4. 9. 15.	OUDERDOM	Lt Gen Sir H.C.O. Plumer inspected Battn.	
4. 9. 15	CANAL I33.	Took over trenches from 5th Bn (27. 28. 29. 30S & R11)	
11. 9. 15		LONDON GAZETTE. Corpl W.A. Lyttle to be Sec. Lieut 17. 9. 15.	
22. 9. 15		Bn relieved by 5th Bn & moved to Bivouac. Casualties:- Killed. O.R. 7 Wounded:- 2/Lt J. Sampson (6. 9. 15) Lt D. Storrs 7 or 9. 9. 15 & 11 Other Rks.	
24. 9. 15		Bn stood-to until 25th in consequence of attack by 5th Corps.	
25. 9. 15.		2/Lt W.L. BROWN killed in action	
28. 9. 15		Bn inspected by Major Gen Stuart Wortley.	
28. 9. 15.		Took over trenches from 5th Bn (27. 28. 29. 30S & R11)	
30. 9. 15.		Enemy shelled very heavily SPOIL BANK & trenches in afternoon and at 6.35pm exploded a mine under trench 29 & right of Angle Trench. Casualties resulting from this were:- KILLED 4 Other Rks. MISSING, BELIEVED KILLED 1 Off. (2nd Lt L.G. DICKINSON) & 12 Other Rks. WOUNDED 24 Other Rks. Continuous shelling of all our trenches	
30. 9. 15		Bn relieved by 7th LINCOLNS & 7th E YORKS and moved into bivouac at Transport Lines. Casualties, other than those above stated:- WOUNDED 3 Other Rks (including 1 accidental).	

139th Inf.Bde.
46th Div.

6th BATTN. THE SHERWOOD FORESTERS (NOTTINGHAMSHIRE AND DERBYSHIRE REGIMENT).

O C T O B E R

1 9 1 5

Instructions regarding War Diaries and Intelligence Summaries are contained in F. S. Regs., Part II. and the Staff Manual respectively. Title pages will be prepared in manuscript.

WAR DIARY or ~~INTELLIGENCE SUMMARY.~~ 6/Sherwood Foresters

(Erase heading not required.)

Army Form C. 2118.

Hour, Date, Place	Summary of Events and Information	Remarks and references to Appendices
6.30pm 1. 10. 15. ABEELE	Battn (less transport) entrained for FOUQUEREUIL.	G.D.G.
9.30pm " FOUQUEREUIL	Detrained and marched into BETHUNE and billeted in French Barracks. Division now joined 1st ARMY, 11th CORPS, the latter comprising GUARDS and 12th and 46th Divisions under Lt Gen. HAKING C.B.	G.D.G.
3. 10. 15	Battn moved to Billets at HINGES.	G.D.G.
4. 10. 15 HINGES	Bn (less details) embussed for SAILLY LA BOURSE, and from there marched to trenches N. of LOOS, where the Bn was employed converting old German trenches. Casualty:- 1 man killed.	G.D.G.
5. 10. 15 HINGES	Details proceeded to MAZINGARBE, and joined Bn who came out of trenches and billeted in MAZINGARBE	
6. 10. 15 MAZINGARBE	Bn moved to billets at FOUQUEREUIL. 2nd Lt H.W. HIGHAM joined for duty.	G.D.G.
8. 10. 15 FOUQUEREUIL.	Lt T. L. DARBYSHIRE to Hospital sick. Ordered to stand to 7pm. Stand down 11pm. (Counter attack on Guards' Division)	G.D.G.
9. 10. 15 "	Lt J.D.B. SYMONDS transferred to A.S.C. with effect from 19/8/15.	G.D.G.
11. 10. 15 "	2Lt J.G.J. HUTTON joined for duty.	G.D.G.
12. 10. 15 "	Capt E.B JOHNSON to Hospital sick. Capt C.T. WHEATCROFT to command "D" Coy.	G.D.G. G.D.G.

Instructions regarding War Diaries and Intelligence Summaries are contained in F. S. Regs., Part II. and the Staff Manual respectively. Title pages will be prepared in manuscript.

WAR DIARY

or ~~INTELLIGENCE~~ SUMMARY. Continued 6th Sherwood Fosters

(*Erase heading not required.*)

Army Form C. 2118.

Hour, Date, Place	Summary of Events and Information	Remarks and References to Appendices
12. 10. 15. FOUQUEREUIL	Bn (less details) moved out in fighting order and occupied support trenches East of VERMELLES branching off GORDON ALLEY and HULLUCK ALLEY.	E.B.J.
13. 10. 15	46th DIVISION attacked enemy trenches on a line from DUMP TRENCH to North of HOHENZOLLERN REDOUBT. 137th Brigade on Right 138th Brigade on Left 139th Bde in Reserve. At 12 noon Battalion came under orders of 137th Brigade to which it was in immediate support. Artillery opened at noon – gas attack at 1.0 pm Infantry attacked at 2 pm. ~~B~~ A Company (Capt. V.O. Robinson) moved to front line trenches B (Capt. Dick) & D (Capt. Wheatcroft) ordered to push on to DUMP supporting S. STAFFORDS but MAJOR BLACKWALL found attack unsuccessful & kept them in trenches. All Companies (less 3 platoons & M.G.) eventually in front line and immediate support trenches. Great congestion in trenches owing to evacuation of wounded & carriage of S.A.A. & bombs. Battn Remainder under 2/Lt LYTLE then attacked BIG WILLIE but attack unsuccessful.	E.B.J.
~~14. 10. 15.~~ 14. 10. 15	Battn. relieved by GUARDS and ordered to take over HOHENZOLLERN REDOUBT West face which had been captured. Owing to lateness of relief only 3 platoons & 3 M. Gun teams ~~[illegible]~~ arrived before dawn & these were kept with 5th Bn S.F. who took over. Capt. HEATHCOTE with them	E.B.J.
15. 10. 15.	Major J.E. BLACKWALL took over ~~to~~ command of 8th Sherwood Foresters vice Lt Col. G.H. FOWLER (killed in action)	
15. 10. 15.	Total casualties Officers wounded 2. (2/Lts PERCIVAL & GARDNER) O. Ranks killed 13 missing believed killed 1 wounded 48. Bn moved to billets at VERQUIN.	E.B.J.
16. 10. 15. VERQUIN	Details joined Bn. CAPT. E.M.B. TAYLOR to command C Coy.	E.B.J.
17. 10. 15 "	Draft of 50 N.C.O's & men joined from Entrenching Bn.	E.B.J.
18. 10. 15 "	2Lt W.H. HOLDERNESS joined for duty.	E.B.J.
18. 10. 15 "	Bn addressed by Maj. Gen. STUART WORTLEY.	E.B.J.
19. 10. 15	Capt E.B. JOHNSON rejoined.	E.B.J.
	Moved to LAPUGNOY.	E.B.J.

(9 29 6) W 3332—1107 100,000 10/13 H W V Forms/C. 2118/10.

Instructions regarding War Diaries and Intelligence Summaries are contained in F. S. Regs., Part II. and the Staff Manual respectively. Title pages will be prepared in manuscript.

WAR DIARY
or
~~INTELLIGENCE~~ SUMMARY.

(*Erase heading not required.*)

6 Sherwood Foresters.

Army Form C. 2118.

Hour, Date, Place	Summary of Events and Information	Remarks and References to Appendices
21. 10. 15 LAPUGNOY.	120 men & 10 Officers forming part of Brigade fatigue party under Capt E. H. HEATHCOTE proceeded in Busses to LA BOURSE and were billeted at SAILLY LA BOURSE, and were employed in removing gas apparatus from trenches.	
24. 10. 15	Lt Col G. D. GOODMAN to temp Command of 139th Bde. Capt F. M. DICK to Command Bn.	[illegible]
25. 10. 15 "	Fatigue party relieved by a similar party.	[illegible]
	CAPT A. J. HOPKINS & Lt J. TOLSON joined for duty.	[illegible]
26. 10. 15 "	CAPT A. J. HOPKINS took command of Bn.	[illegible]
	Bn moved to new billets in BETHUNE.	[illegible]
28 10 15 BETHUNE "	H.M. King inspected 1st Army. Bn provided 1 full Company & 1 full platoon towards 139th Bde representative Bn, which was commanded by Lt Col G. D. GOODMAN.	[illegible]
29. 10. 15 "	His Majesty's horse reared & fell at inspection of ROYAL FLYING CORPS. 2nd Fatigue party returned	[illegible]
30. 10. 15 "	T. Lt K. H. BOND joined for duty. Draft of 15 N.C.O's & men arrived from No 2 Entrenching Bn.	[illegible] [illegible]

(9 29 6) W 3332—1107 100,000 10/13 H W V Forms/C. 2118/10.

139th Inf.Bde.
46th Div.

6th BATTN. THE SHERWOOD FORESTERS (NOTTINGHAMSHIRE AND DERBYSHIRE REGIMENT).

N O V E M B E R

1 9 1 5

Attached:

Appendix I.

Instructions regarding War Diaries and Intelligence Summaries are contained in F. S. Regs., Part II. and the Staff Manual respectively. Title pages will be prepared in manuscript.

WAR DIARY
of 6th Bn Sherwood Foresters

~~INTELLIGENCE SUMMARY.~~
(Erase heading not required.)

Army Form C. 2118.

Hour, Date, Place	Summary of Events and Information	Remarks and References to Appendices
BETHUNE 1. 11. 15.	2Lt. W D JAMIESON reported for duty.	GBh
" 3. 11. 15.	Draft of 35 Other ranks arrived.	GBh
" 4. 11. 15.	Bn moved into Billets at PACAUT.	GBh
PACAUT 5. 11. 15.	Notification received that Capt Y O ROBINSON had been awarded the MILITARY CROSS for conspicuous gallantry at HOHENZOLLERN REDOUBT between the 13th & 15th Oct. The award is announced in the Supplement to the London Gazette of 18. 11. 15.	GBh
" 6. 11. 15.	Bn moved into Brigade Reserve at LA COUTURE, the 46th Divn having taken over the trench line on the right of NEUVE CHAPELLE.	GBh
" 6. 11. 15.	Capt E. B JOHNSON proceeded to Base Depot and relieved Capt G.S. Heathcote 8th Bn Sherwood Foresters	GBh
LA COUTURE 9. 11. 15.	Bn relieved 3rd LONDON REGT in BACK POSTS in rear of RIGHT SECTOR.	GBh
" 9. 11. 15.	Bn provided working party of 7 Officers & 250 Other Ranks for the repair of the OLD BRITISH FIRE TRENCH	GBh
" 10. 11. 15.	Draft of 16 Other Ranks arrived.	GBh
" 10. 11. 15.	Bn relieved 5th SHERWOOD FORESTERS in RIGHT SECTOR. (RIGHT SUBSECTION)	GBh
" 13. 11. 15.	Bn was relieved by 5th LEICESTERS, and moved into billets as follows:- A B & D Coy & details to LA COUTURE. C Coy remained in the line. Casualties - O.R. Killed 1 Wounded 1	GBh
14. 11. 15.	C Coy relieved by 7th Sherwood Foresters and joined Bn at LA COUTURE.	GBh
14. 11. 15.	2Lt T GRIMSHAW & 20 Other Ranks arrived.	GBh

Army Form C. 2118.

Instructions regarding War Diaries and Intelligence Summaries are contained in F. S. Regs., Part II. and the Staff Manual respectively. Title pages will be prepared in manuscript.

WAR DIARY of 6th Bn Sherwood Foresters. INTELLIGENCE SUMMARY.

(*Erase heading not required.*)

Hour, Date, Place	Summary of Events and Information	Remarks and References to Appendices
LA COUTURE. 17. 11. 15	2/Lt Y. T. G. HORE reported for duty.	E.B.L.
17. 11. 15	Bn relieved 7th SHERWOOD FORESTERS in LEFT SECTOR about 300 yds S. of ESTAIRES – LA BASSEE ROAD.	E.B.L.
20. 11. 15	Bn relieved by 7th SHERWOOD FORESTERS ~~[illegible]~~ in LEFT SECTOR and moved into Billets at LA COUTURE. Casualties. Wounded. OR. 2.	E.B.L.
23. 11. 15.	Bn relieved 8th SHERWOOD FORESTERS in RIGHT SECTOR	E.B.L.
23. 11. 15	Capt E. H. HEATHCOTE attached to 8th SHERWOOD FORESTERS for duty	E.B.L.
25. 11. 15	Major E HALL reported for duty. from England	E.B.L.
25. 11. 15	Bombing enterprise undertaken by 2/Lt M. A. LYTLE + bombers on German Trenches. See report herewith.	E.B.L. Appendix No I
27. 11. 15.	Bn relieved by 7th SHERWOOD FORESTERS and moved into Billets at VIELLE CHAPELLE. Casualties. – OR Killed 3 Wounded 7.	E.B.L.
VIELLE CHAPELLE. 28. 11. 15	2/Lt N. H. HOLDERNESS to Hospital sick.	E.B.L.
30. 11. 15.	Bn relieved 7th SHERWOOD FORESTERS in RIGHT SECTOR	E.B.L.

(9 29 6) W 3332—1107 100,000 10/13 H W V Forms/C. 2118/10.

A P P E N D I X   I.

War Diary Nov 1915
Appendix No 1

REPORT ON BOMBING ENTERPRISE.

Reference.
TRENCH MAP.

From, O.C. 6th Battalion, Sherwood Foresters.

To,

Headquarters,

139th Infantry Brigade.

I beg to report that in accordance with Operation Order No. 32 of 26th instant, ~~an~~ Bombing enterprise was undertaken by grenadiers of my Battalion under 2/nd Lieut. W.A.LYTLE on the evening of that day, the objective being the small German Salient about S.16.a.2.7. adjoining the BOAR'S HEAD Trench.

On the previous evening the North & South sides of this salient had been reconnoitred by 2 N.C.O's patrols it being the intention if possible to attack from both sides simultaneously. The patrol on the North however reported that on that side the enemy's wire was good and the parapet sound.

It was therefore decided to attack only from the South where the N.C.O. No. 1631, Lance Sergt M.LIMB reported that the wire had been very well cut and that there were several gaps in the parapet. This report was found to be accurate in every particular.

Shortly before 7.30 p.m. on the 26th inst. 2/nd Lieut. LYTLE'S party was formed up at S.16.a.2.5. It consisted of 10 Grenadiers, each carrying 10, and 10 bayonet men each carrying 5 Mills ~~Grenadiers~~ Grenades together with a Machine Gunner to dismantle a Machine Gun if found.

All the party wore steel helmets.

A Machine Gun had been firing on the broken wire from S.16.a.2.5. since 5 p.m. In addition to the usual garrison of BOARS HEAD, 8 extra grenadiers were stationed there to render any needful assistance - under an Officer - while the Company ~~Grenadiers~~ Commander moved up to the Telephone station at S.16.a.0.6 inorder to supervise.

At 7-30 p.m. the attacking party left the trench. A Corporal and 2 men were sent to ascertain that the German wire was still passable while the remainder followed in single file moving along the S.E. side of the BOARS HEAD. The moon was rising and the night was bright. The going was very bad - the ground being very bad and wet, cut up with ditches and shell holes and about 20 bodies lying about. When the party arrived at about 20 yards fromthe German wire, the patrol reported that the wire was passabl -ble. At 8-45 p.m. the whole party lay opposite the enemy's trench at about S.16.a.4.6½. They could hear whistling and talking from about 3 sentries who were standing up, and other men who were in the trench.

At a given signal, all rose and doubled across the German wire which was about 15' from the trench. As soon as the wire was crossed a Sentry challenged in English "Halt, who goes there?" This caused a moments hesitation but German voices were heard the men threw their bombs (all landing in the trench) and rushed at the parapet. Immediately the enemy threw about 6 bombs which were mostly high. 2/Lieut.LYTLE and 2 N.C.O's were knocked down and partly stunned by the explosion but were unhurt and rejoined their comrades.

Nearly all the party reached the top of the parapet and two got into the trench. Three Germans were bayonetted. Most of our men ran about the parapet throwing in bombs and the trench was a mass of flame. The enemy ran towards both ends of the trench "Squealing"- many of them without arms or equipment. Gradually they formed parties on the flanks and threw a consid--erable number of bombs and as there did not seem to be a reasonable chance of doing further damage without suffering serious loss, our party withdrew, returning for the lost part by the way they came though a few lost direction and got into the British Line further South.

From a check taken of the bombs that remained it appears that over 95 bombs were thrown by our men, and from the comparatively crowded state of the trench 2/nd Lieut. LYTLE is satisfied that the enemy must have suffered considerable loss.

Our casualties consisted of 1 man missing - he was last seen in the trench throwing bombs - and 3 men wounded (2 slightly)

The enemy were obviously taken by surprise but had a considerable number of bombs at hand which they were able to seize at once on an attack. It seems clear that they rely almost exclusively on these - There was hardly any rifle fire and no Machine Guns fired on our party, in fact some of the party walked back after clear of the German Trench. They did not run and were not fired upon.

A man who got into the Enemy's trench reports that the bottom of the trench was knee deep in mud, but there were good fire steps. He observed no Dug-outs. There were at least 6 fires in braziers in the length of trench attacked.

2/nd Lieut. LYTLE reports that none of our grenades were defective. He noticed that the German Grenade had a much greater explosive force but that they are not so effective as the Mills Grenade, there being fewer splinters. He had noticed the samething at BIG WILLIE in October. He was struck on the head with one splinter, but was saved from any ill effect by his stell helmet, which appears to be a most valuable article of equipment.

The Artillery carried out their part of the programme most effectively. As the attack took so much longer to develop than was expected (owing to the bad going) I requested the Batteries to continue their fire, which they did until the party returned at about 9.30 p.m.

I should like to bring the name of 2/Lieut.W.A.LYTLE to the favourable notice of the G. O. C. He organised the attack with ability and diplayed great coolness throughout. I also consider that he shewed good judgement in withdrawing at a point when he would otherwise have sustained a serious loss. I have previously mentioned his name in connection with the attack on BIG WILLIE on the 13th/14th October last when he displayed great coolness and disregard of danger in leading his grenadiers.

The following N.C O's and men have also done excellent work :-

No.1631 L/Sergt.M.LIMB.

No.3627 L/Cpl.M.C.RUST.

(the above were in charge of the patrols on the previous night and shewed great gallantry in the attack)

No.1920 L/Cpl.B.KENSEY.

No.1891 Pte. P.MARPER.

No.3065 Pte. J.BROWN (missing)

No.4316 Pte. J.CROXHALL.

/sd/ G.D.GOODMAN.Lieut-Col.

Commanding, 6th Sherwood Foresters. (T.F.)

3 a.m.

27/11/15.

139th Inf.Bde.
46th Div.

6th BATTN. THE SHERWOOD FORESTERS (NOTTINGHAMSHIRE AND DERBYSHIRE REGIMENT).

D E C E M B E R

1 9 1 5

Instructions regarding War Diaries and Intelligence Summaries are contained in F. S. Regs., Part II. and the Staff Manual respectively. Title pages will be prepared in manuscript.

WAR DIARY of 6th Bn SHERWOOD FORESTERS
INTELLIGENCE SUMMARY.
(*Erase heading not required.*)

Army Form C. 2118.

Hour, Date, Place		Summary of Events and Information	Remarks and references to Appendices
3.12.15	LACOUTURE	GAZETTE. Major J.E. BLACKWALL of 6th Bn Sherwood Foresters is transferred to the 8th Bn Sherwood Foresters dated 16th Oct 1915 & promoted temp Lt Col.	G.D.G.
3.12.15	TRENCHES	Battn relieved in RIGHT SECTOR by 9th WELSH REGT, and went into billets at RICHEBOURG the 46th Division being under orders for EGYPT	G.D.G.
4.12.15	RICHEBOURG & LACOUTURE	Battn marched into billets at ROBECQ, with HQrs at P.22.C.0.3 (Map BETHUNE Comb Sheet). In addition the usual transport the Battn had the use of 2 motor lorries for the conveyance of the men's fur coats, clean clothing &c.	G.D.G.
6.12.15	ROBECQ	2/Lt T.H. CASH reported for duty from 3rd Entrenching Battn	G.D.G.
7.12.15	ROBECQ	G.O.C. Division inspected the Battalion	G.D.G.
		Christmas gifts from the people of Nottingham distributed to the Officers and men of the Battalion	G.D.G.
		Draft of 53 Other Ranks arrived from 4th Entrenching Battn	G.D.G.
8.12.15	ROBECQ	Fur coats handed in to ordnance, together with all special issue winter clothing	G.D.G.
		2nd Lt G.F. GARDNER and 13 other ranks arrived from Base	G.D.G.
12.12.15	ROBECQ	Draft of 5? Other Ranks arrived from Base	G.D.G.
16.12.15	ROBECQ		G.D.G.
23.12.15	ROBECQ	Battn moved into billets at BOESEGHEM	
24.12.15	BOESEGHEM	GAZETTE. 2/Lt W.A. LYTLE awarded MILITARY CROSS for Conspicuous Gallantry on 25.11.15 at BOARS HEAD. Plum puddings given by the Daily News issued to the troops.	G.D.G.
25.12.15	BOESEGHEM	£20 given by 2nd Line Battalion toward Xmas dinner. CHRISTMAS DAY Xmas dinners arranged for the men by Coys & Details	G.D.G.
26.12.15	BOESEGHEM	Battn moved to ISBERGUES and occupied billets vacated by 5th Bn NORTH STAFFS REGT.	G.D.G.
29.12.15	ISBERGUES	Observed as a Holiday throughout the Brigade	G.D.G.
30.12.15	ISBERGUES	PROMOTION No [illegible] C.S.M. BROWNE, 6th Sherwood Foresters to be 2nd Lieut in the 2nd Bn Sherwood Foresters d/- [illegible]	G.D.G.

G.D. Goodman Lt Col.

(9 29 6) W 3332—1107 100,000 10/13 H W V Forms/C. 2118/10.

1

Army Form C. 2118.

Instructions regarding War Diaries and Intelligence Summaries are contained in F. S. Regs., Part II. and the Staff Manual respectively. Title pages will be prepared in manuscript.

WAR DIARY
of 6th Bn Sherwood Foresters
~~INTELLIGENCE SUMMARY.~~
(Erase heading not required.)

Hour, Date, Place		Summary of Events and Information	Remarks and references to Appendices
1. 1. 1916	ISBERGUES.	Observed as a Holiday throughout the Brigade	GDG
2. 1. 1916	"	Notification received that {Lt Col G.D. GOODMAN, Capt. V.O. ROBINSON, Regl Sr H.H. JACKMAN, Pte J. HAMER} had been mentioned in Sir John French's despatches.	GDG
4. 1. 1916	PROMOTIONS	CQMS J.E. BARKER & Cpl F.W.A STUBBS to be 2nd LIEUTS dated 18.12.15.	GDG
6. 1. 1916.	ISBERGUES.	Battn less Regt Transport entrained 10.41pm at BERGUETTE STATION	GDG
7. 1. 1916		2/Lt H.W. HOLDERNESS granted 3 weeks sick leave to England.	GDG
9. 1. 1916	MARSEILLES.	Battn less Transport detrained at 8 am and marched into SANTI CAMP	GDG
9. 1. 1916	"	Capt E.B JOHNSON rejoined for duty with Bn from Base.	GDG
LONDON GAZETTE:- of 6. 1 1916		Capt A.J. HOPKINS to be Tempy Major d/- Oct 23rd	
		Lieut H.H. JACKSON to be Tempy Captain d/- Oct 23rd	
of 7. 1. 1916		Capt E.H HEATHCOTE to be Tempy Major d/- Sept 13rd	GDG
		Lieut F.B. ROBINSON} Lieut J. TOLSON} to be Tempy Captains d/- 3rd Sept	
		To be Tempy Lieuts:- 2nd Lt C.A BROWN. 30th Aug	
		" A.B. WALLIS 17th Sept.	
		" G.F. GARDNER 21st Sept.	
		H.W. HIGHAM 17th Oct.	
		C.E.V. CREE. 20th Oct	
10. 1. 16.	ISBERGUES	Regt Transport entrained at BERGUETTE Station	GDG
~~11. 1. 16~~	~~MARSEILLES.~~	~~Rev S M WHEELER reported for duty as Chaplain~~	GDG
13. 1. 16	LONDON GAZETTE	No 2006 Pte A. WRIGHT awarded Distinguished Conduct Medal for gallantry.	GDG
13. 1. 16	"	Transport arrived and detrained and were camped at BORELI CAMP.	GDG
14. 1. 16	"	2nd Lts R. EVANS, M.R.K BION, F.W. HIPKINS, & G.H. KNOWLES joined from 3/6th Bn for duty	GDG
14th & 15th		Battn (Officers & other Ranks) vaccinated. Percentage vaccinated 97%.	GDG

Instructions regarding War Diaries and Intelligence Summaries are contained in F. S. Regs., Part II. and the Staff Manual respectively. Title pages will be prepared in manuscript.

WAR DIARY II
of 6th Bn Sherwood Foresters
~~INTELLIGENCE~~ SUMMARY.
(*Erase heading not required.*)

Army Form C. 2118.

Hour, Date, Place	Summary of Events and Information	Remarks and references to Appendices
26.1.16 MARSEILLES	Batn, complete with Transport entrained 8.55 pm at GUIBAL Station	G.D.G.
28.1.16 PONT REMY	Bn detrained at 4 am and marched into billets vacated & handed over by 5th Bn S. LANCS Regt at COULONVILLERS, having joined the 14th Corps commanded by Lt Gen the Earl of Cavan.	G.D.G.

G. D. Goodman Lt Colonel
Cdg 6th Bn Sherwood Foresters

(9 29 6) W 3332—1107 100,000 10/13 H W V Forms/C. 2118/10.

Army Form C. 2118.

Instructions regarding War Diaries and Intelligence Summaries are contained in F. S. Regs., Part II. and the Staff Manual respectively. Title pages will be prepared in manuscript.

WAR DIARY
of 6th Bn Sherwood Foresters.
~~INTELLIGENCE~~ SUMMARY.
(Erase heading not required.)

Hour, Date, Place	Summary of Events and Information	Remarks and references to Appendices
3. 2. 16. COULONVILLERS.	Brigade Ceremonial Parade at GORENFLOS. 4 Lewis Guns received for Lewis Detachment.	
	LONDON GAZETTE (Supplement). d/- 14. 1. 1916. – No 2006 Private WRIGHT. A, 1/6th Bn Nottinghamshire & Derbyshire Regt (T. F). AWARDED DISTINGUISHED CONDUCT MEDAL.	E.H.
4. 2. 16 COULONVILLERS.	2nd Lt S. G. J. HUTTON to Hospital.	E.H.
10. 2. 16 COULONVILLERS.	Bn marched into Billets at BEAUMETZ.	E.H.
10. 2. 16 BEAUMETZ.	Letter of thanks received by Lt Col GOODMAN (through the Foreign Office) from FRAU ROSER, wife of CAPTAIN ROSER who fell from a German Aeroplane by SANCTUARY WOOD on 25th JULY 1915 and was buried by the Battalion, his flight badge having been sent to his Widow.	E.H. See War Diary for JULY 1915.
11. 2. 16 BEAUMETZ.	2/Lt W. H. HOLDERNESS rejoined on expiry of sick leave in England.	E.H.
12. 2. 16 BEAUMETZ.	2Lt V. T. G. MORE to Transport Course HAVRE.	E.H.
13. 2. 16 BEAUMETZ.	Capt E. TOLSON, Capt M. H. JACKSON & 1 Sergt to 3rd ARMY SCHOOL of INSTRUCTION.	E.H.
14. 2. 16 BEAUMETZ.	LIEUT D. S. FOX arrived from England, and took over command of Lewis Gun Detachment.	E.H.
16. 2. 16 BEAUMETZ.	Lt G. F. GARDNER, 2Lt T. GRIMSHAW & 36 Other Ranks from Bn Machine Gun Section proceeded to join 139th Bde M. G. Company.	E.H.
19. 2. 16 BEAUMETZ	Bn moved into Billets at PUCHEVILLERS	E.H.
19. 2. 16 BEAUMETS	Lts C. E. V. CREE & A. B. WALLIS to 46th Divl SCHOOL of INSTRUCTION.	E.H.

Army Form C. 2118.

Instructions regarding War Diaries and Intelligence Summaries are contained in F. S. Regs., Part II. and the Staff Manual respectively. Title pages will be prepared in manuscript.

WAR DIARY II
of 6th Bn Sherwood Foresters
~~INTELLIGENCE~~ SUMMARY.

(*Erase heading not required.*)

Hour, Date, Place	Summary of Events and Information	Remarks and references to Appendices
20. 2. 16 to 28 2. 16. PUCHEVILLERS.	The Battn provided an average of 360 men per day, with complement of Officers and NCOs for fatigue and working parties under R.E. on the new line (Sector CANDAS - BELLE EGLISE)	E.H.
25. 2. 16 PUCHEVILLERS	2/Lt J.E. BARKER proceeded to BOULOGNE for Dental Treatment	E.H.
27. 2. 16. PUCHEVILLERS	Lt Col G.D. GOODMAN proceeded to advanced Officers Course at FLIXECOURT.	E.H.
29. 2. 16 PUCHEVILLERS.	Bn moved to Billets at BEAUVAL.	E.H.

E Hall Major
Comdg 6th Bn Sherwood Foresters

(9 29 6) W 3332–1107 100,000 10/13 H W V Forms/C. 2118/10

Appendices to War Diary of 6th Bn Sherwood Foresters for March 1916

A. Instructions for attack

B Orders for attack

C. Message from G.O.C.

Instructions regarding War Diaries and Intelligence Summaries are contained in F. S. Regs., Part II. and the Staff Manual respectively. Title pages will be prepared in manuscript.

WAR DIARY

of 6th Bn Sherwood Foresters.

~~INTELLIGENCE SUMMARY~~.

(*Erase heading not required.*)

Army Form C. 2118.

Hour, Date, Place		Summary of Events and Information	Remarks and references to Appendices
BEAUVAL.	6. 3. 1916.	Battn moved into Billets at IVERGNY.	G.D.G.
IVERGNY	6. 3. 1916.	Lt V.T.G. HORE rejoined from Transport Course at HAVRE.	G.D.G.
	7. 3. 1916	SHROVE TUESDAY football in village. Football presented by Ashbourne Committee, 1st goal by Private Robinson 'C' Comp'y	G.D.G.
IVERGNY	8. 3. 1916	Battn moved into Billets at MAIZIERES.	
MAIZIERES.	9. 3. 1916.	Battn moved into Billets at MONT ST ELOY.	G.D.G.
MONT ST ELOY	10. 3. 1916	Bn proceeded to trenches and relieved the 125th Regiment (Lt Col MADELIN) (FRENCH ARMY) in the RIGHT SECTOR. (opposite LA FOLIE FARM). Flanks:- ~~6th Bn Somerset Regt~~ 50th French Regt on right. 5th Bn SHERWOOD FORESTERS on left.	G.D.G.
MONT ST ELOY.	13. 3. 1916	Capts TOLSON & JACKSON rejoined Bn from 3rd Army School.	
MONT ST ELOY.	14. 3. 1916	Capt C.J. WHEATCROFT proceeded to CENTRAL TRAINING SCHOOL, ROUEN, and Capt E.M. BROOKE-TAYLOR took over command & payment of "C" Company	
MONT ST ELOY.	16. 3. 1916.	Draft of 142 men arrived as re-inforcements from 3rd line.	G.D.G.
MONT ST ELOY.	20. 3 1916	Q.M. Stores & Transport lines moved to CAPPEL FERMONT.	G.D.G.
TRENCHES.	22. 3 1916	Bn relieved by 5th SHERWOOD FORESTERS in trenches, and marched into Billets & Hutments at ACQ. 12 days tour. Casualties during tour of duty:- KILLED ... O.R. 3. DIED OF WOUNDS O.R. 1. WOUNDED ... O.R. 11	G.D.G.

(9 29 6) W 3332–1107 100,000 10/13 H W V Forms/C. 2118/10.

Army Form C. 2118.

Instructions regarding War Diaries and Intelligence Summaries are contained in F. S. Regs., Part II. and the Staff Manual respectively. Title pages will be prepared in manuscript.

WAR DIARY II
of 6th Bn. Sherwood Foresters. ~~INTELLIGENCE SUMMARY~~.

(*Erase heading not required.*)

Hour, Date, Place	Summary of Events and Information	Remarks and references to Appendices
ACQ. 25-3.16.	A & B Companies under Capts E.B. JOHNSON & J. TOLSON proceeded to trenches for 6 hours work in marching order without packs. On arrival at the trenches they were detained as the 5th Battalion had attempted to seize the near lip of a crater caused by enemy mine explosion early that day, and had been driven back by enemy bomb attack. About 11 pm. Lt Col. GOODMAN was ordered to proceed to the trenches and organise an attack with these two Companies. Capt DICK, 2 Lieuts BOND & LYTLE with Bn. Grenadiers & Scouts also proceeded to the trenches. Brig. Gen. SHIPLEY C.B. and the Brigade Major were also there. It was found impossible to launch ~~before~~ the attack before dawn & on reference to the Division it was postponed.	
TRENCHES 26-3-16	The attack was organised in accordance with instructions. Greatcoats were sent up for the men in the evening also a hot meal. Owing to unavoidable delays in carrying meal the attacking party did not commence to dig until about 2 pm. Operations were conducted with the utmost quietness and by dawn a trench 3' deep had been dug ~~at~~ on the near lip of the crater linking up existing trenches, and this without a single casualty. It was snowing at times & the men throughout the 48 hours bore great discomfort very cheerfully. The Bn. Lewis guns arrived under Lt FOX.	G.D.G. Appendix A Instructions for attack. B Orders for attack C Message from G.O.C.
ACQ. 27-3-16.	The detachment returned to billets in the evening.	G.D.G.
ACQ. 27-3-16	2/Lt R. EVANS to 46th Div School.	G.D.G.
ACQ 27-3-16	Bn relieved 5th SHERWOOD FORESTERS in RIGHT SECTOR.	
FERMONT CAPPEL 31-3-16	Draft of 122 Other Ranks arrived from 3rd line as re-inforcements.	G.D.G. G.D. Goodman Lt Col. Comdg 6th Sherwood Foresters.

(9 29 6) W 3332—1107 100,000 10/13 H W V Forms/C. 2118/10.

"C" Form (Duplicate). Army Form C. 2123.

MESSAGES AND SIGNALS. No. of Message ....

AB KG RYB BRS	Charges to Pay. £ s. d.	Office Stamp.
Service Instructions. Priority JdL		

Handed in at .... Office 10.30p m. Received 10.55p m.

TO: Advanced KJB

Sender's Number	Day of Month	In reply to Number	AAA
G830	26th		

The G.O.C. considers disposition for attack excellent and relies on 6th Sherwood Foresters to retrieve the situation knowing the excellent work always performed by them

FROM: 46th Divn

PLACE & TIME: 10.30pm

Wt. 9771/4004. 75,000 Pads. 10/15. McC. & Co., Ltd., London. Forms/C.2123.

A

SECRET.
******

Instructions issued verbally to Lieut-Colonel G.D.GOODMAN, 6th Battalion Sherwood Foresters, and other Officers concerned.

---

1. Two Companies of the 6th Battalion Sherwood Foresters under command of Lieut-Colonel GOODMAN will attack and occupy the near lip of the Crater adjacent to the end of BIRKIN COMMUNICATION TRENCH tonight the 26th/27th March.

2. The exact hour for the attack will be fixed by the Officer above mentioned.

3. The following will co-operate in this attack and are placed under the command of Lieut-Colonel GOODMAN.

    (i) 2 Guns, Z.46th Trench Mortar Battery.

    (ii) 139/1 Light Trench Mortar Battery.

4. The Centre Group R.F.A. will co-operate in the attack by

    (a) Firing intermittent Salvoes on the Crater, commencing at 6.30 p.m. until up to half an hour of the attack.

    (b) Covering Fire in rear of the Crater as soon as the Infantry attack is launched.

    (c) Creating a Barrage on points already arranged whenever called on.

5. Two Companies of the 8th Battalion Sherwood Foresters will form a Reserve in the QUARRIES, ready to move at once any time after an hour which will be communicated to them.

6. Reports will be sent to the Battalion Headquarters RIGHT BATTALION in the QUARRIES where the Brigadier General Commanding 139th Infantry Brigade will be.

----------oOo-----------

(69)

Secret.

ORDERS

by

LIEUT COL. G.D. GOODMAN

for

ATTACK ON CRATER OPPOSITE FIRKIN C.T.

26/3/196

ENEMY. 1. Are believed to be entrenched on far lip of crater which is linked with their first line by old C.T's

OBJECTIVE. 2. Our object is to establish touch on the near lip of the crater so as to link up the disconnected portions of our front trench (DURAND)

ATTACK. 3. "B" Coy. 6th S.F. will be organised in 3 platoons 1 platoon with 4 grenadiers on each flank will occupy the forward retrenchment near the crater. At 11p.m. this party will advance as quietly as possible and occupy the near lip of the crater from trench to trench. This party will carry picks and shovels also wire netting rolled and fixed to stakes as already prepared. The latter they will at once fix as securely as possible so as to obtain protection from hand grenades and then dig a deep and narrow trench in rear of the palisade. Each man will carry two grenades.

Capt. J. Tolson
6th S.F.

FLANK. 4. The flanks will be protected by 2 parties

(a) Right.

Capt. Dick
6th S.F.

1. In COMMON C.T. in advance of DURAND.
   2 rifle grenadiers 6th S.F.
   4 grenadiers 6th S.F.
   1 Lewis gun 5th S.F.
2. In old C.T. running forward on right of COMMON.
   4 grenadiers 6th S.F.
   1 Lewis gun 5th S.F.
3. In trench running up to crater
   4 grenadiers 5th S.F.
4. In front line (DURAND) 1 platoon "B" Coy. 6th S.F.

(b) Left.

2/Lt. Parker
6th S.F.

1. In and near forward sap left of crater
   2 rifle grenadiers 6th S.F.
   1 Lewis gun 5th S.F.
2. In front line (DURAND)
   5 grenadiers 6th S.F.
   1 platoon "B" Coy 6th S.F.

SUPPORT. 5. "A" Coy. 6th S.F. in retrenchment between GRANBY and FIRKIN C.T's

Capt.
E.E. Johnson

RESERVE GRENADIERS. 6. Battn. grenadiers 6th S.F. in [illegible].75

ARTILLERY. 7. The 3rd N.Mid.Bde. will fire at intervals during the evening.
On an enemy counter attack they will establish a barrage on enemy's first line trenches.

TRENCH MORTARS. 8. At 5p.m. the Medium T.M.Batty and 139/1 T.M. Batty bombarde the crater.
On a counter attack these batteries will place a barrage on enemy's front line trenches and head of C.T. opposite crater.

RECONNAISSANCE. 9. At dusk the battn.Scouts 6th S.F. will reconnoitre flanks of crater and report on enemy's positions and communications.

MOVE. 10. "A" Coy. 6th S.F. will move from QUARRY trench at 9p.m. by GRANGE and file into retrenchment.
Left flanking party will move from same place at 9.15 p.m. by GRANGE to front line (DURAND).
Right flanking party will move from same place at 9.35 p.m. by GRANGE P.75 and BIRKIN.
Attacking party will move from same place at 10p.m. by GRANGE, P.75 and BIRKIN, filing into forward retrenchment.
8th.Battn grenadiers will follow last party into P.75.
O.C. 5th S.F. will please arrange for a free passage through P.75 so that his men in BIRKIN and beyond move forward with the right along front trench (DURAND)

RATIONS. 11. A day's rations will be carried and a hot meal provided for 6th S.F. before moving.

REPORT. 12. O.C's detachments willreport arrival in positions and will render constant reports by runners.

7.30 p.m. 13. I shall be at telephone on left of BIRKIN C.T.

G. D. Goodman Lt.Col.
Comdg 6/Sherwood Foresters

Copy No 1 to 5th Sherwood Foresters
- 2 - 139th Infy Brigade
- 3 - Retd to officers comdg parties

Instructions regarding War Diaries and Intelligence Summaries are contained in F. S. Regs., Part II. and the Staff Manual respectively. Title pages will be prepared in manuscript.

WAR DIARY
of 6TH BN SHERWOOD FORESTERS
~~INTELLIGENCE~~ ~~SUMMARY.~~
(*Erase heading not required.*)

Army Form C. 2118.

Hour, Date, Place	Summary of Events and Information	Remarks and references to Appendices
2. 4. 16. CAPPEL FERMONT	CAPT E.B. JOHNSON to 3rd Army School of Instruction for 1 month	G.D.G.
3. 4. 16 TRENCHES.	Bn relieved by 5th Bn Sherwood Foresters & moved into Huts & Billets at ACQ. Casualties during tour - Killed - 2. Other Ranks Wounded - 2/Lt F.W.A STUBBS } slightly, at Duty 2/Lt J.E. BARKER } 4. Other Ranks	
5. 4. 16 ACQ	CAPT E.M.B TAYLOR to 46th DIVISION as Divl Bomb Officer	G.D.G.
	CAPT J. TOLSON to command "C" Coy	G.D.G.
8. 4. 16 ACQ	Lt & QM. W.N BROOMHEAD to Hospital sick.	G.D.G.
8 4 16	2/Lt G.W. KNOWLES invalided to England.	G.D.G.
9. 4. 16 ACQ	2/Lt F.W.A STUBBS to 46th Divl School	G.D.G.
9. 4. 16 ACQ	Bn relieved 5th Bn Sherwood Foresters in Trenches	G.D.G.
9. 4. 16 ACQ	Band proceeded to 3rd Army School of Instruction. See letter from Lt Col Brownlow, Rifle Brigade, Commandant, Appendix	Appendix I
16. 4. 16 CAPPEL FERMONT	Lt F.W. HIPKINS & 5 men proceeded to Lewis Gun Course, CAMIERS for 1 week's course.	G.D.G.
Night of 16/17th apl.	The French miners exploded two mines (1) at head of GRANGE C.T. at 11.55 P.M. & (2) at head of BIRKIN C.T. (under old crater) at 11.59 P.M. 2/Lt W.H. HOLDERNESS killed & 1 other rank 3 O.R. wounded. 2/Lt HOLDERNESS had served in S. Africa ~~had~~ resided in PARIS and had been most useful as an Interpreter for the Battalion.	Appendix II. Bde Operation Orders " III Memo re II " IV Bn Operation Orders " V Message from 139th Bde " VI Report on operation G.D.G.

Instructions regarding War Diaries and Intelligence Summaries are contained in F. S. Regs., Part II. and the Staff Manual respectively. Title pages will be prepared in manuscript.

Army Form C. 2118.

WAR DIARY of 6th Bn Sherwood Foresters. II
INTELLIGENCE SUMMARY.

(*Erase heading not required.*)

Hour, Date, Place	Summary of Events and Information	Remarks and references to Appendices
17. 4 16 Divl School	2/Lt F.W.A. STUBBS to Hospital Sick.	G.D.G.
17 4 16 TRENCHES	Relieved by 5th Bn Sherwood Foresters. Casualties for tour other than mine { Killed 2. O.R / Wounded 11. O.R / Died of Wounds 2. O.R	G.D.G.
18 4 16	Lt & QM W.N. BROOMHEAD invalided to England.	G.D.G.
19 4 16 ACQ	Bn moved into billets as follows – Bn H.Q. C & D Coys. & Details MAROEUIL (Billets); 1 B Coy & ½ A Coy ANZIN; ½ A Coy ROCLINCOURT } (Dug-outs)	G.D.G.
	and relieved 3rd WORCESTER REGT, who took over Huts & Billets at ACQ.	
19. 4 16 to 29 4. 16 (inclusive)	Battn provided mining fatigues on 51st (HIGHLAND) DIVISIONAL front for 181 & 185 Coys RE & 7/1 FRENCH GENIE (latter on 25th Divl front)	G.D.G.
23. 4 16 ANZIN	2/Lt R EVANS to Hospital sick.	G.D.G.
24 4 16 MAROEUIL	Lt E.M. JELLICOE & 2/Lt J.E. BARKER to Divl School	G.D.G.
29. 4. 16. MAROEUIL ANZIN & ROCLINCOURT	Bn relieved by 4th Lincs, who took over mining fatigues.	G.D.G.
	Bn marched to PENIN & took over Billets vacated by 5th LINCS	
	Lt Col G.D GOODMAN to temporary command of 139th Inf Bgde, during absence on leave of BRIG-GENl C.T. SHIPLEY C.B	
	Major E HALL to temporary command of Battn.	G.D.G.
	During the month 416 steel Helmets were issued to the Battn	G.D.G.

G.D. Goodman Lt Col
Cdg 6th Bn Sherwood Foresters

(9 29 6) W 3332—1107 100,000 10/13 H W V Forms/C. 2118/10.

SECRET. II

Operation Order No. 53.

Copy No 1

-by-

Brig-General. C.T. Shipley C.B.

Commanding 139th Inf Brigade

Reference TRENCH MAP 1/5,000.

April 16th, 1916.

1. The following mines will be exploded tonight the 16th/17th instant at 12 midnight:-

(a) P.75."P" at point of BIRKIN.

(b) P.75."O" at point of GRANGE.

2. These Operations will be under the Command of the following Officers.

(a) BIRKIN MINE. Lieut-Colonel GOODMAN, 6th Battalion Sherwood Foresters, Commanding the RIGHT SECTOR.

(b) GRANGE MINE. Lieut-Colonel BLACKWALL, 8th Battalion Sherwood Foresters, Commanding the LEFT SECTOR.

3. These Officers will be responsible that:-

(a) An area of 100 yards from each mine is cleared by 11:45 pm. That is, in the Outpost Line, from a point 100 yards south of its junction with BIRKIN up to its junction with DUFFIELD, and in the Retrenchment Line from a point 40 yards South of the new C.T. TIDSA to DUFFIELD.

(b) That in each case, parties are told off ready, to seize the near lip, consolidate the position & protect the flanks, in accordance with the orders already approved for mine Explosions.

(c) That the required R.E. material is ready in the adjacent Emergency Dumps.

4. On the mines being exploded:-

(a) The Field Artillery will form a barrage of fire on each flank and onto the German Support Trenches in rear.
The 4.5" Howitzers & the Heavy Artillery will also bombard the enemy's Support Trenches & C.Ts.
The exact details of these barrages will be issued when received from the C.R.A.

(b) The Trench Mortars (one 2" & one Stokes at each mine) will support the Infantry as follows:-

(i) <u>At the BIRKIN MINE.</u>
The 2" will fire into the enemy's trenches, 100 yards ~~South~~ ~~immediately [illegible]~~ of the Crater, and the Stokes on to the enemy's front line Trenches 100 yards South of COMMON, but will be ready to take on any Machine Gun firing on our attacking Infantry.

(ii) <u>At the GRANGE MINE.</u>
The 2" will fire on the German Crater LABRIGOT. N, and the Stokes on the enemy front line Trenches opposite DUFFIELD, but will be prepared to fire on any Machine Gun firing on our attacking party.

(c) One West Bomb Thrower in rear of BIRKIN CRATER will act against the enemy first line trenches N. of BIRKIN CRATER, & the other in DUFFIELD will act against the German front line Trenches opposite that C.T.

(d) ~~The~~ 3 grenade ~~s~~ rifle-stands in rear of each Crater will come into action under orders of Officers Commanding at these Craters.
The Brigade Bomb Officer will assist in the operations under (c) & (d)

(e) OC Machine Gun Company will arrange to bring fire on enemy's rear & communication trenches.

5. With the idea of taking advantage of the Commotion which will ensue in the enemy's trenches when the mines are sprung, the Officers Commanding at each Crater, will evolve a small enterprize with the object of reaching the enemy's trenches, getting in with the Bayonet & bringing back a prisoner.

(i) At the BIRKIN CRATER, the Southern side would appear to offer the best chance of success.

(ii) At the GRANCE CRATER, the Northern side & new trench which the enemy is now digging would appear to give a good opportunity.

Parties in these schemes should be kept small, a definite limit must be given. & men should be instructed to use their Bayonets.

The outer flanks of both these enterprizes should be protected by Lewis Gun fire from our Outpost Line Trench.

6. Watches will be synchronised from Advanced Brigade Headquarters at 9 pm tonight

7. Acknowledge by wire.

Major
Bde Major, 139th Bde.

Issued at 7-30 pm to:—

Copy No 1 O.C. 6th Battn S.F.
" " 2 O.C. 8th Battn S.F.
" " 3 "246" T.M Btty & 139/1 T.M. Battery
+ Bde [illegible] Coy

8. The Company of the 5th Battn S.F. from the CHEMIN DES PYLONES is placed at the disposal of the RIGHT Commander as a Support, & the Working Coy. of the 7th Batt. S.F. in the Trenches this evening is placed at the disposal of the Left Commander for a similar purpose.

III Secret

O.C. 6th Bn. Sherwood Foresters

—

1 With reference to Para 4(a) of Operation Order No. 53 the following are the details of the Artillery Barrages referred to:-

2 (a) The 4th + 5th Staffs: Batteries will form a Barrage 100 yards behind the line joining the two craters + 100 yards to the SOUTH + 50 yards to North of COMMON + DUFFIELD respectively

(b) The 3rd Lincs: Battery will barrage the Enemy's front line trenches for 150 yards to the South of the 4th Staffs Battery Barrage

(c) The 6th Staffs: Battery will barrage the Enemy's front line trenches for 150 yards to the North of the 5th Staffs Battery barrage

3 (a) All the above Batteries will open fire as soon as a Mine goes up, with Section fire 20 seconds, and continue at that rate for 5 minutes, after which they will reduce their rate of fire to Section fire 30 seconds for another 5 minutes after which they will continue at Sect: fire 1 minute until information is obtained from the Infantry that fire is no longer required or can be reduced.

(b) All batteries must be prepared to quicken their fire on application from the Infantry.

(c) The 2nd Derby Battery will fire on selected Registered points behind "P" Sector, Section fire 1 minute. The 1st Derby Batt'y firing on similar targets behind the left of O Sector.

(d) The Remainder of the Div: Artillery will be ready for any eventuality.

4. The Corps artillery will cooperate by firing at selected points, opening fire as soon as a mine goes up + continuing for an hour or longer if the enemy undertakes any offensive –

5. Please acknowledge by wire

~~Signed~~

W. W. Watson [illegible] Major

Bde Major

139th Inf Bde

16/4/16

IV

Copy.

Operation Order No 1
by Lt Col G D Goodman, Commanding
6th Bn Sherwood Foresters

Reference. Trench map

16.4.16

1. It is intended to explode mines opposite (a) BIRKIN (b) GRANGE
The near lip of the craters will be occupied. (a) by 6th Sherwood Foresters (b) by 8th Sherwood Foresters. Each Bn will also send out a raiding party (a) S. of BIRKIN crater. (b) N of GRANGE crater.

2. O.C. Lt 'D' Coy will clear the Outpost line and Retrenchment Line by 11.45 pm. and O.C. 'C' Coy the Outpost line from COMMON for 50 yards south at the same time

3. Covering Party.- This party will consist of 2 groups each of 2 grenadiers and 2 bayonet men furnished by Lt D Coy 6/Sherwood Foresters. They will be stationed to the extreme left of the RETRENCHMENT, Right of BIRKIN by 11.45 pm. Immediately on the explosion these parties will move by BIRKIN to the forward retrenchment and occupy the near edge of the craters. The first party moving towards left of crater the second towards the right. Bayonet men will carry shovels and will dig O.P on lip similar to that at present in BIRKIN crater. They will at once be followed by 2 parties of [illegible] grenadiers each who will move up Birkin and establish themselves: First party by forward retrenchment to L, second to R. on the flanks of covering and digging parties, and if possible on the outpost line L & R of the crater

4. Digging Party (2/Lt Holdness) Digging party of 30 NCOs & men from D Coy will be formed up on the right of P 75 at 11.45 pm. This party will draw tools & material in advance from the special dump in BIRKIN and on the mine explosion will at once move in rear of the parties previously mentioned up BIRKIN into the forward retrenchment, advancing from there to dig the trenches close up to the near lip of the crater in accordance with plans issued in case of an enemy mine explosion.

5. Raiding Party - (2nd Lt Evans) This party consisting of 4 Bomb throwers and 8 Bayonet men from Lt B Coy will be assembled on the outpost line 50 yds to the R of COMMON by 11.30 pm. This party will, on the mine explosion proceed up the extension of COMMON towards the enemy trenches. It will raid the enemy barricade at the top of COMMON & the adjacent trench using the bayonet and will endeavour to bring back at least 1 prisoner. It must act as quickly as possible, with the idea of taking advantage of the confusion caused by the explosion of the mine and it is essential that the retirement should be conducted in a similar way.
This party will be supported by a patrol of 2 bombers and 2 bayonet men of Lt B Coy in the sap leading out of our outpost line to the right of COMMON.

6. Flanking Parties (a) Left. 2/Lt [illegible] This party will consist of 2 bombers 12 bayonets & Lewis Gun No L from left P 75 and will be formed up

in P.95 to left of digging party at 11.45 pm. This party will follow digging party into BIRKIN and move to the forward retrenchment and occupy outpost line N of BIRKIN crater.

(b) Lieut Brown (i) This party will consist of 2 bombers and 20 bayonet men of "C" Coy and will be formed up at 11.45 pm in outpost line to the L of VERNON. On the mine explosion they will occupy outpost line on R of COMMON with the object of ensuring the safe return of the raiding party. Every opportunity will be seized of keeping down enemy's fire.

2nd Lt D S [illegible] (ii) Lewis Gun Officer will place 3 Lewis Guns at suitable intervals in the outpost line to R of COMMON. They will be employed in keeping down enemy's rifle fire and dealing with his M.G.s

7. Support (2nd Lt [illegible]) 2 platoons "D" Coy will occupy the retrenchment R & L of BIRKIN moving into position from P.95 after the other parties have gone forward.

8. Reserve (i) "A" Coy 6th Sherwood Foresters under Capt [illegible] will occupy P.S.94 at 11.30 pm and will be prepared to move by COMMON into P.95 on receiving orders

(ii) The Coy 1st Wiltshire Regt in [illegible] St and QUARRY will be prepared to move on receipt of orders.

9. Artillery On the mines being exploded the Field Artillery will form a barrage of fire on each flank and into the German support trenches in rear. The [illegible] Howitzers and the Heavy Artillery will also bombard the enemy's support trenches & C.T.s. The exact details of these barrages will be issued when received from the C.R.A.

10. Other Troops Remainder of 6th S.F. will cease work & stand to at 11.45 pm.

11. Bn H.Qrs The C.O. will be at "D" Coy H.Q. in P.95 from 11 pm.

(sd) [illegible] Johnson

Capt & Adjt

6th Sherwood Foresters.

Issued at 9.15 pm

Copy No 1 to 139th Bde

2 " 8th [illegible]

3 Retd to Bn Copy & files.

"A" Form. Army Form C. 2121.

MESSAGES AND SIGNALS. No. of Message

Prefix .... Code .... m.	Words	Charge	This message is on a/c of:	Recd. at .... m.
Office of Origin and Service Instructions.	Sent		.... Service.	Date
	At .... m.			From
	To			
	By		(Signature of "Franking Officer.")	By

TO O.C. 6 Bn Sherwood Foresters

Sender's Number	Day of Month	In reply to Number	AAA
* N 347	17		

Following wire received from Division G begins AAA The G.O.C. wishes me to convey to you his appreciation of the work done by your Brigade last night AAA Whilst deploring the casualties which must necessarily occur he is very satisfied with the manner in which the operations were arranged and carried through. ends AAA The Bdg Comdr is very pleased to convey the above message to you & in doing so adds his own appreciation for the work done by the units engaged –

From Bde 139 Bde

Place

Time 7.40 PM

The above may be forwarded as now corrected. (Z) [illegible signature]

Censor. Signature of Addressor or person authorised to telegraph in his name.

* This line should be erased if not required.

292146—W. & S. Ltd., London.—W 14142/641—20,000—4/15. Forms C 2121/10.

VI

From:- O.C. 6th Sherwood Foresters

To:- H.Q. 139th Bde.

Reference 139th Bde Operation Order No 53 I beg to attach a copy of my operation orders, and to report as follows:-

The trenches specified in Bde Orders were cleared by 11.45 pm and at 11.52 pm it was reported to me that all parties were in position. At 11.58 pm a shock was felt which proved to be the explosion of the GRANGE mine before the given time. This tended to cause confusion. However at 11.59 pm the second shock was felt and the artillery were directed to start firing. At 12.10 am 2/Lt HALDERNESS reported that his digging party were enfiladed from the right and unable to get out to dig. I sent CAPT JACKSON forward and by 12.18 am received a further report that the digging party were being posted. Ultimately a trench was dug a few feet in rear of the original crater trench, linking up the outpost line as before. An observation post was not fully completed. Shortly before 4 am I regret to say that 2/Lt HALDERNESS was badly wounded while engaged in fixing wire palisades, and I regret to say that he died. An inspection of the crater from the observation post showed that it was about 30 yards inside diameter and about 15 feet deep. It must have carried away the enemy loophole posts, barricades and a good deal of his front line trench. It is of an unusual length and the ground to the south is covered with chalk. The new crater projects to the right of the old outpost line and it is a question whether it is desirable to make a short trench joining the new crater trench with a portion of COMMON CT. beyond our present line. Both ends of the new crater trench are occupied by bombers.

I attach 2/Lt Evans' report on his attempted raid. I directed him to make a second attempt if he saw any way of doing it successfully, as I thought he had mistaken the direction first time. Fortunately, although his party came under a heavy rifle fire, he was able to withdraw without loss. On viewing the ground at daybreak I saw that ~~at any~~ the attempt could not have succeeded. Apparently the post we intended to seize and the adjacent position was obliterated and it would have been practically impossible to cross the chalk without being seen. Our Shrapnel appeared to burst very effectively. Unfortunately the 2" Trench Mortar and the Stokes Gun could not fire. The former had not registered owing to shortness of notice and the latter was defective at the time. My Lewis Guns did good work. One of the 3 on the right took on the German Gun that was enfilading the crater trench, & eventually silenced it. The total casualties are, Killed 1 Officer 1 Other Ranks. Wounded 4 Other Ranks.

(Sgd) G. D. Goodman Lt Col

17.2.16
6.30 am.

Cdg 6th Sherwood Foresters

Instructions regarding War Diaries and Intelligence Summaries are contained in F. S. Regs., Part II. and the Staff Manual respectively. Title pages will be prepared in manuscript.

6th Battn Sherwood Foresters.

WAR DIARY

~~INTELLIGENCE SUMMARY~~.

(Erase heading not required.)

Army Form C. 2118.

1/6 Notts & Derby

Vol 16

Hour, Date, Place	Summary of Events and Information	Remarks and references to Appendices
2.5.16. PENIN.	Battn practised smoke attack with 139th Bde,(less 5th Bn) at TINQUES.	
3.5.16. "	CAPT V.O.ROBINSON to 3rd Army School of Instruction	
5.5.16. "	LT EM.JELLICOE & 2/LT J.E.BARKER rejoined from 46th Divl School of Instruction.	
6.5.16. "	Battn marched in to Billets at IVERGNY.	
6.5.16. IVERGNY.	2/LT F.W.A.STUBBS rejoined from Hospital	
7.5.16. "	Battn marched into Billets and huts at HUMBERCAMPS.	
9.5.16.HUMBERCAMPS.	Re-inoculation of Battn commenced.	
13.5.16. "	CAPT R.SAXBY, LIEUT J.TAYLOT, LIEUT G.S.RIVINGTON and LIEUT A.H.GOODALL rejoined from England.	
13.5.16. "	CAPT R.SAXBY took over command and payment of Lr "C" Company.	
14.5.16 "	2/Lt H.SIMPSON joined from Reserve Battn.	
17.5.16. "	2/Lt G.GLOSSOP rejoined from England.	
10th to 18th.	During this period the Battn dug communication trenches West of FONQUEVILLERS.	
19.5.16.FONQUEVILLERS.	The Battn relieved the 6th Battn South Staffs Regt in the CENTRE SECTOR trenches, with Battn H.Qrs at FONQUEVILLERS, the billets in HUMBERCAMPS being taken over by the relieved Battn.	
19.5.16.HUMBERCAMPS.	2/LT W.A.LYTLE to Hospital for Dental treatment.	
20.5.16. "	Transport & Q.M.Stores moved into Billets vacated by 6/S.Staffs Regt at SOUASTRE.	
27.5.16.FONQUEVILLERS.	Draft of 42 Other Ranks arrived from 8th Entrenchg Bn.	
27.5.16. "	2/LT K.H.BOND with patrol went out at 1.15 a.m. and spent the day in a trench in SUCRERIE on the GOMMECOURT ROAD, returning at night with an enemy cap.	
27.5.16. "	Relieved by 8th Bn Sherwood Foresters from support and moved back in to Brigade support at FONQUEVILLERS. Casualties for tour:- Killed, 1 O.R. Accidentally Killed. 1 O.R. Wounded 18 O.R., 2 of whom have since died of wounds. Accid.Wounded 1.	
30.5.16. "	150 men under CAPTS R.SAXBY & J.TOLSON dug advanced trench 250 yards linking up with 37th Dinv on left. 50 men under CAPT E.B.JOHNSON wired.	Appendix 1.

Lt Col
Comdg,
6/Sherwood Foresters.

165

(9 29 6) W 3332–1107 100,000 10/13 H W V Forms/C. 2118/10.

Instructions regarding War Diaries and Intelligence Summaries are contained in F. S. Regs., Part II. and the Staff Manual respectively. Title pages will be prepared in manuscript.

II.

WAR DIARY

6th Sherwood xx Foresters.

~~INTELLIGENCE SUMMARY.~~

(*Erase heading not required.*)

Army Form C. 2118.

Hour, Date, Place	Summary of Events and Information	Remarks and references to Appendices
30.5.16.	LONDON GAZETTE. The following is an extract from the London Gazette d/- 30th May 16. Major,(tempy Lt Col) G.D.GOODMAN to be Lieut Col. Captain,(tempy Major) A.J.Hopkins to be Major (May 22nd) Lieutenant,(tempy Capt) B.DARBYSHIRE to be Captain (Oct 16th). Lieutenant,(tempy Capt) C.B.JOHNSON to be Captain (May22nd) 2/Lieutenant,(tempy Capt) J.Tolson to be Lieut,(tempy Capt) (Oct 16th) 2/Lieutenant,(tempy Capt) H.H.JACKSON to be Lieut,(temp capt) (May 22nd)	G.D.G.
		G. D. Goodman

(9 29 6) W 3332—1107 100,000 10/13 H W V Forms/C. 2118/10.

I.

3 Army Inf School

Dear Colonel Goodman

I am just writing you a line to thank you most heartily for the loan of your splendid band it was most thoroughly appreciated and every one remarked on its playing. It is a great thing for the students having one here & bucks them up tremendously. Again many thanks

yours sincerely

G. V. Bramley

WAR DIARY. APPENDIX "A" Form. I. Army Form C. 2121.

MESSAGES AND SIGNALS.

No. of Message

Prefix SM Code DAS m.	Words	Charge	This message is on a/c of:	Recd. at 4.15 m.
Office of Origin and Service Instructions	Sent		31.5.16 Service.	Date
R N	At m.			From R N
	To			
	By		(Signature of "Franking Officer.")	By Pte Lund

TO R. N. C

Sender's Number	Day of Month	In reply to Number	
* SC 271	31		AAA

46th Div wires begin aaa GOC wishes to congratulate 6th SF on the very good work performed last night aaa Please convey these congratulations aaa Ends

From

Place R. N

Time

The above may be forwarded as now corrected.

Censor.

(Z)

Signature of Addressor or person authorised to telegraph in his name.

* This line should be erased if not required.

(15491) S. & Co. Ltd. W 14142/641. 90,000. 4/15. Forms C 2121/10.

1/6 Notts & Derby Vol 17

Army Form C. 2118.

Instructions regarding War Diaries and Intelligence Summaries are contained in F.S. Regs., Part II. and the Staff Manual respectively. Title pages will be prepared in manuscript.

WAR DIARY
of 6th ~~Sherwood~~ Foresters
~~INTELLIGENCE SUMMARY.~~
(Erase heading not required.)

Hour, Date, Place	Summary of Events and Information	Remarks and references to Appendices
3rd June 16	LONDON GAZETTE Lt Col G.D. GOODMAN appointed C.M.G.	
	Sgt M.J. UNWIN (2230) awarded "Military Medal"	G.D.G.
FONQUEVILLERS 4.6.16.	Lt J. TAYLOR for 3 days instruction in Sniping.	G.D.G.
	Lt R.D. WHEATCROFT rejoined from England.	G.D.G.
" 5/6.6.16.	Bn relieved by 4th LINCOLNS in support and marched into Billets at HUMBERCAMPS.	G.D.G.
HUMBERCAMPS. 6.6.16	Draft of 72 men arrived from Base.	G.D.G.
	Lt Col G.D. GOODMAN on reconnaissance of VII Corps line.	G.D.G.
	2/Lt C.H.C. COUSINS & 2/Lt F.R. OLIVER joined from England.	G.D.G.
	Bn marched into Billets vacated by 5th S. STAFFS Regt at SUS. ST. LEGER.	G.D.G.
SUS. ST. LEGER. 7.6.16.	Bn Bomb Section joined Bde Bomb Section for Instruction.	
	Lt C.A. BROWN from 46th Divl School.	G.D.G.
" 8.6.16	Capt H.H. JACKSON from Hospital.	G.D.G.
" 9.6.16.	2/Lt J.L. ROBINSON joined from England.	G.D.G.
" 11.6.16.	2/Lts W.G. WOOD, W.T. STEPHENS & A.E. SYLVESTER joined from England.	G.D.G.
	Lt C.A. BROWN & C.S.M. SLATER to 3rd Army School of Instruction.	G.D.G.
13.6.16.	Lt A.W. HIGHAM to C.T. School ROUEN for duty.	G.D.G.

Instructions regarding War Diaries and Intelligence Summaries are contained in F. S. Regs., Part II. and the Staff Manual respectively. Title pages will be prepared in manuscript.

WAR DIARY
or II
~~INTELLIGENCE~~ ~~SUMMARY~~.
(Erase heading not required.)

Army Form C. 2118.

Hour, Date, Place	Summary of Events and Information	Remarks and references to Appendices
15. 6. 1916	LONDON GAZETTE:- mentioned in despatches by C-in-C. for gallant & distinguished conduct in the field:- Lt. Col. G.D. GOODMAN CAPT. C.B. JOHNSON. 158 C.S.M. W. GODDARD. 456 " H.H. HOLLAND. 2388 Sergt T. HUNTER 1464 " W. LONGSON. 1644 Drummer J. CHATTERTON.	8D.L
SUS. ST LEGER. 18/19 6. 16	Marched to FONQUEVILLERS & relieved 4th Lincs in SUPPORT. Q.M. Stores & Transport lines to LA BAZIQUE FARM.	8D.L
" 17. 6. 16	139th Bde practised attack near LUCHEUX ~~xxxxx~~ FOREST in presence of Corps Commander & G.O.C. Division. 6th Battn in Support.	8D.L
TRENCHES. 22/23. 6. 16	Bn began to dig advanced trench on Brigade front. (Total length with all C.T's about 1.300 yards) 7th Battn furnished covering party & reserve diggers. Bn wired head of saps & C.T's.	appendix 1. 8D.L
" 23/24. 6. 16	Bn continued digging advanced trench with 7th Bn finding covering party & reserve diggers. Rather heavy M.G fire and shelling	8D.L

(9 29 6) W 3332—1107 100,000 10/13 H W V Forms/C. 2118/10

Instructions regarding War Diaries and Intelligence Summaries are contained in F. S. Regs., Part II. and the Staff Manual respectively. Title pages will be prepared in manuscript.

WAR DIARY ~~or INTELLIGENCE SUMMARY.~~ III

(Erase heading not required.)

Army Form C. 2118.

Hour, Date, Place	Summary of Events and Information	Remarks and References to Appendices
	Owing to the heavy rain the trench, although linked up was not finished in depth. See appendix.	GDG
24.6.16.	Bn marched into Huts on the GAUDIEMPRE–PAS ROAD. Every man wet through & covered with mud from digging	appendices II & III GDG
GAUDIEMPRE 23.6.16	CAPT. C.J. WHEATCROFT rejoined from Base	GDG
" 24.6.16	Lt T.L. DARBYSHIRE rejoined from England	GDG
" 26.6.16	2/Lt E. KERSHAW joined from England	GDG
" 28.6.16	2/Lt L.N. JOHNSON & 2/Lt A.J. COOKE joined from England	GDG
FONQUEVILLERS. 28.6.16	Capt Parberry Sanitary officer ordered isolation & inoculation of 65 men prior to joining Bn pending operations Bn relieved 5th Sherwood Foresters in trenches (LEFT SECTOR)	GDG GDG
FONQUEVILLERS 30-6-16	Bn relieved in fire trenches by 5th & 7th Bns. & drew stores preparatory to attack on German trenches	GDG appendix IV. Please place with April diary

G. D. Goodman Lt Col
Comdg 6th Sherwood Foresters

COPY

I

6TH BATTAN SHERWOOD FORESTERS.

Detail of Working Parties 22/23rd June 1916.

No.	Officer Comdg.	Digging Strength.	Commn Trench.	Firing Trench.	Wiring Strength.	Trench.	Move by.
1.	Capt V.O.Robinson.	231.	C-186.x	276.x	10.	C.T"C."	STAFFORD AVENUE.
2.	Capt E.B.Johnson.	60.	-	120.x	10.	SAP 3.	ROTTEN ROW.
3.	Capt F.M.Dick.	156.	D-168.x	144.x	10.	C.T"D"	ROTTEN ROW immediately in rear of No 2 Party
4.	Capt J.Tolson.	120.	E-144.x	96.	10.	C.T"E"	ROBERTS AVENUE.
5.	Capt H.H.Jackson.	108.	-	216.	10.	SAP 4.	REGENT STREET.

TIME TABLE:-

10 p.m. Digging parties to be at Head of C.T's.

10.15 p.m. Move up to gaps in fire trench where R.E.guides will meet parties.

10.30 p.m. Digging parties go out followed by wiring parties.

10.45 p.m. Work commences.

1.45 a.m. Digging and wiring parties return.

One scout will meet each party at C.Trench and guide the parties to gaps.
This scout will remain with party and take reports to H.Q. ROBINSON LANE.

(sd) C.B.Johnson.
Capt & Adjutant.
6th Batt Sherwood Foresters.

II

COPY

6TH BATTN SHERWOOD FORESTERS.

DETAIL OF WORKING PARTIES 23/24TH JUNE 1916.

			C.T.	F.T.	
1.	Capt V.O.Robinson.	280 men.	"C"186.[x]	276.[x]	STAFFORD AVENUE move out by "C" Sap or Sap 3.
2.	Lieut F.W.Hipkins.	25 men.	-	120.[x]	ROTTEN ROW.
3.	Capt F.M.Dick.	200 men.	"D"168[x].	144[x].	ROTTEN ROW.
4.	Capt R.Saxby.	75 men	"E"144[x].	96.[x]	ROBERTS AVENUE.
5.	2/Lt G.Glossop.	40 men.	-	216[x]	REGENT STREET.

TIME TABLE:-

10 p.m.	Digging parties to be at head of C.T's.
10.15 p.m.	Move up to gaps in F.T's.
10.30 p.m.	Digging parties to go out followed by wiring parties.
10.45 p.m.	Work commences.
1.45 a.m.	Digging and wiring parties return.

O.C.parties must ascertain that the covering party is out before moving.

(2) POINT OF BIRKIN

(a) Officer responsible. O.C. No 3 Company.
(b) Covering party from P 75 by BIRKIN.
(c) Digging party from P 74 by BIRKIN.
(d) Right flanking party, grenadiers and bayonet men from P 74 moving by COMMON- Lewis gun moving from OUTPOST line of P 74.
(e) Left flanking party from RETRENCHMENT No 4 Company, Lewis gun from P 75 (left) by GRANGE.
(f) Supports to move from P 74 into RETRENCHMENT right and left of BIRKIN trench.
(g) Special dump is in BIRKIN trench by RETRENCHMENT.

(3) POINT OF ALBANY.

(a) Officer responsible. O.C. No 1 Company.
(b) Covering party from P 73 by ALBANY.
(c) Digging party from P 73 2nd sap by ALBANY.
(d) Right flanking party, grenadiers and bayonet men & Lewis gun from right of P 73 moving by CHASSERY.
(e) Left flanking party, grenadiers and bayonet men from No. 2 Company P 73 moving by VERNON. Lewis gun already in OUTPOST line.
(f) Supports to move from P 73 1st sap into P 73.
(g) Special dump is in ALBANY.

5. Commanders of all parties will be warned on every relief.

6. Battalion Grenade Officer will be responsible for refilling forward reserves of Grenades.

(Signed) G.D.GOODMAN. Lt.Colonel.

2nd April, 1916. Commanding, RIGHT SECTOR.

III

Wt. W. 1789-1402. 5/15. 36,000 Pads. L. S. & Co.

"B" Form

Army Form C. 2122.

MESSAGES AND SIGNALS.

No. of Message

Prefix SM Code 11 p m.		Received	Sent	Office Stamp.
Office of Origin and Service Instructions.	Words.	At 11.20 p. m.	At m.	RNC
TDF	58	From TDF	To	23/6/16
		By ohayft	By	

TO { 6th Batt. S. F.

* Sender's Number	Day of Month	In reply to Number	AAA
E 28	23rd		

Major General commanding wishes to congratulate all ranks of the Battalions concerned on their good work in advancing the line last night also to those who marked out the line previously aaa The result has been most satisfactory and has been obtained with a minimum of casualties

From 46th Div

Place

Time 9 40 p.m

* This line should be erased if not required.

IV

S E C R E T.
-:-:-:-:: -:-:

RIGHT SECTOR.
-:-:-:-:-:-:-:-

ACTION TO BE TAKEN IN CASE OF AN ENEMY MINE EXPLOSION.

1. In the event of a crater being formedby enemy's mine explosion in any point of our front, the near lip of the crater will immediately be occupiedand should the enemy have gained a footing in any part of our line, he will be ejected by grenade & bayonets. The covering party will hold the lip while a second party digs.

The new trench must be dug on solid ground close up to the near lip of the crater. It should be narrow and deep and protected by wire palisading, with a small trench in front to take the explosion of grenades. A post must always be constructed to enable a sentry to overlook the interior of the crater. The new trench will link up existing trenches.

The work should be conducted quietly.

2. The Company Commander or Officer on duty in the trench affected will at once take the following steps:-

(a) Send a report to Battalion Headquarters and send message to Artillery "Mine blown up opposite......... please give covering fire".
(b) Send covering party to hold near lip.
(c) Send digging party who will draw tools and materials from the nearest special dump, which contains 1000 Sandbags, 2 rolls barbed wire, 25 shovels, 5 picks, 40 stakes or corkscrews, wire palisade, and 4 trench ladders.
NOTE:- This party should nor exceed 1 man for each 5 feet of proposed trench.
(d) Send two parties of 4 grenadiers each for each flank of digging party.
(e) Send out independent flanking parties, each consisting of one Lewis gun, 2 rifle grenadiers, 4 grenadiers, and 12 bayonet men under one Commander.
(f) Bring up support.
(g) Send constant information to Battalion Headquarters.

3. Battalion Headquarters will if necessary fill the place of troops moved from the defensive line by a company from the Reserve Battalion.

4. The following measures will be taken in the event of an enemy crater being formed at the following points:-

(1) POINT OF GRANGE
(a) Officer responsible. O.C. No 4 Company.
(b) Cover party will be furnished by platoon in RETRENCHMENT
(c) Digging party from P 75 (left).
(d) Right flanking party, grenadiers and bayonet men from P 75 will move up by BIRKIN trench and Lewis gun if not already in OUTPOST line will be moved from P 75 (left) by BIRKIN trench.
(e) It has been arranged that left flanking party shall be furnished by LEFT SECTOR Battalion, butO.C. No 4 Company must satisfy himself that his party gets into position.
(f) Supporting party will be moved from P 75 into RETRENCHMENT.
(g) Special dump is in GRANGE W. of RETRENCHMENT.

Army Form C. 2118.

Instructions regarding War Diaries and Intelligence Summaries are contained in F. S. Regs., Part II. and the Staff Manual respectively. Title pages will be prepared in manuscript.

WAR DIARY of ~~INTELLIGENCE~~ ~~SUMMARY~~. 1/6th Bn Sherwood Foresters

(Erase heading not required.)

Vol 18

Hour, Date, Place		Summary of Events and Information	Remarks and References to Appendices
FONCQUEVILLERS.	1.7.16.	139th Bde attacked on a front from N.E. corner of GOMMECOURT WOOD to point of LITTLE Z. 5th & 7th Bns assaulted in 4 waves of 3 coys, remaining coys of each Bn carrying Bombs, S.A.A. & ~~[illegible]~~ material. The 6th Bn also carried – A & B on front in 2 waves to follow 5th & 7th Bn carrying coys, and D & C in two waves to remain in old front ~~trench~~ & retrenchments until ordered to advance.	Appendix I (Battn operation orders)
		The 1st 3 waves of assault carried 1st, & to some extent 2nd & 3rd German trenches under partial cover of smoke, but owing to very muddy state of our trenches, part of 4th wave and greater part of 5th & 7th Bn carrying companies could not get away before smoke lifted, and all attempts to advance by these and 6th A & B coys were met by heavy artillery and machine gun Barrage. The attack (as also that of 137th Bde against GOMMECOURT WOOD) therefore failed with heavy losses to assaulting Battns, but the main object was achieved of containing enemy forces near GOMMECOURT.	
		About 8 pm, the Bn was relieved in trenches by 8th Bn Sherwood Foresters, and remained the night near LEFT BATTN HD QRS, FONCQUEVILLERS.	
		– Casualties –	
		KILLED. Officers:- LIEUT E.M. JELLICOE.	
		Other Ranks:- No 158 C.S.M. GODDARD, 1443 L/Sgt ALLCOCK, & 2206 L/Sgt S. SHARMAN and 17 others.	
		WOUNDED:- Officers:- CAPT F.M. DICK, CAPT & ADJT C.B. JOHNSON, CAPT V.O. ROBINSON (at duty) CAPT F.B. ROBINSON (att. 139th Bde M.G. Coy) died of wounds 3.7.16. LIEUT R.D. WHEATCROFT, died of wounds 2.7.16. 2nd Lt H. SIMPSON. died of wounds 2nd Lt F.W.A. STUBBS. 2nd Lt T.F. RADFER 2/Lt F.R. OLIVER (at duty)	

(9 29 6) W 3332—1107 100,000 10/13 H W V Forms/C. 2118/10.

Army Form C. 2118.

WAR DIARY II
of 6th SHERWOOD FORESTERS
~~INTELLIGENCE SUMMARY~~.

(Erase heading not required.)

Instructions regarding War Diaries and Intelligence Summaries are contained in F. S. Regs., Part II. and the Staff Manual respectively. Title pages will be prepared in manuscript.

Hour, Date, Place	Summary of Events and Information	Remarks and References to Appendices
	WOUNDED, Other Ranks, 140.	
	Total casualties 170.	G.B.G. Appendix II (C.O's report)
FONCQUEVILLERS 2.7.16	Bn marched into H.Q.s at WARLINCOURT. CAPT TOLSON to command "B" vice Capt Dick. Lt G.K.K. MAUGHAN appointed ADJUTANT vice Capt C.B. JOHNSON	G.B.G.
WARLINCOURT. 3.7.16	Bn marched into billets vacated & handed over by 5th N Staffs Regt (Divl Reserve) at BAILLEULMONT.	G.B.G. Appendix III (C. in C's message published in Div. R.O. of 17-7-16)
	Officers rejoined :- CAPT. W. SEATON from England.	
	Officers joined :- 2/Lt W.L. COOPER, 2/Lt F.S. ROWLAND from England.	G.B.G.
	Draft of 54. O.Rks joined from Base	G.B.G. G.B.G.
BAILLEULMONT. 4.7.16	Draft of 8 O.Rks joined from Base.	G.B.G.
SAULTY 5.7.16	Maj Gen The Hon E.J. STUART-WORTLEY C.B. CMG said goodbye to Officers who came out with Division.	G.B.G.
BAILLEULMONT. 3.7.16	Capt W. SEATON to command "D" coy. - Capt JACKSON to be 2nd in command.	G.B.G.
" 8/9.7.16.	Bn carried Gas accessories to trenches. of 137th Inf Bde	G.B.G.
" 9/10.7.16	Bn carried Gas accessories to trenches. " " "	G.B.G.
" 9.7.16	CAPTS R. SAXBY & C.J. WHEATCROFT to THIRD ARMY SCHOOL. CAPT. C.B. JOHNSON to Command "C" Coy vice Capt Saxby. CAPT W. SEATON attached to 7th Bn Sherwood Foresters.	G.B.G.
" 10.7.16	LIEUTS T.L. DARBYSHIRE & G.S. RIVINGTON attd to 7th Bn Sherwood Foresters.	G.B.G.
" 11/12 7 16.	Bn marched to trenches and relieved 5th Bn SOUTH LANCASHIRE REGT in RIGHT SECTOR. Transport & QM Stores to BAILLEULVAL.	G.B.G.
" 12.7.16	Draft of 8 Other Ranks arrived from Base, under 2/Lt E. Jones.	G.B.G.
" 15.7.16	Hrs C & D Coys were relieved by 2 Coys 5th N. STAFFS Regt, A & C Coy relieving a coy of 8th S.F. on left, & D Coy going into Bn reserve in BELLACOURT.	G.B.G.
" 15.7.16	Preliminary patrol of TALUS under 2/Lt E. KERSHAW	G.B.G.

Instructions regarding War Diaries and Intelligence Summaries are contained in F. S. Regs., Part II. and the Staff Manual respectively. Title pages will be prepared in manuscript.

WAR DIARY
or
INTELLIGENCE SUMMARY.

(Erase heading not required.)

Army Form C. 2118.

Hour, Date, Place	Summary of Events and Information	Remarks and references to Appendices
BELLACOURT. 16.7.16	2/Lt B.N. PARKER joined from England	G.D.G.
17.7.16	Lieut D.S. FOX to Transport Course, HAVRE. 2/Lt HIPKINS to be L. Gun Officer	G.D.G.
17.7.16	Preliminary patrol of TALUS under 2/Lt E. KERSHAW.	G.D.G.
17.7.16	Bn relieved by 5th S.F. in RIGHT SECTOR & went into Bde SUPPORT in village of BELLACOURT, providing Garrisons of BOUNDARY BURNT FARM, STAR FISH & ORCHARD POSTS. 'A' Coy remained in support of 5th Battalion	G.D.G.
18.7.16	Officers joined from England:- CAPTS C.V.H.C. BLACKWALL, E.S. HOOD 2/Lieuts R. EVANS, - V.H. ARMITAGE, - C.L. CROUCHER - A.B. DAVIES, - A.P. STONER.	G.D.G.
19.7.16	G.O.C. inspected Bn (Maj Genl N. THWAITES) & said he was pleased with the appearance of the men.	G.D.G.
20.7.16	Very heavy bombardment of trenches by enemy. 'A' Coy under Capt V.O. ROBINSON moved up to reinforce within 1 minute of receiving order from OC 5th Battn. 2/Lt C.E.V. CREE & 3 OR killed, 15 OR wounded	
21.7.16	Preliminary patrol of TALUS under 2/Lt F.R. OLIVER.	G.D.G.
23.7.16	Bn relieved 5th in RIGHT SECTOR, 'A' Coy being in Bn reserve in village	G.D.G.
24.7.16	A patrol of 2/Lts E. KERSHAW & F.R. OLIVER & 3 OR penetrated gap in TALUS wire & lay on bank. Whilst there they were challenged by a German patrol who fired, severely wounding 2/Lt OLIVER. Pte Webb missing. Others got back with valuable information.	G.D.G.
27.7.16	2/Lt M.R.K. BIRN to Hospital	G.D.G.
28.7.16	Raid on TALUS, see appendices	Appendices IV, V & VI
29.7.16	Bn relieved by 5th in RIGHT SECTOR, the Bn moving into Billets handed over by 5th in BAILLEULVAL	G.D.G. Instructions to Raiding party. Report.
30.7.16	Draft of 59 OR arrived	G.D.G. G.O.C.'s message.
31.7.16	2/Lt B.N. PARKER to Div Bomb School.	

G. D. Gordon ? Lt Col
Cmdg 6/Sherwood Foresters

(9 29 6) W 3332—1107 100,000 10/13 H W V Forms/C. 2118/10

S E C R E T. I No 2. Copy No 7

OPERATION ORDERS No 2 BY LIEUT COLONEL G.D.GOODMAN C.M.G
COMMANDING
6TH BATTALION SHERWOOD FORESTERS.

30th June 1916.

1. The Battn will be distributed (on the front of attack) as follows:-

(a). LETTER "A" COMPANY. In 1st SUPPORT LINE with RIGHT on STAFFORD AVENUE.
To move into position via ROBERTS AVENUE.

(b). LETTER "B" COMPANY. In 1st SUPPORT LINE with left on RAYMOND AVENUE.
To move into position via REGENT STREET.

(c) BOMBERS............ In 1st SUPPORT LINE on RIGHT of Lr "B" Company.
To move into position via ROBERTS AVENUE.

(d) 4 BRIGADE M.GUNS.... In 1st SUPPORT LINE on RIGHT of Bombers.
To move into position via ROBERTS AVENUE.

(e). LETTER "D" COMPANY. In 3rd SUPPORT LINE with RIGHT on STAFFORD AVENUE.
To move into position via ROBERTS AVENUE.

(f). LETTER "C" COMPANY. In 3rd SUPPORT LINE with LEFT on RAYMOND AVENUE
To move into position via REGENT STREET.

(g). BATTALION RUNNERS AND SIGNALLERS In 3rd SUPPORT LINE on RIGHT of Lr "C" Coy.
To move into position via ROBERTS AVENUE.

(h). BATTALION H.Q.... In dugout at junction of ROBERTS AVENUE and [illegible] ROAD.
At about –60 Battn H.Q. will move up to H.Q. LEFT BATTALION in GREEN STREET.

Companies will move into position in the above order, unless definite orders to the contrary are received from Battn H.Q. All troops will be in their allotted positions by 2 am.
Orders for the movement of Companies from their present position to their assembly trenches and for drawing the necessary S.A.A., bombs and material will be issued under separate cover.

2.(a). At ZERO Letters "A" & "B" Companies, bombers, the 4 Brigade M.Guns and Battalion H.Q. will commence to move up to the OLD BRITISH FRONT LINE.
Letter "A" Coy will use ~~STAFFORD AVENUE~~, ROTTEN ROW and ROBERTS AVENUE.
Letter "B" Company will use REGENT STREET and RAYMOND AVENUE.
Bombers and 4 Brigade Machine Guns will use REGENT STREET. These details will first allow Letter "B" Company to go up in advance of them, and then follow up to old FRONT LINE.
Signallers, Battalion Runners will use REGENT STREET in rear of Bde Machine Guns.

(b). On arrival at the heads of the above C.T's Companies will file into the old BRITISH FRONT LINE TRENCH. As soon as the last man of each Company reaches his position, Companies will move out by half Companies, through the gaps in our wire, and deploy as soon as possible. Companies will move across to the GERMAN FIRST LINE TRENCH using the following as guides as to direction:-

LETTER "A" COMPANY. RIGHT will move on new C.T. from STAFFORD AVENUE to NEW FRONT LINE.
LEFT will move a little to the left of No 3 Russian sap.

LETTER "B" COMPANY. LEFT will move on No 4 Russian sap.
RIGHT will be between "D" C.T. and No 3 Russian sap

These

These Companies will check on arrival at NEW FRONT LINE, correct their dressing and then advance across the Trench to the FIRST GERMAN LINE.

(c). As soon as the Battn runners and signallers arrive at the LEFT BATTALION H.Q., Battn H.Q. will move across in rear of the Bombers and Machine Guns to the FIRST GERMAN FIRST LINE TRENCH, and establish themselves in the vicinity of ORINOCO C.T.

(d). As soon as the troops in the 2nd SUPPORT LINE have moved out:-

<u>LETTERS "D" & "C" COMPANIES</u> will move up and line the OLD BRITISH FRONT LINE TRENCH.

Letter "D" Company will move by ROTTEN ROW and ROBERTS AVENUE.

Letter "C" Company will use REGENT STREET and RAYMOND AVENUE.

As the opportunity occurs, men will be sent forward in small parties to fill up the NEW FRONT LINE TRENCH, until half of each Company has gone forward. An officer from each Company will god with the first group of men.

Letters "D" & "C" Companies will not move forward unless ordered to do so by Battn or Brigade H.Q.

3. The 2nd in Command and the Assistant Adjutant will remain in the Headquarters LEFT BATTALION until their services are required.

4. In addition to the stores already enumerated in previous orders, there will be 70 trench grids for the Battn stacked at the MAIN STREET END of the C.T's. These will be picked up en route and placed in the trenches for the men to stand on.

5. Arrangements for a hot drink and an issue of rum on arrival at the trenches will be given out later.

6. ACKNOWLEDGE.

C B Johnson
Captain & Adjutant.
6th Battn Sherwood Foresters...

Issued at 1.15pm

Copy No. 1. WAR DIARY
2. FILE
3. C.O.
4. ADJUTANT
5. O.C. A Coy
6. O.C. B Coy
7. O.C. C Coy
8. O.C. D Coy
9. Lewis Gun Officer.
10. Bomb Officer.
11. Signalling Officer.

II

Corrections. To.

Headquarters,
139th Infantry Brigade,

In accordance with Brigade Operation Orders my Battn was, in the early morning of the 1st inst disposed as follows:- "A" &"B" Coys in 1st Support Line with some bombers, remainder of bombers and 4 Brigade Machine Guns in a small trench behind. The remaining two Companies "C" & "D"occupied 3rd Support Line in order from right. Owing to the muddy state of the trenches it took considerably longer than had been expected to get this wave into position and it was not completed before 3.15 a.m.

read "D" & "C"

At 5.45 a.m. I moved to LEFT ADVANCED HEAD QRS (7th Battn).
About 7 a.m. Mjor HIND, his Adjutant and Medical Officer left. He stated he was going to new front trench to watch the waves out and then go himself.

At 8.45 a.m. I and my Adjutant went along GREEN STREET towards REGENT STREET to watch my leading Companies advance and to follow them.

7.45 a.m.

I found GREEN STREET congested and waited a long time trying to get men forward but found it impossible as the front line was blocked. During this time the enemy's bombardment was very heavy with shrapnel and H.E., the latter being distributed round advanced Headquarters of both Battalions. My Adjutant was wounded beside me.

At 7.45 a.m. Capt ROBINSON, Commanding my Right ("A") Coy had a report from his runners that the 5th Battn Carrying Company was moving. He lead his Company forward but was checked by the 5th Carring Coy who said theywere checked by the 4th Wave who had not cleared. It was 8.45 a.m. before the head of my "A" Coy was in the old front line trench and partially ready to move. (All the men could not get into this trench.)

xAt 8.45 a.m. Lieut Wheatcroft at head of his platoon crossed our wire. All but Sgt Wagg being hit, and withdrew to old sap.

Capt ROBINSON reported the block to Major CHECKLAND who pushed on 5th Carrying Company. By this time the smoke had almost gone.

xsee above.

xThe left platoon of "A" Coy (or most of them) then got over the parapet under Lt R.D.WHEATCROFT and the right of the Company endeavoured to advance up No 3 sap and "C" C.T.

The Barrage was very heavy and Lt Wheatcroft was almost at once badly wounded. There were many casualties and the men withdrew for shelter to the saps and other trenches.

The same thing happened on the left when my "B" Company was kepy back by the 7th Carrying party. Capt F.M.DICK Commanding my Company was hit in the leg as soon as he got over the parapet and his Coy Sergt Major was killed at his side. The survivors accordingly took cover.

When I found it was impossible to get my men forward owing to the congestion I returned to left HEADQUARTERS about 9.30 a.m. and reported by telephone to Brigade. At my request the Assistant Adjutant 7th Battn went to the new front trench for information and I received a verbal message from Capt SCOTT. M.O., 7th Battn that he was in that trench with a good many men.
I understand he remained there all day taking charge in the absence of a combatant officer and attending

I sent messages to Coy Commanders to organise men in old front trench and retrenchments.

9.45 a.m. received telegraphic message from Brig Genl that Naylor of 5th in German front line trench required help. I sent message to Capt Robinson to organise advance from new Front line trench and went to No 3 sap where I conferred with Capts KERR & ROBINSON who said Naylor was back and advance impossible.

The

The enemy's fire (chiefly rifle) on that (new front) trench was very heavy and accurate. No 3 Sap (to which I went) was covered by enemy's rifle fire.

About 12.30 p.m. I received orders to attack with two Companies of my Battalion at 1.15 p.m. under cover of smoke. There was no smoke however and I did not attack. Another attack was ordered for 2.30 p.m. also under cover of smoke which however was not ready, and orders were received to the effect that the smoke would be at 3.25 p.m. and I was to advance at 3.30 p.m.

Read 3.30 and 3.35 p.m. 1.200 men of 137th Bde were also attacking.

A Staffird Officer came to confer and I settled that my right should advance on ORKNEY, my left on OUSE C.T.'s A small carrying party was organised and bombers collected. About 3.30 p.m. a small film of smoke appeared but in no way interfered with the view of the enemy trenches. I accordingly at 3.35 p.m ordered the men not to go over the parapet.

There was a very heavy and extremely accurate barrage and also considerable rifle fire. I was and am, quite satisfied that there was no possible chance of reaching the objective and no result could have been achieved. As a matter of fact, owing to a mistake. a party of 20 did leave the trench, most of them were struck down at once.

/sd/ G.D.Goodman. Lt-Col

3/7/16. Commanding 6th Battalion Sherwood Forester

-:-

From:- O.C.6th Sherwood Foresters.
To:- H.Q., 139th Infantry Brigade.

I shoud like to add to my report of this morning a statement with regard to the smoke and state of our trenches on the 1st inst.

1. I had anticipated that the state of the trenches would add materially to the time required by the rear waves for deploying into the open. Shortly before 8.30 a.m. I sent a message to the right of the line (to Capt Robinson) that the smoke must be prolonged if required and was subsequently informed that Major Checkland had given orders to the Officer in charge of the Smoke party. However, when shortly after, I was waiting in GREEN STREET for my carrying party to move up I found a small party of LINCOLNS with an Officer coming down the trench. They said they had orders to go back. I ordered them back to continue the smoke. and they complied but I believe ther was not much material left. All reports agree that the smoke has practically gone when the 4th wave was about to start.

2. The greatest difficulty was the mud in the trenches. The C.T's were even more difficult to pass than on the preceding days as the water was subsiding and thick mud being formed. It was immensely difficult for the carrying Companies to get along with their loads and the men were much fatigued.

But the men were all very keen and did their utmost, and I am confident that all would have gone well had they not been impeded by the condition of the trenches.

/sd/ G.D.Goodman, Lt-Colonel.
Comdg 6th Battn Sherwood Foresters.

3.7.16.
3.15 p.m.

III

EXTRACT FROM 46TH DIVISIONAL ROUTINE ORDERS
dated 17th July 1916.

1775. COMPLIMENTARY.

The G.O.C. has great pleasure in publishing the following Communication from the Chief of the General Staff dated 15th July 1916.

The Commander in Chief directs me to confirm in writing the verbal message already delivered by an A.D.C. to General Snow, conveying his appreciation of the gallant efforts made at GOMMECOURT on the 1st & 2nd July by the 46th & 56th Divisions of the VII Corps.

While deeply deploring the losses suffered by these Divisions he is glad to be able to assure them that their vigorous and well sustained attack proved of material assistance in the success of the general plan of operations.

True Extract
G.D. Goodman Lt Col
Cr 6/Sherwood Foresters
8/9/16

III

Copy No. 4

S E C R E T.

I N S T R U C T I O N S   T O
R A I D I N G   P A R T Y.

-:-:-:-:-:-:-:-:-:-:-:-:-:-

ENEMY. 1. In advance of the enemy's main line and lying in a hollow screened from direct observation, is a bank, (or sunk fence) 200 yards long, known as the TALUS. (See plan) This bank is 200 yards distant from No 14 SAP and rather more from No 15, from which saps it is approached by a downward slope devoid of cover. There is apparently no bank on our side, and the TALUS is in the nature of a sunk fence, with a drop of 6 ft to 8 ft towards the enemy. A path below runs along the bank. This path is floorboarded and entirely open to the enemy's front line. At intervals there appears to be steps or short fire bays. On the top of the Bank are bushes. There are none for perhaps 20 yards on SOUTH portion of bank. The TALUS is connected at its SOUTH end with enemy's front line by a C.T. some 200 yards long. About 120 yards down this C.T. is a circular work probably a Machine Gun dug-out or emplacement marked "D". In front of the TALUS are two depths of wire, each about 10 yards deep with an interval between them of some 10 yards. At a point apparently 15 yards from SOUTH end of TALUS is a gap 10 to 15 yards wide (marked A - B on plan) Both sides of the C.T. are strongly wired and there is also much wire between the TALUS and the enemy's front trench, and on the NORTH (open) flank which latter is protected by the BLOCKHOUSE. Apparently it is the enemy's custom to patrol the TALUS from time to time. His patrols also use the gap A - B to approach our line, and there is often a working party on the wire in the neighbourhood.

OBJECTIVE. 2. It is proposed to make a raid on enemy's advanced posts in the TALUS with the object of taking prisoners and securing identification, also of taking any machine guns at "D" and of inflicting as much injury on the enemy as possible.

PARTIES. 3. RAIDING PARTY. Under 2nd Lieut R. EVANS will consist of 20 N.C.O's and men of Letter "B" Company with 8 Bombers. This will be divided into:-

(i) BLOCKING PARTY of 2 Bombers (1 N.C.O.) and 3 men.
(ii) 1 N.C.O. 2 Bombers and 2 men.
(iii) 1 Officer, 1 N.C.O., and 11 men with 1 R.E. carrying Explosive.
(iv) 1 N.C.O., 2 Bombers and 1 man.
SCOUTS under 2/Lieut E. KERSHAW - 7 Scouts.

DRESS. 4. SCOUTS will wear their usual equipment, remainder will not wear their equipment but will carry 10 rounds in pocket-magazines charged with safety catch closed and 2 bombs per man in pockets. ~~If wind is favourable, Gas helmets will not be carried.~~ Socks will be drawn over boots. All badges and marks of identification will be removed.

RAID. 5. After dark, the parties will be assembled near 14 SAP. A party of Scouts will leave 14 SAP and will reconnoitre the gap in enemy's wire, to ascertain if it is clear. 2 Scouts will remain at entrance to gap, and two will return to guide party. The raiding party will then leave 14 SAP in their proper order. On passing through gap, Blocking party will turn to left, and take up positions by nearest bush on TALUS, marked "C". This party will remain there on top with two bayonet men below and will be responsible for this flank until raiding party returns, when they will protect the rear.

Should

RAID (contd) Should any of the enemy's patrols approach (any such would probably come from NORTH along TALUS) they will be dealt with by the Bayonet. This party must not use Bombs unless absolutely necessary.

The RAIDING PARTY will get into TALUS as quickly as possible and proceed in three parties to the Right until they come to the C.T. turning down it to the left. Short intervals (not exceeding 10 yards) will be kept between parties. If any enemy patrols are met with they should be bayoneted or taken prisoners without noise. Any prisoners should be disarmed and sent back at once under escort. On arrival at "D" the leading party will block the trench beyond "D". Any dug-outs must be bombed and search made for a Machine Guns, which if found must be brought back. The party will not proceed further than "D", but having accomplished its task will immediately return by the TALUS and gap in wire followed by BLOCKING PARTY and SCOUTS. During the operations the Scouts will remain in the vicinity of the TALUS and wire to direct the return of the various parties. Care must be taken to indicate position of steps from below TALUS.

RETURN. 6. On leaving gap in enemy's wire all parties will make for No 9 SAP keeping their right shoulders up. The direction of the SAP will be given by flares. O.C. "B" Coy will arrange to send a succession of flares from this spot and will have two men lying out to show gap in our wire.

WEAPON. 7. The success of the operation depends largely on surprise. All ranks must therefore understand that the bayonet is the proper weapon and bombs should only be used for bombing dug-outs, except in case of absolute necessity.

ARTILLERY.8. B/231 Battery will have its guns laid on the enemy front line NORTH and SOUTH of the TALUS gap (leaving a gap at the gap) and an F.O.O. will be on duty with telephone near No 18 SAP. On receiving an order from the Commanding Officer, slow fire will be opened, and the Battery will be prepared to increase the rate of fire on being called up-on to do so.

G. D. Goodman Lieut Colonel.

30th July 1916. Commanding 6th Battn Sherwood Foresters.

Copy No 1 Brigade
2 2/Lt [illegible]
3 C.O.
4 File

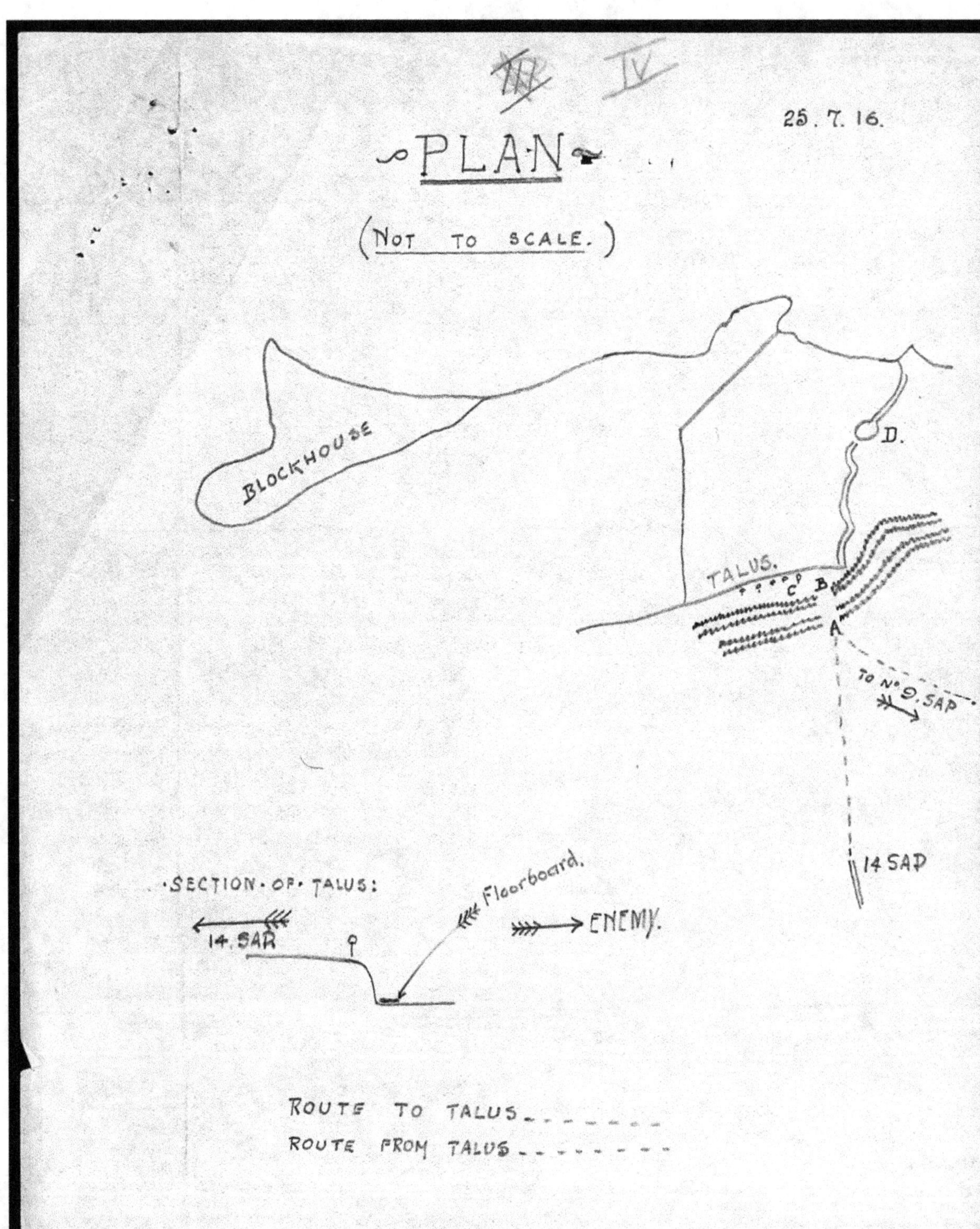
IV
25. 7. 16.
PLAN
(NOT TO SCALE.)
BLOCKHOUSE
D.
TALUS.
C
B
A
TO No 9. SAP
14 SAP
·SECTION · OF · TALUS:
Floorboard.
14. SAP
ENEMY.
ROUTE TO TALUS
ROUTE FROM TALUS

V

From:- Officer Commanding,
6th Battalion Sherwood Foresters

To:- Headquarters,
139th Brigade.

I beg to report as follows on the attempted raid of last night (28/29th)

At 10.30 p.m. 2/Lt KERSHAW and the Scouts left No 15 SAP taking with them a reel of tape, one end of which was made fast to a stake. This party has orders to find the gap in the TALUS wire and to reconnoitre it as far as the 2nd belt of wire. At 11.50 p.m. 2 scouts returned to the Sapt and took 2/Lt Evans and his party out. This party was made up according to the instructions and included 3 R.E's with explosives. By keeping to the tape they joined the Scouts at 12.15 a.m. and then passes throught the gap and got into the TALUS, the blocking party going to the bush on the left and the Scouts remaining on the Bank. So far the plan worked up to the most sanguine expectations but on proceeding to the right under the TALUS Bank, 2/Lt Evans found the position quite different to what he had expected. On moving along he found his way barred by 2 separate belts of wire stretching right across from the enemy front line trench to the TALUS. His party managed to cross these and went for quite 100 yds when, as there was no sign of the Sap he decided to return. He noticed that bullets (evidently unaimed) were striking the bank from the German front line trench and he considered that if he proceeded much further he would have to run the gauntlet of this fire on his return, there being absolutely no cover from it of any kind. The party therefore returned and got through the gap without accident or observation by the enemy.
In the meantime the two Scouts who had led 2/Lt Evans party from No 15 Sap had reeled up the tape and laid it again from outside the gap in the direction of No 9 sap. Consequently the whole of the party with scouts were able to return without loss of direction or time to our lines at this sap. When near the sap 1 N.C.O. and 1 man were wounded by Maching Gun fire.
In moving along the TALUS about 4 or 5 "T" headed saps were observed facing our lines and in one of them was an empty box probably used for flares. This and an empty cartridge case were all that was noticed.
There were no floorboards such as 2/Lt Kershaw is sure were in use on the 23rd inst: This might lead ~~him~~ to suppose that he struck a different gap on this occasion but white stones marked it as before. Nothing was left behind and the enemy were obviously unaware of the visit. It might be possible to lie up for a German patrol in this part of the TALUS, but it does not seem feasible to attack the sap from such a distance.
As there was no attack the guns did not open fire.

29/7/16. /sd/ G.D.Goodman. Lt Col.
Comdg 6th Batt Sherwood Foresters.

File VI

139th Infantry Brigade.

****

Although the operation carried out by the 6th Sherwood Foresters on the night of 28th/29th did not result in any capture of prisoners, the G.O.C considers the arrangements made and the method they were carried out in reflects great credit on all concerned.

The G.O.C wishes these remarks passed to all who took part in arranging or carrying out the operation.

T. Rose Capt. [illegible]
for Lieut-Colonel,
General Staff, 46th Division.

30/7/1916.

HEADQUARTERS
No. 6/7.
Date 30/7/16.
139th INFANTRY BRIGADE

2.

O.C. 6th Sherwood Foresters.

Forwarded for your information & attention please.

[illegible] Capt.
A/de Bgde Major 139th Inf Bde.

30/7/16.

Instructions regarding War Diaries and Intelligence Summaries are contained in F. S. Regs., Part II. and the Staff Manual respectively. Title pages will be prepared in manuscript.

WAR DIARY
6th Battalion, Sherwood Foresters.
INTELLIGENCE SUMMARY.
(*Erase heading not required.*)

Army Form C. 2118.

Vol 19

Hour, Date, Place	Summary of Events and Information	Remarks and References to Appendices
2.8.16. BAILLEULVAL.	2/Lt A.L.DENT & 2/Lt R.F.BRIGGS joined.	
4.8.16. BAILLEULVAL.	Inter Company Competitions in Bayonet Fighting and Gas helmet drill Winners, Bayonet fighting, "A" Coy. Gas helmet drill, Bombers.	
4.8.16. BAILLEULVAL.	Relieved 5th Sherwood Foresters in RIGHT SECTOR.	
6.8.16. BELLACOURT.	Capts SAXBY and WHEATCROFT rejoined from Third Army School.	
7.8.16.	1680 Sergt R.WAGG awarded D.C.M. for gallantry in connection with the operations of the 1st July.	
8.8.16. BELLACOURT.	Capts C.V.H.C.BLACKWALL and E.S.WOOD to Third Army School.	
10.8.16. TRENCHES.	Relieved by 5th Battn in RIGHT SECTOR and moved into Brigade Reserve at BELLACOURT.	
11.8.16. BELLACOURT.	Capt E.B.JOHNSON to Hospital.	
18.8.16. BELLACOURT.	I Officer and 15 other ranks 1st DRAGOON GUARDS attached for instruction.	
16.8.16. TRENCHES.	Relieved 5th Battalion in RIGHT SECTOR. MAJOR E.HALL to Hospital.	
16.8.16.	2/LT W.G.WOOD transferred to England.	
19.8.16. BELLACOURT.	Enemy shelled village about 12.15 a.m. 17 other ranks wounded, and 1 killed and 1 wounded attached 139th Trench Mortar Battery.	
22.8.16. TRENCHES.	Relieved by 5th Battn and moved into Divl Reserve in BAILLEULVAL.	
26.8.16. BAILLEULVAL.	Battn ceremonial drill and inspection by G.O.C.Division.	
26.8.16. BAILLEULVAL.	Battalion sports held.	
28.8.16. TRENCHES.	Relieved 5th Battalion in RIGHT SECTOR.	
28.8.16. BELLACOURT.	Draft of 11 Signallers and 15 Lewis Gunners arrived.	
31.8.16. BELLACOURT.	Capt W.SEATON rejoined from 7th Battalion.	

G. D. Goodman

Lieut Colonel.
Commanding 6th Battalion Sherwood Foresters.

195

(9 29 6) W 3332—1107 100,000 10/13 H W V Forms/C. 2118/10.

SECRET. Copy No

INSTRUCTIONS TO

RAIDING PARTY.

-:-:-:-:-:-:-:-:-:-:-:-:-:-:-

ENEMY. 1. In advance of the enemy's main line and lying in a hollow screened from direct ~~xiex~~ observation, is a bank (or sunk fence) 200 yards long, known as the TALUS.(See plan). This bank is 200 yards distant from No 14 SAP and rather more from No 15, from which saps it is approached by a downward slope, devoid of cover. There is apparently no bank on our side and the TALUS is in the nature of a sunk fence with a drop of 6ft to 8 ft towards the enemy. A path below runs along the bank. This path is floorboarded and entirely open to the enemy's front line. At intervals there appears to be steps or short fire bays. On the top of the Bank are bushes. There are none for perhaps 20 yards on the SOUTH portion of the Bank. The TALUS is connected at its SOUTH end with the enemy's front line by a C.T. some 200 yards long. About 120 yards down this C.T. is a circular work probably a machine gun dug-out or emplacement marked "D". In front of the TALUS are two depths of wire each about 10 yards deep with an interval between them of some 10 yards. At a point apparently 16 yards from the South end of TALUS is a gap 10 to 15 yards wide (Marked A-B on plan). Both sides of the C.T. are strongly wired and there is also much wire between the TALUS and the enemy's front line trench and on the NORTH (open) flank which latter is protected by the BLOCKHOUSE. Apparently it is the enemy's custom to patrol the TALUS from time to time. His patrols also use the gap A - B to approach our line, and there is often a working party on the wire in the neighbourhood.

OBJECTIVE. 2. It is proposed to make a raid on the enemy's advanced posts in the TALUS with the object of taking prisoners and securing identification, also of taking any machine guns at "D" and of inflicting as much injury on the enemy as possible.

PARTIES. 3. <u>RAIDING PARTY</u> under 2/Lt R.Evans will consist of N.C.O's and men of Letter "B" Coy with 7 Bombers and R.E.
This will be divided into:-

(i) BLOCKING PARTY of 2 Bombers (1 N.C.O.) and 3 men,
(ii) 1 N.C.O 2 Bombers and 2 men.
(iii) 1 Officer, 1 N.C.O. 1 bomber and 5 men with 3 R.E.
(iv) 1 N.C.O. 2 bombers and 1 man.

<u>SCOUTS</u> under 2/Lieut E.Kershaw. - 7 Scouts.

DRESS. 4. Scouts will wear their usual equipment, remainder will not wear their equipment but will carry 10 rounds in pocket - magazines charged with safety catch closed and 2 bombs per man in pockets. Socks will be drawn over boots. All badges and marks of identification will be removed.

RAID. 5. After dark the parties will be assembled near 15 SAP. A party of Scouts will leave 15 SAP and will lay tape and reconnoitre the gap in enemy's wire to ascertain if it is clear. 2 Scouts will remain at entrance to gap and two will return to guide party. The raiding party will then leave 15 SAP in their proper order. On Passing through gap, Blocking party will turn to left and take up positions by nearest bush on TALUS marked "C". This party will remain there on top with two bayonet men below and will be responsible for this flank until the raiding party returns when they will protect the rear. Should any of the enemy's patrols approach (any such would probably come from NORTH along TALUS) they will be dealt with by the bayonet. This party must not use bombs unless absolutely necessary.
The raiding party will get into the TALUS as quickly as possible and proceed in three parties to the RIGHT until they come to the C.T.

RAID (Contd). C.T. turning down it tothe left. Short intervals (not exceeding 10 yards) will be kept between parties. If any enemy patrols are met with they should be bayoneta or taken prisoners without noise. Any prisoners should be disarmed and sent back at once under escort. On arrival at "D" the leading party will block the trench beyond "D". Any dugouts must be bombed and search made for a machine gun, which, if found must be brought back. The party will not proceed further than "D", but having accomplished its task will immediately return by the TALUS and gap in wire followed by BLOCKING PARTY and SCOUTS, During the operations the Scouts will remain in the vicinity of the TALUS and wire, to direct the return of the various parties, and will lay tape to No 9 SAP. Care must be taken to indicate position of steps from below TALUS.

RETURN. 6. On leaving gap in the enemy's wire all parties will make for No 9 SAP along the tape keeping their right shoulders up. ~~The direction of the SAP will be given by flares.~~ O.C. "A" Coy will arrange to send up a succession of flares from this spot and will have two men lying out to show gap in our wire.

WEAPON. 7. The success of the operation depends largely on surprise. All ranks must therefore understand that the bayonet is the proper weapon and bombs should only be used for bombing dug-outs, except in case of absolute necessity.

ARTILLERY. 8. B/231 Battery will have its guns laid on the enemy front line NORTH and SOUTH of the TALUS SAP and a F.O.O. will be on duty with the telephone at head of CHURCH STREET. On receiving an order from the Commanding Officer, slow fire will be opened and the battery will be prepared to increase the rate of fire on being called upon to do so.

C.O. 9. The C.O. will be at the head of CHURCH STREET (Junction of front line trench)

G. D. Goodman

Lt Colonel.

31st August 1916. Commanding 6th Battn Sherwood Foresters.

Copy No 1. War Diary

" " 2. 2/Lt Evans

" " 3. 2/Lt Kershaw

31·8·1916.

PLAN

NOT TO SCALE

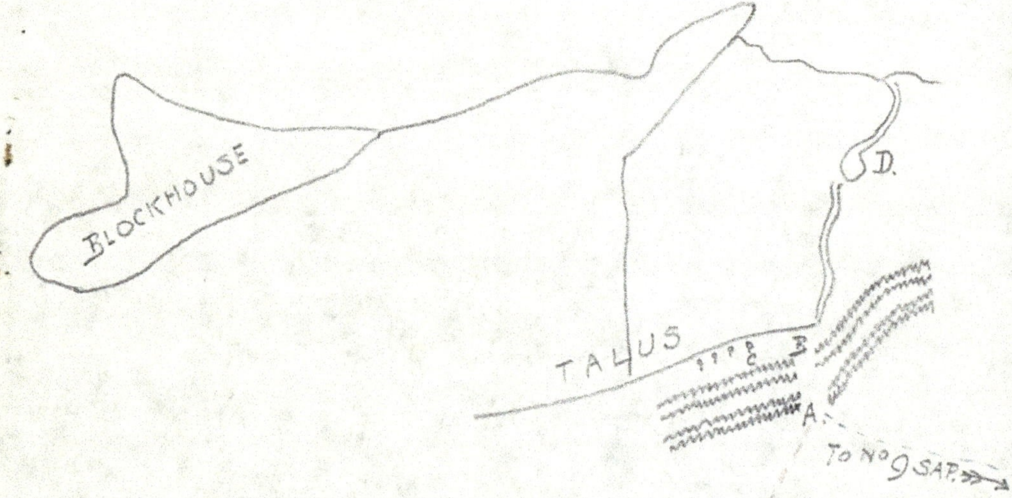

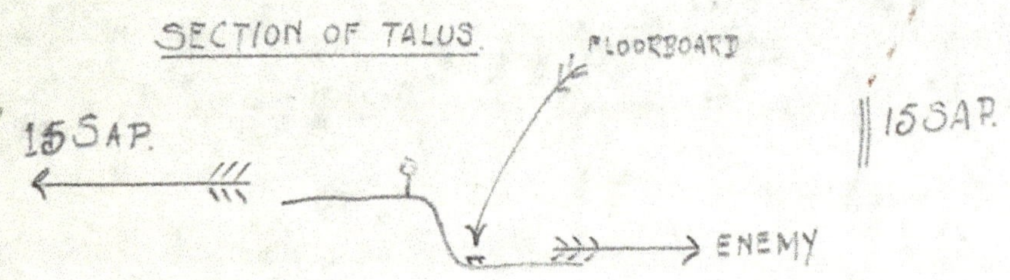

ROUTE TO TALUS - - - - - - -

ROUTE FROM TALUS. - - - - - - -

Instructions regarding War Diaries and Intelligence Summaries are contained in F. S. Regs., Part II. and the Staff Manual respectively. Title pages will be prepared in manuscript.

Army Form C. 2118.

WAR DIARY

6th Battalion Sherwood Foresters.

~~INTELLIGENCE SUMMARY.~~

(Erase heading not required.)

Vol 20

Hour, Date, Place		Summary of Events and Information	Remarks and references to Appendices
Trenches.	1.9.16.	Raid on TALUS. which was checked by wire & party withdrew	App I.
Trenches.	3.9.16.	Relieved by 5th Battalion in RIGHT SECTOR and on relief occupied Billets in BELLACOURT, furnishing garrisons of strong posts.	
LONDON GAZETTE.	7.9.16.	NOTTS & DERBY REGT. The Precedence of the undermentioned 2/Lts (Tempy Lieuts) to be as notified against their names, & not as previously stated. G.K.K.MAUGHAN 4th June 1915. C.A.BROWN. 5th June 1915. J.L.PERCIVAL. 6th June 1915. A.B.WALLIS. 7th June 1915. H.W.HIGHAM. 14th June 1915. Second Lieutenants to be Temporary Lieutenants:- R.W.CASH with precedence from 8th June 1915 (March 2) G.GLOSSOP with precedence from 9th June 1915. (Feb 12.)	
BELLACOURT.	7.9.16.	2/LIEUT L.N.JOHNSON rejoined from Hospital.	
Trenches.	7.9.16.	Battalion relieved 5th Battalion in RIGHT SECTOR. CAPT E.B.JOHNSON rejoined from Hospital.	
	10.9.16.	MAJOR E.HALL discharged from Hospital and proceeded to England on Special leave.	
Trenches.	15.9.16.	Battalion relieved by 5th Battalion and moved back into Divisional Reserve, occupying Billets at BAILLEULVAL.	
BAILLEULVAL.	16.9.16.	Draft of 22 other ranks arrived.	
BAILLEULVAL.	17.9.16.	CAPT W.SEATON & LIEUT J.TAYLOR to Third Army Infantry School.	
BAILLEULVAL.	17.9.16.	CAPT J.TOLSON to Hospital.	
BAILLEULVAL.	18.9.16.	CAPT R.SAXBY took over Command of the Battalion during the absence of LIEUT COLONEL G.D.GOODMAN C.M.G on short leave.	
	17 ~~18~~.9.16.	2/LIEUT W.B.DAVIES died in Hospital.	
Trenches.	20.9.16.	Battalion relieved 5th Battalion in RIGHT SECTOR.	
LONDON GAZETTE.	22.9.16.	7TH (ROBIN HOOD) BATTALION SHERWOOD FORESTERS. 2/Lts(Tempy Lieuts) G.S.RIVINGTON (from 6th Battn Sherwood Foresters) to be 2/Lt. 10.7.16. T.L.DARBYSHIRE(from 6th Battn Sherwood Foresters) to be 2/Lt. 10.7.16. 2/Lt G.S.RIVINGTON to be Tempy Lieut 10.7.16. 2/Lt T.L.DARBYSHIRE to be Temp Lieut 10.7.16.	
Trenches.	26.9.16.	Battn relieved by 5th Battn in RIGHT SECTOR & moved to BELLACOURT.	
BELLACOURT.	27.9.16.	LIEUT G.GLOSSOP & 10 other ranks arrived from Base.	
BELLACOURT.	27.9.16.	All long rifles withdrawn and replaced by short rifles.	
BELLACOURT.	30.9.16.	Lt Col G.D.GOODMAN C.M.G resumes Command of the Battalion.	

G.D. Goodman Lt Colonel.
Commdg 6th Batt Sherwood Foresters

Instructions regarding War Diaries and Intelligence Summaries are contained in F. S. Regs., Part II. and the Staff Manual respectively. Title pages will be prepared in manuscript.

WAR DIARY

6th Battalion Sherwood Foresters.

~~INTELLIGENCE SUMMARY~~

(Erase heading not required.)

Army Form C. 2118.

Vol 21

Hour, Date, Place	Summary of Events and Information	Remarks and references to Appendices
1.10.16. Trenches.	Relieved 5th Batt Sherwood Foresters in RIGHT SECTOR.	
3.10.16. Trenches.	Enemy attempted to raid 14 SAP but were driven off, leaving 2 wounded prisoners in our hands.	
5.10.16. BELLACOURT.	LIEUT HIGHAM rejoined Battalion from the Base.	
5.10.16. BASSEUX.	CAPT C.J.WHEATCROFT joined 139th Bde H.Q. as Assistant Staff Captain.	
7.10.16. Trenches.	Relieved by 5th Battalion Sherwood Foresters and moved back into Billets at BAILLEULVAL. (Divisional Reserve).	
11.10.16. BAILLEULVAL.	MAJOR E.HALL rejoined Battalion from Sick leave. + took over command	
11.10.16. BASSEUX.	LIEUT COLONEL G.D.GOODMAN C.M.G to temporary Command of 139th Bde.	
12.10.16. LONDON GAZETTE.	CAPT R.SAXBY to be Temporary Major d/- 5/9/16.	
13.10.16. Trenches.	Relieved 5th Battalion in RIGHT SECTOR.	
15.10.16. BELLACOURT.	CAPT SEATON & LIEUT TAYLOR rejoined from Third Army School.	
15.10.16. BELLACOURT.	LIEUT G.K.K.Maughan to Third Army Infantry School.	
16.10.16. Trenches.	LIEUT C.A.BROWN to be Acting Adjutant.	
19.10.16. Trenches.	Relieved by 5th Battn and went back into Bde Reserve at BELLACOURT.	
22.10.16. BELLACOURT.	2/LIEUT J.G.J.HUTTON rejoined with 4 other ranks from Base.	
24.10.16. BELLACOURT.	MAJOR SAXBY to Hospital.	
25.10.16. BELLACOURT.	LT COL G.D.GOODMAN C.M.G. returned from Divisional School. Relieved 5th Bn in RIGHT SECTOR	
26.10.16. BELLACOURT.	CAPTAIN & ADJUTANT C.B.JOHNSON rejoined from England.	
30.10.16. Trenches.	Relieved in Trenches by 2nd Battalion Royal Scots Fusiliers, 90th Brigade and moved to BAILLEULVAL in the morning, and at 5.30 p.m. the Battalion marched into Billets at SUS ST LEGER. (5 men casualties)	

G. D. Goodman Lieut Colonel.
Commanding 6th Batt SherwoodForesters.

21 S

Instructions regarding War Diaries and Intelligence Summaries are contained in F. S. Regs., Part II. and the Staff Manual respectively. Title pages will be prepared in manuscript.

WAR DIARY
of 6th Bn Sherwood Foresters
INTELLIGENCE SUMMARY.
(*Erase heading not required.*)

Army Form C. 2118.

Vol 22

Hour, Date, Place	Summary of Events and Information	Remarks and references to Appendices
1. 11 16. SUS ST. LEGER	Battalion marched into Billets at BARLY.	E.H
3. 11 16. BARLY.	Battalion marched into Billets at COULONVILLERS.	E.H
5. 11 16 COULONVILLERS	2/Lt A P STONER proceeded to Base pending transfer to England for attachment to R.E's	E.H
11. 11 16 COULONVILLERS	Battalion moved into Billets at GAPENNES, taking over from 6th Bn N. STAFFS REGT, billets at COULONVILLERS being handed over to 9th Bn S.F.	E.H
13 11 16 GAPENNES.	All Company Imprest accounts merged into 1 central account the Adjutant being the Imprest Holder.	E.H
14. 11. 16 GAPENNES.	LIEUT. G. GLOSSOP to Third Army School.	E.H
15. 11. 16 GAPENNES.	2/Lt J. G. J. HUTTON, 2/Lt J. L. ROBINSON, 2/Lt A. F. BRIGGS, 2/Lt A. L. DENT, 2/Lt H. T. STEPHENS & 2/Lt W. L. COOPER despatched to join 11th Bn K.R.R.C, & struck off strength.	E.H
20. 11. 16 GAPENNES.	Lt COL G. I. GOODMAN C.M.G. V.D proceeded to command 52nd Infantry Brigade, and to be Tempy BRIGADIER-GENERAL. MAJOR E. HALL took over the command of the Battn	E.H
21 11. 16. LONDON GAZETTE.	W D JAMIESON from 6th Sherwood Foresters to be QUARTERMASTER & HON LIEUT. dated 17th Oct 1916.	E.H
6. 11 16/21. 11. 16	Battn underwent training in the St RIQUIER training area.	E.H
22. 11. 16 GAPENNES.	Battn marched into Billets at AGENVILLE.	E.H
23. 11. 16. AGENVILLE.	Marched into Billets at BARLY.	E.H
25. 11. 16. BARLY.	Marched into Billets at SUS ST LEGER.	E.H
26. 11. 16 SUS. ST LEGER	MAJOR. R. SAXBY rejoined from Hospital.	E.H
30 11 16 SUS. ST LEGER	MAJOR E HALL authorized to wear badges of Lt COLONEL pending promotion appearing in LONDON GAZETTE.	E.H

E. Hall Lieut Colonel
Comdg 6th Bn Sherwood Foresters

F. Abraham

22. 6

(9 29 6) W 3332—1107 100,000 10/13 H W V Forms/C. 2118/10.

Instructions regarding War Diaries and Intelligence Summaries are contained in F. S. Regs., Part II. and the Staff Manual respectively. Title pages will be prepared in manuscript.

WAR DIARY or ~~INTELLIGENCE SUMMARY~~. 6th Bn Sherwood Foresters

(Erase heading not required.)

Army Form C. 2118.

Vol 23

Hour, Date, Place	Summary of Events and Information	Remarks and references to Appendices
1.12.16 SUS. ST LEGER	LIEUT D.S. FOX proceeded on leave.	E.H.
2.12.16 SUS. ST LEGER	CAPT C.B. JOHNSON vacates appt of ADJT.	E.H.
	LIEUT G.K.K. MAUGHAN appd A/ADJT.	E.H.
	G.O.C. DIVISION inspected BRIGADE & expressed his satisfaction at the soldierly appearance & steadiness of the Bn on parade & congratulated the Bn on the "MARCH PAST", also presented MILITARY MEDAL ribbons to the a/m:-	E.H.
	570 C.S.M. DAKIN G.W., 71 SGT HOPKINS W., 1450 SGT. WOOLLEY C.W. 1464 SGT LONGSON W. 2323 CPL. STREYAN A. 1936 L/CPL SMITH V.S. 1644 DMR CHATTERTON J. 1790 PTE DAWES S.	E.H.
3.12.16 SUS. ST LEGER	LT. COL E. HALL proceeded to Commanding Officers Conference at 3RD ARMY SCHOOL at AUXI-LE-CHATEAU.	E.H.
	CAPT. C.B. JOHNSON assumed Command of Battalion.	E.H.
	MAJOR R. SAXBY appd TOWN MAJOR of SUS. ST LEGER. (PAS-DE-CALAIS)	E.H.
4.12.16 SUS. ST LEGER	2 Lewis Guns issued to Battalion	E.H.
	2101 TPR. P. BOSHER 2/2ND COUNTY LONDON YEOMANRY who had been attached to Battn. for instruction appd to Commission in 11th Battn BORDER REGT.	E.H.
	LIEUT HIGHAM H.W. to THIRD ARMY SCHOOL	E.H.
5.12.16 SUS. ST LEGER	Formation of H. Qrs. L.G. Detachment.	E.H.
	CAPT H.H. JACKSON proceeded on leave.	E.H.
6.12.16 SUS. ST LEGER	DIVISION took over GOMMECOURT Sector of trenches from 49TH DIVISION.	E.H.
	Battn moved from SUS-ST-LEGER (PAS-DE-CALAIS) into new billets at SOUASTRE (SOMME) & was in DIVISIONAL RESERVE.	
9.12.16 SOUASTRE	LIEUT B.E. JOHNSON proceeded on leave	E.H.
10.12.16 SOUASTRE	LIEUT A.M. GOODALL Commands BDE. Dug-Out Company.	E.H.
11.12.16 SOUASTRE	LIEUT. COL. E. HALL returned from Commanding Officers Conference & took over Command of Battalion vice CAPT C.B. JOHNSON to 2nd in Command.	E.H.
	Battalion found working parties in SOUASTRE during Divisional Reserve	E.H.

23.S

(9 29 6) W 3332—1107 100,000 10/13 H W V Forms/C. 2118/10

Instructions regarding War Diaries and Intelligence Summaries are contained in F. S. Regs., Part II. and the Staff Manual respectively. Title pages will be prepared in manuscript.

WAR DIARY ~~or~~ of 6th II Batt SHERWOOD FORESTERS
INTELLIGENCE SUMMARY.

(*Erase heading not required.*)

Army Form C. 2118.

Hour, Date, Place		Summary of Events and Information	Remarks and references to Appendices
12.12.16	SOUASTRE	Batt relieved 5th Batt in RIGHT SECTOR (X1 Sub Sector) trenches. (GOMMECOURT). Disposition of Batt as under	
		L "C" Coy LEFT Sub-Sector. Lt "B" Coy CENTRE Sub Sector Lt "A" Coy RIGHT Sub-Sector BLUFF Lt "D" Coy. H. Qrs THORPE St.	
		Relief completed by 12.20 pm	EH
		~~[illegible]~~	
		2 LIEUT. F.W. HIPKINS to DIVISIONAL INFANTRY SCHOOL	EH
13.12.16	TRENCHES.	LIEUT. D.S. FOX rejoined from leave	EH
14.12.16	"	LIEUT D.S. FOX to Brigade School as L.G. Instructor	EH
15.12.16	"	LIEUT H.W. HIGHAM rejoined from 3RD ARMY SCHOOL	EH
18.12.16	"	Batt relieved by 5th Batt & moved into Brigade SUPPORT billets 2 Coys moving to SOUASTRE. 2 Coys staying in FONQUEVILLERS & H Qrs	EH
		Casualties during Tour 4. OR. W.	EH
		Batt finding fatigue parties during Brigade Support.	EH
22.12.16	SOUASTRE	LIEUT. A.H. GOODALL & 2nd Lieut V.T.G. HORE proceeded to join the Branch Machine Gun Corps.	
		Casualties during Brigade Support 2. OR Wounded	EH
		Batt relieved 5th Bn in same Sector trenches. Distribution of Coys Lt "A" Coy SUPPORT. Lt "B" Coy Centre Sub Sector "C" Coy LEFT Sub Sector Lt "D" Coy RIGHT Sub Sector	EH
24.12.16	Trenches	Draft 40 OR from Base (25 OR old 7th Bn & 15 OR old 8th Bn)	EH
26.12.16	SOUASTRE	Batt relieved by 5th Batt & moved to billets at SOUASTRE into DIVISIONAL reserve.	EH
		Casualties for tour Nil	
		During rest Company dinners were held in Y.M.C.A. hut SOUASTRE	EH
30.12.16	SOUASTRE	Batt relieved 5th Batt in same sector, distribution of Coys as under	
		Lt "A" Coy Support (Bluff dug-outs). Lt "B" Coy Centre Sub Sector Lt "C" Coy LEFT Sub Sec. "D" Coy RIGHT Sub Sec H. Qrs THORPE ST.	EH

(9 29 6) W 3332—1107 100,000 10/13 H W V Forms/C. 2118/10

Instructions regarding War Diaries and Intelligence Summaries are contained in F. S. Regs., Part II. and the Staff Manual respectively. Title pages will be prepared in manuscript.

WAR DIARY III ~~or~~ of 6/Sherwood Foresters
~~INTELLIGENCE SUMMARY.~~

(*Erase heading not required.*)

Army Form C. 2118.

Hour, Date, Place		Summary of Events and Information	Remarks and references to Appendices
28 12 16	SOUSTRE	Capt BLACKWALL C.V.H.C. to 2nd in Command. Div. School	EH
		LIEUT B.E. JOHNSON rejoined from leave.	
30 12 16.	SOUASTRE	2/LIEUT R EVANS to 3rd ARMY SCHOOL	EH
31. 12. 16.	TRENCHES	CAPT V.O. ROBINSON rejoined from duty at the I.B.D.	EH
		2/LIEUT F.W.A. STUBBS rejoined as reinforcement from England	EH
		2/LIEUT F.W. HIPKINS. rejoined from Div. School	EH

Edward Hall Lieut-Col.
Cdg 6th Sherwood Foresters

1/6th Battalion Sherwood Foresters

Vol 24

Army Form C. 2118.

Instructions regarding War Diaries and Intelligence Summaries are contained in F. S. Regs., Part II. and the Staff Manual respectively. Title pages will be prepared in manuscript.

WAR DIARY or INTELLIGENCE SUMMARY.

(*Erase heading not required.*)

Hour, Date, Place	Summary of Events and Information	Remarks and references to Appendices
1.1.17	Gazette Lt Col. E. HALL to be a Companion of the Distinguished Service Order	
	1453 Sgt W MARCHINGTON awarded D.C.M.	EH
	Despatches The follg were mentioned in the Despatches of Field Marshal Sir D. HAIG'S	
	LIEUT COL E. HALL, D.S.O, SURG MAJOR A W SHEA	
	CAPT. E M B. TAYLOR 508 Drmr A. ASKEY.	EH
3.1.17	Bn relieved by 5th Battn. & moved back to Bde Reserve.	EH
7.1.17	Relieved 5th Bn in Right Sector	EH
	Draft of 180 ORs (160 partly trained) joined Battn & sent to Bde Training Depot	EH
11.1.17	Relieved by 5th Bn & moved back into Divl Reserve.	
	Lieut A.H. GOODALL & 2nd Lieut V.T.G HORE seconded for duty with Heavy Branch Machine Gun Corps. d/- 23-12-16.	EH
12.1.17	Appointments Capt C.B. JOHNSON Appd a/Major d/- 13-12-16	
SOUASTRE	Village shelled by enemy. 2374 L/Sgt T. LAND wounded in A. & eventually died of W.	EH
13.1.17	Major C.B. JOHNSON assumed Temy Comd. of Bn vice Lt Col E. HALL, D.SO, on short leave to England	EH
15.1.17	Bn relieved 5th Bn in X1 Sub Sector.	EH
18.1.17	2/Lts. T A MABBOTT & A.L. PALMER joined Battn.	
	Surg Major A.W. SHEA on 1 months leave	EH
19.1.17	Relieved by 5th Bn & moved to Bde Reserve	EH
23.1.17	Relieved 5th Bn	EH
24.1.17	Lt. G. GLOSSOP struck off strength, being sick in England	EH
27.1.17	Relieved by 5th Bn & moved to Divl Reserve	EH
31.1.17	Relieved 5th Bn & took over Right. Coy. Sector of X2 Sector	EH

E Hall Lieut Col
Comdg. 1/6 Sherwood Foresters

24

(9 29 6) W 3332—1107 100,000 10/13 H W V Forms/C. 2118/10.

Instructions regarding War Diaries and Intelligence Summaries are contained in F. S. Regs., Part II. and the Staff Manual respectively. Title pages will be prepared in manuscript.

WAR DIARY
of 6th Bn Sherwood Foresters
~~INTELLIGENCE~~ SUMMARY.
(Erase heading not required.)

Army Form C. 2118.

Vol 25

Hour, Date, Place		Summary of Events and Information	Remarks and references to Appendices
4.2.17	Trenches	Relieved by 5th Bn in RIGHT SECTOR & moved back to Divisional Res. in SOUASTRE.	a/a
6.2.17	SOUASTRE	Bn moved into Huts in HALLOY & commenced special training.	a/a
7.2.17	HALLOY	160 other ranks joined Bn from Brigade Depot.	a/a
13.2.17	C in C's list No 121.	LIEUT G.K.K. MAUGHAN appointed Adjutant d/- 28.11.17.	a/a
18.2.17	HALLOY	Bn moved to BEAUDRICOURT.	a/a
19.2.17	BEAUDRICOURT	Lt Col E. HALL. D.S.O. appointed VII Corps area Commandant & vacated command of the Battn.	a/a a/a
20.2.17	BEAUDRICOURT	MAJOR A.L. ASHWELL D.S.O. 8th Bn Sherwood Foresters assumed command of the Battn.	a/a
		2/Lt K.H. BOND rejoined from 139 Bde HQ.	
22.2.17	BEAUDRICOURT	SERG-MAJ A.W. SHEA returned from Special leave.	a/a
26.2.17	BEAUDRICOURT	Bn marched to SIMENCOURT.	a/a
27.2.17	SIMENCOURT	Bn marched to ACHICOURT.	a/a
28.2.17	ACHICOURT	Bn marched to FOSSEUX.	a/a a/a

A. L. Ashwell Major
Comdg 6th Sherwood Foresters

25.S

Army Form C. 2118.

Instructions regarding War Diaries and Intelligence Summaries are contained in F. S. Regs., Part II. and the Staff Manual respectively. Title pages will be prepared in manuscript.

WAR DIARY
of 1/6th Bn Sherwood Foresters
INTELLIGENCE SUMMARY.
(Erase heading not required.)

Vol 26

Hour, Date, Place			Summary of Events and Information	Remarks and references to Appendices
1.3.17.	FOSSEUX		Battn marched to HALLOY (HQ at GRENAS)	CBS.
2.3.17.	HALLOY.		Bn marched to SOUASTRE & billeted in HUTS.	CBS.
3.3.17	SOUASTRE		Moved into Billets vacated by 4th Leicesters.	CBS.
4.3.17	SOUASTRE.		HQrs. "A" & "D" Coys moved to FONQUEVILLERS with HQrs at the BREWERY 2/Lt A.L. PALMER wounded.	CBS.
5.3.17.	FONQUEVILLERS	5.30am.	HQrs; B & C Coys moved into GOMMECOURT.	CBS
6.3.17.		10.pm	Bn relieved 8th Bn Sherwood Foresters in LEFT GOMMECOURT SECTOR. HQrs in old German 3rd line, E29A.8.3. "B" & "C" in Front line, "A" in support (PIGEON TRENCH) & "D" in reserve in LANDSTURM GRABEN. (FONQUEVILLERS Trench Map)	CBS
7.3.17.			Front line held by "B" & "C" Coys was E23.d.7.9 — E23.d.9.7 — E23.d.40.45 — E23.d.5.2 — BRAYELLE GRABEN to E30.a.6.9 — E30.b.2.5 — E30.b.3.5. (FONQUEVILLERS Trench Map).	CBS.
8.3.17		11 pm.	2nd B & C Coys attacked KITE COPSE & the BURG.	CBS
9.3.17.		12.50 am.	"B" Coy holding KITE COPSE & trenches running S.W from corners. BURG strongly held by enemy.	CBS
9.3.17.		3.5 am.	MAJOR A.L. ASHWELL D.S.O wounded in KITE COPSE. Major C.B. JOHNSON assumed command. LIEUT J.S. FOX slightly wounded (at duty)	CBS
9.3.17		5.40 am	KITE COPSE evacuated by us without loss. Identifications of 91st R.I.R obtained.	CBS
10.3.17.		10.10 pm.	Battn relieved by 8th Bn Sherwood Foresters & moved into Bde Reserve in GOMMECOURT. Dispositions:- HQ. at K.4.b.6.3. A Coy Old German second line between STEIN & PILIER GRABEN. C Coy in REIGLE STELLUNG. D Coy in HELMUT TRENCH. Casualties in addition to those already quoted. 2/Lt L.A. Johnson slightly wounded (at duty) 8 other Ranks killed. 2 " " missing. 38 " " wounded.	CBS
13.3.17.	C in C's list		MAJOR R. SAXBY recorded for duty as Town Major AMPLIER MORILLE.	CBS

26.S

Instructions regarding War Diaries and Intelligence Summaries are contained in F.S. Regs., Part II. and the Staff Manual respectively. Title pages will be prepared in manuscript.

WAR DIARY
or
~~INTELLIGENCE SUMMARY.~~
(*Erase heading not required.*)

II

Army Form C. 2118.

6th Sherwood Foresters

Hour, Date, Place		Summary of Events and Information	Remarks and references to Appendices
14.3.17	10 pm.	Battn relieved 8th Bn Sherwood Foresters in LEFT GOMMECOURT Sector. HQrs in PIGEON WOOD. "A" "C" & "D" Coys in front line. "B" in support. Front line – LANDSTURM GRABEN – F.19.c.0.0. – KITE COPSE – E.24.a.5.2 – BRAVELLE GRABEN – E.30.a.6.9 – E.24.c.4.5 – E.29.c.2.9 – E.23.b.9.2. Advanced posts at E.24.a.0.4, E.24.c.80.98, E.24.a.15.50.	CBS
15.3.17		Enemy line held as on day before	CBS
16.3.17		Wire cutting in front of N of BURG continued.	CBS
16.3.17	9.30 pm	Loud explosion heard in ESSARTS. Sound of transport heard in ESSARTS during the night 16/17th	CBS
17.3.17	6 am	Patrols occupied BURG & later whole of HEDGE TRENCH without opposition	
	9 am	Patrols pushed into ESSARTS.	
	2 pm.	Patrols reconnoitred QUESNOY FARM.	CBS
	4 pm.	Small enemy detachment firing machine guns from QUESNOY FARM caused 1 platoon of ours to withdraw.	
	8.30 pm	The Bn occupied & held QUESNOY FARM.	
18.3.17	12 midnight	Bn relieved by 4th Bn LINCOLNS & moved back into Billets at ST AMAND, 2 Platoons remaining at SOUASTRE.	CBS
19.3.17	ST AMAND	Lieut G.H.H. Maughan vacated the appointment of Adjutant. The Divisional Commander presented Military Medal Ribbons to Pte Miles & Pte Taylor.	CBS
20.3.17	ST AMAND.	2/Lt EIKERSHAW appointed Acting Adjutant. Battalion marched into Billets at BAYENCOURT.	CBS
21.3.17	BAYENCOURT	Battalion marched into Billets at COURCELLES.	CBS
23.3.17	COURCELLES.	Capt W. SEATON & Capt C.V.H.C. BLACKWALL rejoined from Divl Depot Bn. Battn marched into Billets at WARLOY-BAILLON.	CBS
24.3.17	WARLOY-BAILLON	Divisional Commander presented Military Cross ribbon to 2/Lt E Kershaw	CBS

Instructions regarding War Diaries and Intelligence Summaries are contained in F. S. Regs., Part II. and the Staff Manual respectively. Title pages will be prepared in manuscript.

WAR DIARY
or
~~INTELLIGENCE SUMMARY~~.
(Erase heading not required.)

111

Army Form C. 2118.

6th Sherwood Foresters.

Hour, Date, Place		Summary of Events and Information	Remarks and references to Appendices
24. 3. 17	WARLOY BAILLON	Battn marched into Billets at VILLERS-BOCAGE.	CBJ
25. 3. 17	VILLERS-BOCAGE	Divisional Commander presented Military Medal Ribbons to Sergt Jackson, L/Cpl Parkes & L/Cpl Hancock.	CBJ
25. 3. 17	VILLERS-BOCAGE	Battn moved to PONT DE METZ by bus.	CBJ
27. 3. 17	BACOUEL	2/Lt R.C.F. DOLLEY joined the Bn	CBJ
28. 3. 17	BACOUEL	The Battn entrained at 3 am.	CBJ
28. 3. 17	BERGUETTE	Battn detrained at 9.30pm & marched into Billets at LIGNY LEZ AIRE.	CBJ

CBJohnson Major
Commdg 1/6th Bn Sherwood Foresters

(9 29 6) W 3332—1107 100,000 10/13 H W V Forms/C. 2118/10.

Instructions regarding War Diaries and Intelligence Summaries are contained in F. S. Regs., Part II. and the Staff Manual respectively. Title pages will be prepared in manuscript.

Army Form C. 2118.

WAR DIARY
of 1/6th Bn The SHERWOOD FORESTERS.
~~INTELLIGENCE SUMMARY.~~
(Erase heading not required.)

Vol 27

Hour, Date, Place	Summary of Events and Information	Remarks and references to Appendices
3.4.17 LIGNY LEZ AIRE	Annual dinner given by remaining Sergeants of the original Sergeants mess to the remaining Officers who were present at the first Dinner at BRAINTREE in Feby 1915.	CBS appendix I
9.4.17. LIGNY LEZ AIRE.	Battn took part in Divisional March Exercise	CBS
13.4.17 LIGNY LEZ AIRE.	Battn marched into Billets at OBLINGHEM.	CBS
14.4.17 OBLINGHEM	Battn marched into NOEUX LES MINES & billeted in huts.	CBS
15.4.17 NOEUX LES MINES	2/Lt F.W. HIPKINS proceeded to 1st ARMY SCHOOL.	CBS
16.4.17. do	CAPT. E.S. WOOD proceeded to Central Training School CALAIS as Instructor	CBS
18.4.17 do	Bn moved into Billets at ANGRES & relieved 12th Bn ROYAL FUSILIERS (24th Divn) in Brigade Reserve.	CBS
19.4.17 do	Qr-Mr Stores & Transport moved to PETIT SAINS	CBS
19.4.17 ANGRES.	Bn relieved 4th Bn NORTHANTS Regt in LIEVIN. (2 Coys A & B Coys in front line, 2 Coys C & D Coys in Support).	CBS
20.4.17 LIEVIN.	The Bn attacked in conjunction with 8th Sherwood Foresters.	Appendix II CBS
22.4.17 PETIT SAINS	2/Lt T G HORE rejoined Bn from Heavy Branch M.G.C.	Appendix III CBS
23.4.17 LIEVIN.	The Bn attacked FOSSE 3 de LIEVIN. See report attached. Casualties in this action:-	Appendix IV CBS Appendix V
	OFFICERS: Wounded & missing Lt C.A. BROWN. Wounded. Capt E.B. JOHNSON, 2/Lt V.H. ARMITAGE, " B.N. PARKER, " W. ARCHER, " L.H. BOND (at duty)	
	OTHER RANKS: Killed 21, Wounded 71 (5 at duty), Missing 2.	
23.4.17 LIEVIN.	Battn relieved by 2/5th Bn Sherwood Foresters & marched into Billets at HARQUEFELES FERME (Divisional Reserve)	CBS

27 S
[illegible]

(9 29 6) W 3332—1107 100,000 10/13 H W V Forms/C. 2118/10.

Instructions regarding War Diaries and Intelligence Summaries are contained in F. S. Regs., Part II. and the Staff Manual respectively. Title pages will be prepared in manuscript.

II

WAR DIARY
of 16th Sherwood Foresters
~~INTELLIGENCE SUMMARY.~~
(*Erase heading not required.*)

Army Form C. 2118.

Hour, Date, Place	Summary of Events and Information	Remarks and references to Appendices
25. 4. 17	Major C B Johnson & Captain W Seaton authorised by G. O. C Division to wear the Badges of rank of LIEUT. COL & MAJOR respectively, pending the announcement in the London Gazette.	CBJ
28. 4. 17 MARGUEFFLES FERME	Bn marched to ANGRES & relieved 8th Bn Sherwood Foresters in Brigade Reserve (H Q at RED MILL)	CBJ
29. 4. 17	Capt C V H C Blackwall proceeded to 1st Corps School as Instructor.	CBJ
30. 4. 17 ANGRES	Battn relieved by 6th S. Staffords & proceeded into Huts & billets at SAINS EN GOHELLE (Divisional Reserve)	CBJ

C B Johnson
Lieut Colonel
Comdg 16th Bn Sherwood Foresters.

(9 29 6) W 3332–1107 100,000 10/13 H W V Forms/C. 2118/10.

Appendix I

List of Officers, Warrant Officers & Sergeants present at the Dinner held on 3rd Jan 1917.

Lieut Colonel J. E. Blackwall. D.S.O. (1st Bn)
Major. C. B. Johnson.
Surg Maj. A. W. Shea.
Capt. W. Seaton.
" V. O. Robinson.
" C. J. Wheatcroft.
" E. V. H. C. Blackwall.
" E. M. Brooke Taylor.
" J. Colson.
" L. H. Jackson.
Lieut R. E. Johnson.
" J. Taylor.
" D. S. Fox.
" & 2nd W. D. Jamieson.
R. S. M. Jackman.
R. Q. M. S. A. Barker.
C. S. M. E. W. Slater.
" G. W. Dakin.
" T. J. Renshall.
C. Q. M. S. S. Bennett.
" J. W. Mycock.
" A. Bacon.
" T. Jackson.
Sergt. J. McMahon.
" W. J. MacFarlane.
" J. Miller.
" W. Kay.
" A. Fox.
" S. Burke.
" A. Bramwell.
" J. Mellor (2nd Bn)
Interpreter M. Heilbronner.
R. S. M. G. A. Eagle. Suffolk Regt.
Staff Q. M. S. C. Parker. A.S.C.
Staff Sgt. A. Fletcher. A.S.C.
Sergt. H. Denton. A.S.C.
C. Q. M. S. D. W. Spiers. M. G. C.

Appendix IV

SECRET To O.C. A Coy B Coy D Coy
To C Coy for information. O.C. 8th S.F. for information

Ref. Map LENS 36c S.W. 1/10000

20th Apr 1917

1. The 6th & 8th Bn Sherwood Foresters will carry out a combined attack to-night.

2 The objectives of the 6th S.F. will be as follows:-

(a) Group of houses M30 c 30.90 and M30 a 45.05.

(b) Road from E corner of Bois de RIAUMONT to cross roads M 30 a 50.75 exclusive

(c) 8th S.F. objective will be Main Road from M30 a 50.75 inclusive to M24 c 90.05 and group of houses immediately S. of cross road M 30 a 50.75.

If objectives (b) of 6th S.F. and whole objective of 8th S.F. is gained 6th S.F. will endeavour to establish themselves in 2 rows of small houses S. of the main road

3 The gaining of objective (a) is allotted to Lt A Coy (Capt. V. O ROBINSON M.C in command) The gaining of objective (b) is allotted to Lt B Coy (Capt. J. TOLSON in command) Latter B Coy will also make good the houses between the BOIS and CITE DE RIAUMONT N of the main road

4 If enemy counter attack Officer

SECRET. APPENDIX IV.

Operation Order No. 1. by Major C. R. Johnson commanding 1/6th Sherwood Foresters

Ref: LENS 1/10000 22nd April 1917.

1. On April 23rd 139 Inf. Bgde will attack the line N25 a. 0.0. — FOSSE 3 DE LIEVIN — ADMIRAL TRENCH — HILL 65 — ADVANCED TRENCH
95th Inf. Bgde are attacking the CENTRAL ELECTRIC GENERATING STATION at the same time.

2. 6th S.F. will attack FOSSE 3. as far NORTH as M.30.b. 5.5. and will consolidate on line N25. c.0.4 — N.25. a 00. 15. — ALMANAC TRENCH — ADMIRAL TRENCH
The trench SOUCHEZ RIVER to M 30. d. 2. 9. will be taken after rest of the objective has been secured. Patrols will be sent S. to gain touch with 95th Inf. Bgde and posts will be established to cover the consolidation of the main line.

3. 8th S.F. will attack HILL 65. and ADVANCED TRENCH between N.19.c. 05. 20. & M.24. d. 90.65 with 2 Coys

4. Lt. C. Coy will carry out the attack supported by Lt. D Coy.

Lr. 'C' Coy will assemble in 1st & 2nd
BIG ROW SOUTH and SWAMP ROW as
soon as possible after dusk
Lr. 'D' Coy will assemble in BOIS ROW

(b) Lr. A Coy will remain in its present position
and will be responsible for the road running
S. from M.30.a. 8.1. They will also find
patrols to 95th Inf. Bgde

5 No. 13. Platoon, Lr. D Coy, will rejoin
the Coy as soon as possible after dusk

6 Lr. 'B' Coy will stand to in their
present position

7 At ZERO Lr 'C' Coy will advance ~~&~~ along
1st & 2nd BIG ROW SOUTH and seize N. end
of FOSSE and continue advance S.E. to
the limit laid down in para. 2.
At Zero Lr. 'D' Coy will send 1 platoon to hold
E end of 1st & 2nd SMALL ROWS until
8th S.F. attack develops: 1 platoon to
hold E end of 1st BIG ROW SOUTH; ½ platoon
to ~~[illegible]~~ establish themselves at trench
junction M.30.b. 5.5. ; ~~1½ platoons should~~
~~[illegible]~~ and to clear up trenches
running N. to either end of ALCOVE
TRENCH.

1½ platoons to establish themselves in 2nd BIG ROW SOUTH ready to support Lt. "C" Coy if required.
The platoon at E end of 1st + 2nd SMALL ROW will move down to 2nd BIG ROW SOUTH as soon as 8th S.F. attack is properly developed.

8 Each N.C.O. + man will carry 2 No. 5 grenades and in the case of Lt. "C" Coy 2 sandbags. Ground flares will be carried. A supply of heavy entrenching tools will be dumped at Lt. A Coy's H.Q.
1 N.C.O. + 2 L.G.'s per platoon will be left at present Coy H.Q.s. Capt. C.V.H.C. BLACKWALL and C.S.M. SLATER will not take part in the attack

7 (a) Artillery bombardment will commence at ZERO minus 8 hours — to cease at Zero minus 7½ hours — to recommence at ZERO minus 6½ hours continuing to ZERO

8 (b) At ZERO the 24th Div Artillery will open on the line M.20.d.20.92 — M.30.b.38.22. to M.30.b.35.52 — M.24.d.21.20 — M.24.d.75.45. — M.24.b.9.4. remaining

on this line for 5 minutes then lifting at the rate of 50 yds per minute to the trench line N.25.a.70.19 N.19.c.28.28. to N.19.c.02.22. — M24 d 90.68. — M24. b. 9.4. Five minutes after this line is reached the barrage will lift off line N19c.28.28 — M24.b. 9.4 to line N.19.c.28.28. — N19.a. 20.48. and remain there till order to cease fire.

The time ZERO minus 7 hours to ZERO minus 6½ hours is left free from bombardment for the discharge of gas by gas projectors if the wind is favourable. 50 drums will be fired on HILL 65. and 50 on FOSSE 3. Only to be fired if wind is between S.S.W and W.

At ZERO minus 7 hours all troops E. of the line M30 a 10.52. to N.1.c 33.35 will put on Box Respirators and retain them for ½ hour.

Two Stokes mortars will be at the disposal of O.C. 'C' Coy

Watches will be synchronised

by telephone or runner with Batt H.Q. at 6.30 p.m - 12.30 p.m - and 2.30 AM night 22nd/23rd.

12 A Contact Aeroplane will call for flares at 7. AM 23rd inst

13 Batt. battle H.Q. will be at M.29. c 65.60.

14 Batt. Aid Post will be in QUARRY.

15 Advanced SAA and Grenade Dumps will be at Battle H.Q.

16 ZERO hour will be 4.45 AM 23rd

17 Acknowledge.

(Sd) E. Kershaw
2/Lt & Adjt.
6th [illegible]

Issued at P.M
Copy No. 1. Adjutant for CO.
2-5 A.B.C.D Coys
6 B.S.F.

APPENDIX V

Report by O.C. 1/6th Sherwood Foresters on the attack on FOSSE 3 DE LIEVIN on 23rd April 1917.

---

1. The attacking force consisted of No. C Coy 6th Sherwood Foresters (Capt. E.B. JOHNSON) with No. D Coy (CAPT. H.H. JACKSON) in support.

2. The attacking force and its supporting Coy were distributed before ZERO as follows:–

No. C Coy as per sketch map. A.
No. D " Coy H.Q. at M30.a.15.
13 Platoon in cellars on either side of Coy. H.Q.
15 Platoon at M.30 a 28.57
14 & ½ 16 Platoons in cellars at M.30.a.40.65.
½ 16 Platoon at corner house M 30.a 52.75.

No. A Coy were close up in reserve as per sketch map A. (map not sent).

3. The objectives of the various platoons were as under:–

C Coy.

9 Platoon. Establish posts on line M 30 c 90.18. to M 30 d 90.40. covering ALMANAC TRENCH

10 Platoon. Make good main group of buildings on FOSSE, moving by S side of 2nd BIG ROW S.

11. Platoon. Make good ALMANAC TRENCH from M.30 c 90 18 to M 30. b 50 50

12. Platoon Buildings on FOSSE about M.30 b 20 10 and thence to clear trench M 30 d. 35. 85 to 20 40 on howitzers ceasing fire.

D. Coy.

13. Platoon. Make good E end of 1st BIG ROW S

15 Platoon. Make good E end of 1st & 2nd SMALL ROWS. S.

½ 16 Platoon. Occupy trench junction at M 30 b 5.5. and clear trenches to N, until ~~touch~~ was gained with 8th SF

14 & ½ 16 Platoon. Occupy 2nd BIG ROW S and act as immediate support to C. Coy

4 At ZERO our advance began. The enemy put down an extremely accurate barrage within 1 minute in response to red lights sent up in pairs from numerous places. This barrage started at the E end of the houses and moved forward for 2 minutes at which time it was on the ~~west~~ W end & remained there. The number of guns employed

in this barrage was not great.
M. Guns fired from ZERO onwards directly down all roads leading to the enemy, and one from the FOSSE obliquely across the spaces between the rows of houses. A M G from M. 30. a. 15 25 enfiladed roads crossing the road near the W end of the houses.

5. The various platoons on advancing progressed as follows:–

<u>C. Coy</u>

<u>9. Platoon</u> Fired on by M G's from E end of 1st BIG ROW. S. and unable to get forward

<u>10 Platoon</u>. Went through gap in wire M. 30. a. 85 20 and along road towards N end of FOSSE. Fired on heavily by M. G's from buildings at E end of road, which were 20 to 30 feet above the level of the road. Came to wall 5' high Lieut. Brown went over and was killed as he did so. Some men who followed found an uncut belt of wire just over the wall. They lay in shell holes till dark. Remainder of platoon forced to withdraw to old enemy gunpits about M. 30 d 80 15. till dark.

1 man of 166 Regt (killed when trying to escape) set fire to house

at M 30 a 72.12 as soon as our men advanced. Resulting flares showed up everyone plainly. Man must have been hidden in house since previous evening. Enemy must have re-occupied houses at E end of Nos 1 & 2 Big Rows S at ZERO. Much sniping and M G fire from these points.

<u>11 Platoon.</u> Found wire in and near trench at M 30 b 10 50 uncut, though this had been specially asked for. 2 sections got round through shell holes about M 30 b 10 40 and pushed on to trench junction M 30 b 35 50. 2 rear sections held up by heavy M G fire from FOSSE. 2 front sections forced to retire by strong German bombing attack from N.

<u>12 Platoon.</u> Platoon came under heavy M G fire from M 30 d 15 70, M 30 b 40 30 and were sniped from house at E end of 2nd BIG ROW S. They took cover in gunpits and their L Guns knocked out enemy M G firing from building M 30 b 40 30.

Capt E B Johnson was wounded by a sniper about 5 AM and 2/Lt Armitage the only surviving officer about 6 AM

D Coy

All platoons quickly gained their objectives except the 2 16 Platoon. These were held up by C Coy's lack of progress, and took cover in a house in 2nd B.C. Row S.

The coy had over 40 casualties in gaining its objectives, all from Shrapnel and M.G. fire.

6 When it was obvious that no progress could be made, every one took what cover was available and remained there till dusk

7 Enemy barrage and M.G fire died down about 6 am

8 I was in touch with 1st D.C.L.I. on my right the whole time.

9 My general conclusions were as follows:

(a) Enemy position was a very strong and well prepared one. There was much wire and trip wires with short lengths of lead piping strung on them at the foot of the slag heaps.

(b) There were prepared M.G. emplace-

-ments in slag heap about M 30.b 20.35 and 15.20. M G's also covered all roads leading to the enemy & the ground between the roads.

(c) The wall marked on the sketch map A with wire in rear of it is an impossible obstacle in the face of M.G fire.

(d) The hostile artillery & M.G barrage was very prompt in coming down & most accurate.

(e) The man who fired the house most materially helped to hold up our attack. He must have been an extraordinary brave man.

(f) Every available position in the FOSSE buildings was occupied by a sniper.

(g) The enemy brought a T.M. into position at M.30.b 35.15 on the 23rd inst.

(h) The enemy must have hidden saps leading out to the houses of most of the rows as he seems to re-occupy them at will.

(i) It was impossible to surmount the obstacles met with quick enough to take advantage of our creeping barrage

24/4/17

Major
6th Bn Sherwood Foresters

A Form. Army Form C.2121
(in pads of 100).

MESSAGES AND SIGNALS.

No. of Message

Code m. | Words | Charge | This message is on a/c of: | Recd. at m.

Office of Origin and Service Instructions.

Sent
At m
To
By

Service.

(Signature of "Franking Officer.")

Date
From
By

TO Head Quarters 70 Inf Bde

Sender's Number.	Day of Month.	In reply to Number.	AAA
* K648	4		

Herewith appendix III for War Diary aaa

From O.C. 11th Sherwood Foresters
Place
Time

The above may be forwarded as now corrected.

Censor.

(Z) [illegible] Lt Col

Signature of Addressor or person authorised to telegraph in his name.

* This line should be erased if not required.

750,000. W 2186—M529. H. W. & V., Ld. 6/16.

APPENDIX. 3

Report by O.C A Coy 6th Sher For
on operations night 21/22 April 1917

On the night 21/22 April A Coy 6 S.F. attacked the groups of houses W of FOSSE 3 de LIEVIN in M 30 a.

The attack was carried out by 3 platoons with 1 platoon in Reserve. The left platoon (Lieut Higham) carried its objective, the W end of the row of houses M 30 a 7.2. at 10 30 P.M. The enemy opened rapid fire & machine gun fire & then ran away.

The centre platoon (Lieut Stubbs) met opposition from an enemy barricade at M. 30 a 5.1. This was rushed at a second attempt under cover of a barrage of rifle grenades from the platoon in Reserve. Following the enemy up, the centre platoon succeeded in causing him casualties with Lewis gun fire as they were getting through the wire in front of FOSSE 3.

The right platoon found the enemy in a house at M 30 c 8.9. bombed him out of the cellar & as they bolted caught the enemy under the fire of men posted outside the house. Two being killed.

They were unable to follow up further on account of our own Lewis gun fire from the centre platoon.

At 11 P.M. the position was consolidated & at 11.15 P.M. a party of enemy attempting to approach from FOSSE 3 were driven back by rifle & Lewis gun fire, six bodies being subsequently found

This operation was successfully carried out under heavy barrage fire & also trench mortar bombardment. Our casualties amounted to one man killed & seven wounded: The enemies casualties being considerably heavier

V. Robinson Capt
O.C. A Coy
6th Sher. Foresters

Instructions regarding War Diaries and Intelligence Summaries are contained in F. S. Regs., Part II. and the Staff Manual respectively. Title pages will be prepared in manuscript.

WAR DIARY
or
~~INTELLIGENCE SUMMARY.~~

Army Form C. 2118.

1/6th Battn (*Erase heading not required.*) Sherwood Foresters.

Vol 28

Hour, Date, Place	Summary of Events and Information	Remarks and references to Appendices
6/5/17 PETIT SAINS	Bn relieved 1/5th Leicestershire Regt. in RIGHT SUBSECTOR of Left Brigade Front, E. of CITÉ ST. PIERRE, M.12d.50.10 to N.1.c.40.35 (Ref. Map. 36c. S.W.1).	CBS
6-5-17 Extract from C in C's List no. 133.	Sherwood Foresters:- 2/Lieut. E. KERSHAW, M.C. to be Adjutant, and to be Temporary Lieutenant whilst so employed, vice 2/Lieut. (Tempy. Lieut) G.K.K MAUGHAN to Regimental Duty 19/4/17.	CBS
8-5-17 TRENCHES	Military Medal awarded to following NCO & men for gallantry on 23rd April at FOSSE 3 DE LIÈVIN. no. 240827 L/Cpl A.E. BEDFORD " 242476 Pte K. BRESSER. 241360 " A. EVANS 240194 " T. WHEATCROFT.	CBS
10-5-17 TRENCHES	2nd LIEUT. F.W.A. STUBBS, M.C., killed in action	CBS
12-5-17 TRENCHES	Bn relieved by 5th Bn. Sherwood Foresters, and moved into Brigade Reserve in dugouts at W. end of CITÉ ST. PIERRE. Casualties:- 4 other Ranks killed, 10 O Ranks wounded.	CBS
13-5-17 TRENCHES	Major W. SEATON assumed temporary command of Battalion vice Lieut. Col. C.B. JOHNSON on short leave to England.	CBS
15-5-17 TRENCHES	Military Medal awarded to following NCO's & men for gallantry on 23rd April at FOSSE 3 DE LIÈVIN:- no. 240076 Sgt. J.G. RAVEY. " 241233 L/Cpl. F.W. HOBBS. " 240981 Pte T. DRABBLE. " 242442 " L. BEASTALL.	CBS
18-5-17 TRENCHES	Following awards made to ~~[illegible]~~ Officers and NCO. for Gallantry on 23rd April at FOSSE 3 DE LIÈVIN:- MILITARY CROSS. 2nd LIEUT. V.H. ARMITAGE. BAR to MILITARY CROSS CAPTAIN. V.O. ROBINSON, M.C. D.C.M 240513 Sergeant. F. LONGSON.	CBS

28

Instructions regarding War Diaries and Intelligence Summaries are contained in F. S. Regs., Part II. and the Staff Manual respectively. Title pages will be prepared in manuscript.

Army Form C. 2118.

WAR DIARY
or
~~INTELLIGENCE~~ SUMMARY.

1/6 Battn (*Erase heading not required.*) Sherwood Foresters.

Hour, Date, Place	Summary of Events and Information	Remarks and references to Appendices
19.5.17. TRENCHES.	Bn. relieved by 1/5th North Staffordshire Regt, and moved back into Divisional Reserve billets at PETIT SAINS.	CBJ
21-5-17. PETIT SAINS	Draft of 21 other Ranks arrived as reinforcements.	CBJ
25-5-17 PETIT SAINS	Bn. relieved 1/5th Leicester Regt. in RIGHT SUBSECTOR of Right Brigade Front.	CBJ
26-5-17 TRENCHES	LIEUT-COLONEL C.B. JOHNSON rejoined from short leave, and resumed command of Battalion.	CBJ
nights 29th/30th, 30th/31st TRENCHES	Attempted raids by enemy on Bn. "A" Coy (RIGHT COY.) successfully repulsed, Sergeants RAVEY and BOAM especially distinguishing themselves.	CBJ
30-5-17. TRENCHES.	Draft of 24 other Ranks arrived as reinforcements.	CBJ
30-5-17 TRENCHES.	LIEUT. G.N.K. MAUGHAN rejoined from short leave to England.	CBJ
30-5-17 MARQUEFFLES FARM	Divisional Commander presented medal ribbons to the following:- BAR to MILITARY CROSS. CAPT. V.O. ROBINSON M.C. D.C. MEDAL 240513 Sergeant F. LONGSON. MILITARY MEDAL. 240076 Sergeant J.G. RAVEY. 242442 Private L. BEASTALL 241360 L/Corporal A. EVANS.	CBJ
31-5-17. TRENCHES	Lieut J.L. PERCIVAL rejoined Bn. from 2nd Entrenching Battalion.	CBJ
31-5-17 TRENCHES.	CAPT. V.O. ROBINSON, M.C. proceeded on 1 month's leave to England.	CBJ
night 31st May/1st June. TRENCHES.	Relieved by 5th Sherwood Foresters and went into Brigade Reserve, with H.Q. at RED MILL M.27.d.75.70 (LENS 36c S.W.1) Casualties during tour:- Killed 5 other Ranks. Gassed 27 other Ranks. Wounded 18 other Ranks.	CBJ

C Bertin Johnson Lieut Colonel,
Comdg. 1/6 Bn. Sherwood Foresters

(9 29 6) W 3332—1107 100,000 10/13 H W V Forms/C. 2118/10

Army Form C. 2118.

Instructions regarding War Diaries and Intelligence Summaries are contained in F. S. Regs., Part II. and the Staff Manual respectively. Title pages will be prepared in manuscript.

WAR DIARY
of 1/6th Bn. Sherwood Foresters
~~INTELLIGENCE SUMMARY.~~
(*Erase heading not required.*)

Vol 29

Hour, Date, Place		Summary of Events and Information	Remarks and References to Appendices
	1. 6. 17.	CAPT V.O. ROBINSON M.C proceeded on 1 month's leave to England. 2/Lt R. EVANS assumed command & payment of "A" Coy, vice Capt Robinson. Lt G.K.K. MAUGHAN assumed command & payment of "C" Coy vice Lt HIGHAM.	CBS.
	2. 6. 17.	Lt & Adj E. KERSHAW. M.C & Lt H.W. HIGHAM on short leave to England. (10 days) Lt J. TAYLOR performed the duties of a/Adj during absence of Lt KERSHAW.	CBS.
LIEVIN SECTOR	3. 6. 17.	2/Lt L.N. JOHNSON M.C killed in action whilst on working party (M.30.c.9.5)	CBS. (Ref map 36 C SW.1).
do.	6. 6. 17.	Bn relieved by 5th Bn LINCOLNSHIRE REGT & moved into Divl Reserve at FOSSE 10. SAINS EN GOHELLE	CBS.
	7. 6. 17.	LONDON GAZETTE. Capt F.H. DICK awarded MILITARY CROSS. C.S.M. H.H. HOLLAND awarded D.C.M.	CBS.
FOSSE. 10 (SAINS EN GOHELLE)	7. 6. 17.	2/Lt K.H. BOND MC transferred to England.	
	9. 6. 17.	Bn inspected by GENERAL Sir W.R. ROBERTSON (Chief of the Imperial General Staff.) The G.O.C. Division expressed his great satisfaction with the work done by the Battalion during the last tour in the trenches.	13 Officers, 463 OR } on parade. CBS.
FOSSE 10.	10. 6. 17.	Lt Col C.B. JOHNSON proceeded to C.O's Conference at BOULOGNE. MAJOR N. SEATON assumed command of the Battn. Battn received a wire of congratulation from 138th Bde on the digging of the advanced trench in RIAUMONT. The assaulting Battn assembled in it without detection.	CBS.
MARQUEFFLES FARM.	11. 6. 17	139th Bde Horse Show. The Bn won Tug of war, 1st in Officers Jumping, 1st in V.C. Race, 2nd in Cross Country race, 3rd in Turnouts.	CBS.
MARQUEFFLES FARM.	13. 6. 17.	Bn inspected by Cdr. Division.	
	15. 6. 17.	Bn relieved 6th S STAFFS Regt in Right Support, ST PIERRE SECTOR. 240584 Lg/Sh Shimwell G awarded MILITARY MEDAL.	CBS
	16. 6. 17.	240333 L/Cpl ADAMS J.L. } 240504 Pte FLETCHER H. } awarded MILITARY MEDAL.	CBS.

29 L.B.S

(9 29 6) W 3332—1107 100,000 10/13 H W V Forms/C. 2118/10.

Army Form C. 2118.

II

Instructions regarding War Diaries and Intelligence Summaries are contained in F. S. Regs., Part II. and the Staff Manual respectively. Title pages will be prepared in manuscript.

WAR DIARY of 1/6th Bn Sherwood Foresters

~~INTELLIGENCE~~ SUMMARY.

(*Erase heading not required.*)

Hour, Date, Place		Summary of Events and Information	Remarks and References to Appendices
FOSSE 10.	18. 6. 17	Lt COL C.B. JOHNSON returned from CO's conference & proceeded to Hospital	CBJ.
	19. 6. 17	Bn relieved 5th S.F. in RIGHT SUBSECTOR. ST PIERRE SECTOR.	CBJ.
	21. 6. 17	Lt COL C.B. JOHNSON rejoined & resumed command of Bn.	CBJ.
	22. 6. 17	2/Lt GLEN. 5th Bn S.F. / 2/Lt 7th Bn S.F. } attached to Bn for duty.	CBJ.
	23. 6. 17	Bn relieved by 5th Bn S.F. & moved into Bde Support dugouts in ST PIERRE.	CBJ.
		2/Lt F. S. ROWLAND awarded Military Cross.	
Bde SUPPORT.	24. 6. 17	2/Lt H.S. PINK & 2/Lt L.Y. BURROWS joined Bn from England.	CBJ.
	27. 6. 17	Bn relieved 5th Bn S.F. in Right SUBSECTOR. ST PIERRE SECTOR	CBJ.
	30. 6. 17	"C" Coy established advanced posts in CORNWALL TRENCH. at N. 7 C. 80.22. N. 7 C. 40.10. (LENS. 36 c S.W. 1. 1/10000).	CBJ.

C Bentin Johnson
~~Lieut~~ Lieut Colonel
Comdg 1/6th Bn Sherwood Foresters

Instructions regarding War Diaries and Intelligence Summaries are contained in F. S. Regs., Part II. and the Staff Manual respectively. Title pages will be prepared in manuscript.

WAR DIARY

1/6th Bn The Sherwood Foresters.

~~INTELLIGENCE SUMMARY.~~

(Erase heading not required.)

139
46

Vol 30

Army Form C. 2118.

Hour, Date, Place	Summary of Events and Information	Remarks and References to Appendices
1-7-17. TRENCHES	In conjunction with rest of Division, 1 Coy attacked German positions W. of LENS. Objective was gained, but was not held. Casualties during the Operation:- 2/Lieut. R.C.F. DOLLEY, Missing; Lieut. J. TAYLOR, 2/Lieut. T.A.D. MABBOTT } Wounded. Other Ranks - 8 killed, 29 wounded, 4 w'ded & missing, 3 missing.	CBJ Map Ref 36c S W 1 1:10000 N13a
2-7-17. FOSSE 10, SAINS en GOHELLE.	2/Lieut. H.T. WOOD joined Battalion from England.	CBJ
3-7-17. TRENCHES.	Battalion relieved by 31st Canadian Battalion. Casualties during whole tour:- 2 O.R. killed, 11 O.R. wounded } in addition to those on 1st. July.	CBJ
Night 3/4th/7/17.	Battalion moved by bus from BULLY to FREVILLERS.	CBJ
4-7-17. FREVILLERS.	Capt. V.O. ROBINSON, M.C. rejoined from 1 month's leave, and assumed command of the "A" Coy.	CBJ
5-7-17. FREVILLERS	Major A.J. HOPKINS, 2/Lieut. K.H. BOND, M.C. } joined Battalion from England.	CBJ
6-7-17. FREVILLERS	Capt. J. TOLSON proceeded on 1 month's leave. Lieut. B.E. JOHNSON proceeded on short leave.	CBJ
6-7-17. FREVILLERS.	2/Lieut. K.H. BOND, M.C., assumed Command of the "B" Coy.	CBJ
8-7-17. FREVILLERS.	Battalion inspected by G.O.C., Division.	CBJ
9-7-17. FREVILLERS.	2/Lieut. H.W. HIGHAM proceeded to join R.F.C. as Observer, on probation. 2/Lieut. A. COATES, " R.W. OAKLEY, " H.H. SHENTON } joined Battalion from England.	CBJ CBJ
11-7-17. FREVILLERS.	Major A.J. HOPKINS proceeded to 46th Divl. Depot Battalion.	CBJ
12-7-17. FREVILLERS.	Battalion Transport inspected by G.O.C., Division.	CBJ

30

(9 29 6) W 3332—1107 100,000 10/13 H W V Forms/C. 2118/10.

Instructions regarding War Diaries and Intelligence Summaries are contained in F. S. Regs., Part II. and the Staff Manual respectively. Title pages will be prepared in manuscript.

WAR DIARY

1/6 Bn. Sherwood Foresters.

~~INTELLIGENCE SUMMARY.~~

(Erase heading not required.)

Army Form C. 2118.

Hour, Date, Place	Summary of Events and Information	Remarks and References to Appendices
14-7-17 FREVILLERS.	Capt. V.O ROBINSON, M.C. attd to 1/5th Sherwood Foresters to be 2nd in Command.	CBJ
	2/Lieut. S.N DEURANCE joined Battalion from England.	
15-7-17 FREVILLERS.	2/Lieut K.H. BOND, M.C to Command the "A" Coy.	CBJ
	" R. EVANS to Command the "B" Coy.	
	2/Lieut V.T.G HORE, " L.V BURROWS } to I Corps Schools	
18-7-17 FREVILLERS.	2/Lieut. H.H. SHENTON to Hospital.	CBJ
	240444 Pte W. GOUGH, the "B" Coy, awarded Military medal for Gallantry on 1st July W. of LENS.	
21-7-17 FREVILLERS.	Battalion held sports in conjunction with 139th M.G. Company & 139th T.M. Battery.	CBJ
21-7-17 FREVILLERS.	No 240935 Cpl. P. KNOWLES awarded Military medal for gallantry on 1st July, W. of LENS.	CBJ
23-7-17 FREVILLERS.	Battalion moved to DROUVIN.	CBJ
24-7-17. DROUVIN.	Battalion relieved 9th SUFFOLK Regt in RIGHT Subsection of the ST. ELIE Sector. Refce map 36c NW3 1:10,000 G12c and d.	CBJ
	Q.M. Stores and Transport to LABOURSE.	
	Major W. SEATON proceeded on short leave.	
26-7-17. LABOURSE.	Lieut & Q.M. W.D. JAMIESON proceeded on short leave.	CBJ
28-7-17 I CORPS SCHOOLS	2/Lt V.T.G. HORE proceeded on short leave.	CBJ
29-7-17 LABOURSE.	2/Lt L.V. BURROWS from I Corps Schools.	CBJ
30-7-17 LABOURSE.	2/Lt. J. MACKAY joined Battalion from England.	CBJ
night 30/31/7/17. TRENCHES	Battalion relieved by 1/5th Sherwood Foresters, & went into support at PHILOSOPHE: 2 Companies remaining in the line in support to 5th Battalion. Casualties during tour :- 8 other Ranks wounded.	CBJ

C Bentin Johnson
Lieut-Col.
Cdg. 1/6 Bn. Sherwood Foresters.

(9 29 6) W 3332—1107 100,000 10/13 H W V Forms/C. 2118/10.

S E C R E T.

From:- Officer Commanding,

6th Sherwood Foresters.

To:- Headquarters,

139th Infantry Brigade.

Ref Map
LENS 1/10.000.

I beg to report as follows on the part taken by my Battalion in the operations subsequent to and on the morning of 1st July:-

1. I attended a conference at Advanced Brigade H.Q at 2 p.m on 29th June when I received a warning that the operations in question would probably take place on 1st July. At 2 p.m. on the 29th my forward posts were on the line CAVALRY-S.W.CORNER of HOSPITAL grounds-N.7.c.10.90-COPPER-N.7.a.20.25.
I received verbal orders from the Brigadier General to advance my posts on the night 29/30th as far as possible to the line M.18.b60.50-CORNWALL-N.7.c.55.45-N.7.a.65.40. If CORNWALL was found to be occupied by the enemy, the line N.7.c.30.20-N.7.c.55.45 was to be consolidated and used as a jumping off place for the attack on the 1st July. I got back to my H.Q. about 4 p.m.and held a conference at the advanced Coy H.qrs at 6.30 p.m. I then ordered Lr "D" Coy (Capt H.H.JACKSON) to push out posts at once to N.7.C.35.85 and N.7.a.20.05. This was done. The posts could not be pushed out further East as the houses are in a very bad condition and the selections of suitable positions for posts required a long and careful reconnaissance. I ordered Lr "C" Coy (Capt G.K.K.MAUGHAN) who were in the right support position to send strong patrols out at dusk along COLLEGE and COMBAT to junction of COLLEGE-CORNWALL and to road junction N.7.c.90.10 respectively. Blocks were to be established at these points. Patrols were then to reconnoitre CORNWALL and if it proved to be unoccupied by the enemy to occupy it and consolidate. The patrols went out at dusk, but owing to the darkness and the very broken state of the houses and trenches they were unable

to.

to find their objectives and finally took up a position on the line N.7.c.48.05 - 40.30 - 50.40. By this time it was too light to move forward again.

2. I attended a second conference at Brigade Advanced H.Q at 9 p.m. on the 29th June and was given verbal instructions as to the general scheme and also informed definitely what my objectives would be, namely:- N.13.a.95.60-COLLEGE-CORNWALL to join up with posts on left. After sume discussion it was settled that I should endeavour to occupy CORNWALL on the night 30th June/1st July as I did not consider that the enemy had any posts there.

3. I spent the morning of the 30th reconnoitring the position, but owing to mist, could see very little. I spent a considerable time in the ruins N of CORNWALL but the ground was so exposed that it was not possible to get near the German line, nor could I see more than a small sector of their line at a time. Capt J.TOLSON accompanied me in this reconnaissance.

4. I attended a third conference at Advanced Brigade H.Q. at 4 p.m. on the 30th to settle all final details. No details of the artillery barrage scheme had been given out up to then. I explained my proposed dispositions to the Brigadier General who approved them. I was then ordered to take CORNWALL before ZERO as the artillery Barrage would open on COWDRAY and not CORNWALL.

5. I held a conferance at a support Coy H.Q. at 6.30 p.m. the 30th to explain in detail the general scheme and dispositions. I ordered O.C."C" Coy to occupy and consolidate CORNWALL as soon as possible after dusk, and O.C. "B" Coy to carry out the main attack. Copy of operation orders is attached.

6. At 11 p.m. 30th strong patrols went out from N.7.c.40.05

to

to find their objectives and finally took up a position on the line N.7.c.42.05 - 40.30 - 50.40. By this time it was too light to move forward again.

2. I attended a second conference at Brigade Advanced H.Q at 9 p.m. on the 29th June and was given verbal instructions as to the general scheme and also informed definitely what my objectives would by, namely:- N.13.a.95.60-COLLEGE-CORNWALL to join up with posts onleft. After sume discussion it was settled that I should endeavour to occupy CORNWALL on the night 30th June/1st Julyas I did not consider that the enemy had any posts there.

3. I spent the morning of the 30th reconnoitring the position, but owing to mist, could see very little. I spent a considerable time in the ruins N of CORNWALL but the ground was so exposed that it was not possible to get near the German line, nor could I see more than a small sector of their line at a time. Capt J.TOLSON accompanied me in this reconnaissance.

4. I attended a third conference at Advanced Brigade H.Q. at 4 p.m. on the 30th to settle all final details. No details of the artillery barrage scheme had been given out up to then. I explained my proposed dispositions to the Brigadier General who approved them. I was then ordered to take CORNWALL before ZERO as the artillery Barrage would open on COWDRAY and not CORNWALL.

5. I held a conference at a support Coy H.Q. at 6.30 p.m. the 30th to explain in detail the general scheme and dispositions. I ordered O.C."C" Coy to occupy and consolidate CORNWALL as soon as possible after dusk, and O.C. "B" Coy to carry out the main attack. Copy of operation orders is attached.

6. At 11 p.m. 30th strong patrols went out from N.7.c.40.05

to

2/Lt R.C.F.DOLLEY (Comdg No 1 party) at 4.30 a.m. This was the first message received. The enemy attacked the left blocking post in force and compelled it to fall back across the cutting, and another blocking post with a Lewis Gun was formed on the W side of the cutting. The enemy made continual attempts to attack this block, but was driven back each time by this Lewis Gun before he could get within bombing distance. The enemy continually fired rifle grenades into our position and caused an increasing number of casualties. 2/Lt DOLLEY kept taking men away from the various sections to reinforce the left blocking post. Sergt HALLAM states that 2/Lt DOLLEY ordered him to prepare the men for an attack with the object of retaking the lost ground E of the cutting: but that at that moment a runner came from LIEUT MARTIN of the 5th S.F. ordering 2/Lt DOLLEY to hold on where he was. The 5th S.F. started to withdraw from trench on E side of cutting on our right front. 2/LT DOLLEY ordered his men to cover their withdrawal by fire. They did so. A party of the 5th S.F. crossed over the trench through 2/Lt DOLLEY's men and went back through the German wire. 2/LT DOLLEY then went along the trench to the right, and SGT HALLAM saw a party of Germans jump in the trench in the direction which 2/Lieut Dolley had gone. Lance Corporal Knowles who was in Command of the left blocking post, states that after the party of the 5th SHERWOOD FORESTERS had gone back through the wire, he saw the Germans advancing towards our men over the top on the East side of the cutting, along the cutting and from the direction of COTTON. He then saw seven or eight men - the garrison of the trench on his right - withdrawing. As it was impossible to hold on any longer without being surrounded, he withdrew with his party, which by now only consisted of two bombers and two Lewis Gunners with their gun.

Return of casualties of Officers and N.C.O's and men

and men who actually took part in the operation:-

	Killed.	Wounded.	Wounded & Missing.	Missing.	Remaining for duty.
Officers.	-	1	-	1	-
Other Ranks.	3	16	5	4	# 26 = 56

Includes Stretcher Bearers, Runners and 4 men who got detached from the Right Party.

Lieut Colonel.

5th July 1917. Comdg 6th Battalion Sherwood Foresters.

Operations &c

139th Infy Brigade

6th Sherwood Foresters

1st – July

Instructions regarding War Diaries and Intelligence Summaries are contained in F.S. Regs., Part II. and the Staff Manual respectively. Title pages will be prepared in manuscript.

WAR DIARY of 1/6th Bn Sherwood Foresters
INTELLIGENCE SUMMARY.
(Erase heading not required.)

Army Form C. 2118.

Vol 31

Hour, Date, Place	Summary of Events and Information	Remarks and references to Appendices
5. 8. 17	2/Lt V. H. ARMITAGE M.C. awarded the Belgian decoration "Chevalier de l'ordre de la Couronne."	W.S.
	6 in G's list No 45 To be captain. Lieut C. J. Wheatcroft To be A/Capts Lieut J. Gibson " H. H. Jackson. To be Lieut 2/Lt D. S. Fox.	W.S.
6. 8. 17. ST. ELIE SECTOR.	Battn relieved 5th Bn in RIGHT SUBSECTION.	W.S.
7. 8. 17	2/Lt W. JACKSON joined Battn from England.	W.S.
	Capt (T. maj) R. Evans (6th S. Staffs) posted to Battn.	W.S.
9. 8. 17.	2/Lt R. EVANS wounded in action & died of wounds.	W.S.
10. 8. 17 ST. ELIE SECTOR.	Relieved by 5th Bn & moved into Bde Reserve at PHILOSOPHE.	W.S.
13. 8. 17 do	2 coys of Battn raided the enemy trenches, inflicting severe casualties on the enemy. The Corps commander expressed his satisfaction with the raid & the preparatory arrangements. 2/Lt K. H. Bond M.C. slightly wounded & Capt H. H. Jackson wounded (to Hospital)	Appendices W.S. 2 & 3
17. 8. 17 PHILOSOPHE	Battn relieved by 4th Lincolns & marched into billets at VAUDRICOURT	W.S.
20. 8. 17	Bn moved into billets at FOUQUIERES.	W.S.
23. 8. 17	Lt & Adt E. KERSHAW. M.C promoted A/Capt whilst Adjutant.	W.S.
24. 8. 17	Lieut B. E. JOHNSON, Lt E. S. HOOD & 2/Lt K. H. BOND authorised to wear Badges of rank of Captain.	W.S.

315

Instructions regarding War Diaries and Intelligence Summaries are contained in F.S. Regs., Part II. and the Staff Manual respectively. Title pages will be prepared in manuscript.

WAR DIARY or INTELLIGENCE SUMMARY.

11

(Erase heading not required.)

Army Form C. 2118.

Hour, Date, Place	Summary of Events and Information	Remarks and references to Appendices
25. 8. 17.	The following were awarded decorations for gallantry in connection with the raid on the 13th August:—	W.S.
	BAR TO MILITARY MEDAL 241233 L/Cpl. F. W. Hobbs	
	MILITARY MEDAL 240138 Cpl. C. W. Spencer.	
	240853 " S. Hatfield.	
26. 8. 17. CAMBRIN SECTOR.	Battn relieved 1st Bn K.R.R.C. in RIGHT SECTOR.	W.S.
27. 8. 17	London Gazette 2nd Lt. M. B. TAYLOR to be Capt. d/f 18.8.17.	W.S.
28. 8. 17	Major W. Seaton assumed temporary command of the Battn during the absence on leave of Lt Col C. B. Johnson	W.S.
28. 8. 17	2/Lt. C. RADFORD joined the Bn from England	

W. Seaton Major
Comdg 16th Bn Sherwood Foresters

(9 29 6) W 3332—1107 100,000 10/13 H W V Forms/C. 2118/10.

Appendix 5

Secret.

I Corps No. 37 (G.O.)
46th Division G.742/83.

46th Division.

The following are the Corps Commanders remarks upon the preliminary report upon raid carried out by 5th and 6th Sherwood Foresters on the night 13th/14th August, 1917 -

"This seems to have been a good raid and well and determinedly executed. It should be impressed on all raiding parties that the taking of live prisoners is one of the objects of raids. Prisoners are better than dead men. Both prisoners and dead men permanently reduce the enemy fighting forces, but prisoners can give valuable information in addition."

15th. August, /17.

sd/ G.V. Hordern, B.G.
General Staff, I Corps..

\- 2 -

139th Infantry Brigade.

For information.

G Thorpe
Lieut-Colonel,
General Staff, 46th Division.

15/8/17.

5/ Sherwood Foresters
Please pass & return.

16.8.17.

Appendix 3

COPY.

139th Bde 411/25/G.

The following lessons can be learnt from the raids successfully carried out by the 5th and 6th Sherwood Foresters last night, and the Brigadier General Commanding wishes them impressed on all ranks:-

1. The value of well planned and well executed raids in increasing the moral of all ranks taking part, in inspiring confidence of the Support of our Artillery, Machine Guns and trench mortars and in improving the superiority of our men in close fighting.
2. The difficulty of those operations on a dark night which can only be overcome by the most careful training and by the ability of junior N.C.O's to take charge of unexpected situations.
3. The necessity of impressing upon N.C.O's and men - particularly recruits - the importance of a close following of our 18 pounder barrage - even at the risk of a few casualties from our shell fire- This lesson is best taught by raids.
4. That every man must be armed with a rifle and bayonet and that the thrower in a bombing squad with his supply of grenades exhausted is defenceless without his rifle.
5. That a power buzzer is of little value unless the raiding party remain at least an hour in the German lines.

15/8/17.

(sd) W.P.Buckley. Captn
Bde Major, 139th Inf Brigade.

Appendix I

I Corps No. 77 (G.O).
46th Division No. G. 742/90.

46th Division.

****

The Corps Commander has made the following note upon your report giving further particulars of the raids carried out by the 5th and 6th Battalions Sherwood Foresters on night 13th/14th August, 1917 -

"A satisfactory raid, which appears to have been well planned and executed."

(sgd) C.E. Clouting,
Captain,
for B.G., General Staff, I Corps.

16th August, 1917.

(2)

139th Infantry Brigade.

****

For information and communication to all concerned.

Lieut-Colonel,
General Staff, 46th Division.....

17th August, 1917.

1/5 Sherwood Foresters

Passed. [illegible] Capt
Bde Major 139 Inf Bde

17.8.17.

Army Form C. 2118.

Instructions regarding War Diaries and Intelligence Summaries are contained in F. S. Regs., Part II. and the Staff Manual respectively. Title pages will be prepared in manuscript.

WAR DIARY
of 1/6th Bn Sherwood Foresters
INTELLIGENCE SUMMARY.
(*Erase heading not required.*)

Vol 32

Hour, Date, Place		Summary of Events and Information	Remarks and references to Appendices
CAMBRIN SECTOR.	1. 9. 17	Battn. relieved in the line by 5th Sherwood Foresters & marched into billets at FOUQUIERES on relief.	BWV
FOUQUIERES	2. 9. 17	CAPT H.H. JACKSON awarded MILITARY CROSS for Gallantry in connection with the raid of 13th August.	BWV
		LONDON GAZETTE Lieut E M B TAYLOR to be CAPTAIN d/ 18. 8. 17	BWV
FOUQUIERES.	5. 9. 17.	CAPT H.H JACKSON M.C relinquishes Acting rank of CAPTAIN.	BWV
"	7. 9. 17.	Battn relieved 5th Battn. S.F in the CAMBRIN SECTOR	BWV
CAMBRIN SECTOR	9. 9. 17	Lt Col C.B. JOHNSON resumes Command of the Battalion	BWV
"	13. 9. 17	Battn relieved by 5th S.F & moved into BRIGADE SUPPORT in ANNEQUIN.	BWV
ANNEQUIN	14. 9. 17.	LIEUTS B.E. JOHNSON & E.S WOOD to be Actg Capts (additional)	BWV
"	20. 9. 17.	Battn relieved by 1st Bn K.R.R.C & marched to billets in LES BREBIS	BWV
LES BREBIS	21. 9. 17	Bn relieved 1st LEICESTERS & 1st W. YORKS in SUPPORT ON HILL TO RIGHT.	BWV
		LIEUT COLONEL C.B. JOHNSON killed in action	BWV
		Major W. SEATON assumed temporary Command.	BWV
HILL TO RIGHT.	22. 9. 17	Bn relieved 2nd D.L.I & 11th ESSEX (4 posts) in front line.	BWV
	23. 9. 17	MAJOR B.W.VANN. M.C. (8th Sherwood Foresters) assumed Command	BWV
"	28/29. 9. 17	Battn relieved by 5th S.F & moved into DIVL RESERVE in MAZINGARBE.	BWV

B.W. Vann Major
Comm'dg 1/6th Bn Sherwood Foresters

(9 29 6) W 3332—1107 100,000 10/13 H W V Forms/C. 2118/10.

File

Secret. G.742/196.

With reference to 46th DIVISION ORDER NO. 254, para. 1., dated 24th October, 1917.

1. The 139th Infantry Brigade raid will be carried out by the 6th Bn. Sherwood Foresters on night 1st/2nd November, 1917.

2. Zero hour will be notified later.

3. ACKNOWLEDGE.

G.R. Sandeman.

Captain,
General Staff, 46th Division.

Issued at 2.30 p.m., 25th October, 1917 to all recipients of D:O: 254.

S E C R E T.

File

Copy No. 22

46TH DIVISION ORDER No. 254.

****

Ref: Maps - CITE ST AUGUSTE (3) and
Secret Trench Maps, 1/10,000.-

24th October, 1917.

1. The 139th Infantry Brigade will raid the enemy's trenches within the points H 32 d 75.30 - H 32 d 80.95 - H 33 c 05.68.
The raid will take place about November 1st; the exact date will be notified later.

2. The object of the raid will be to obtain identifications and do damage.
Special parties will be told off to obtain identifications.

3. Wire cutting will be carried out by 4.5" howitzers and 6" Trench Mortars from now until Z Day.

4. The artillery programme will be drawn up by the C.R.A. to include co-operation by I Corps H.A.

5. O.C., No. 4 Special Company, R.E., will arrange direct with 139th Infantry Brigade for a party to fire a Thermite Bomb signal from advanced battalion headquarters.

6. The D.M.G.O will arrange machine gun barrages during the raid as required by 139th Infantry Brigade.

7. Arrangements will be made with the division on our right to co-operate with machine guns and Stokes Mortars during the raid.

8. Watches will be synchronised at 139th Infantry Brigade Headquarters four hours previous to Zero on Z Day. O.C., No. 4 Special Co, R.E., will send a representative to 139th Infantry Brigade Headquarters at this time.

9. ACKNOWLEDGE.

G.R. Tandman

Captain,
General Staff, 46th Division.

Issued at 8 pm.-

Copy No. 1 to 46th D.A.
2 C.R.E.
3 O.C., Signals.
4 137th Inf: Bde.
5 138th : :
6 139th : :
7 1st Monmouths.
8 178th M.G. Co.
9 A.A. & Q.M.G.
10 D.M.G.O.
11 A.D.M.S.
12 A.P.M.
13 A.D.C for G.O.C.
14 No. 4 Special Co, R.E.
15 11th Division.
16 25th :
17 I Corps H.A.
18 I Corps R.A.
19 I Corps C.B.O.
25 3rd Aust: Tg Co.

Copy No 20/21 to I Corps.
22 File.
23/24 War Diary.
26 Major Evans.

S E C R E T.   Copy No. 16

46TH DIVISION ORDER No. 258.

****

Ref: Maps - CITE ST AUGUSTE (3) and
Secret Trench Maps, 1/10,000.   29th October, 1917.

1. With reference to 46th Division Order No. 254 dated 24th October, 1917. The following machine gun arrangements will be made in connection with the 139th Infantry Brigade Raid.-

137th Machine Gun Company.

(a) 1 gun (G 24 b) enfilade enemy front line from H 26 c 58.78 to H 26 c 74.65.

(b) 1 gun (G 24 d) enfilade enemy front line from H 26 c 78.67 to H 26 d 05.50.

(c) 1 gun (G 24 d) enfilade enemy front line at H 26 d 15.35.

139th Machine Gun Company.

(a) 2 guns, HURDLE Trench, enfilade trench running from H 27 c 13.74 to H 27 c 39.95.

(b) 1 gun (G 36 b) enfilade trench running from H 27 c 40.95 to H 27 a 54.03.

(c) 2 guns (G 36 b) search HUMBUG ALLEY from H 26 d 35.17 to H 26 d 68.20.

(d) 2 guns (G 36 b) flanking barrage from H 32 b 65. 25 to H 33 a 12.27.

(e) 1 gun (G 36 b) trench junction at H 33 a 04.92.

(f) 1 gun (G 32 c) enfilade HYMAN Trench at H 33 d 15.50.

(g) 1 gun (G 32 c) enfilade trench and road at H 27 c 25.00.

178th Machine Gun Company.

(a) 2 guns, 'P' Battery, sweep enemy front line from H 26 d 47.00 to H 32 b 57.57.

(b) 2 guns, 'P' Battery, sweep enemy front line from H 32 b 57.57 to H 32 b 64.25.

(c) 2 guns, 'P' Battery, enfilade communication trench from H 32 d 91.10 to H 33 c 15.05.

(d) 2 guns, 'P' Battery, enfilade enemy front line from H 26 d 25.25 to H 26 d 40.32.

(e) 1 gun (G 30 d) at point H 26 d 50.08.

P.T.O.

2. Machine Guns of 11th Division will co-operate as follows :-

<u>Targets</u>.-

(i) M.G. Post at N 3 a 30.85.

(ii) Enfilade HYMAN Trench from H 33 c 35.38 to H 33 c 92.52.

(iii) Enfilade HYMAN Trench from H 33 d 15.50 to H 33 d 53.66.

3. 1° each way will be allowed for, in all enfilade targets.

4. <u>Rate of fire</u>.-

Zero plus ½' to Zero plus 2½'	-	RAPID.
Zero plus 2½' to Zero plus 5'	-	NORMAL.
Zero plus 5' to Stop - -	-	Intermittent bursts of fire on enfilade targets only.

Cancelled

5. Rate of fire during return of raiders will be arranged between O.C, Raid and D.M.G.O.

6. Acknowledge.

L.B. Sandeman Capt.
for Lieut-Colonel,
General Staff, 46th Division.

Issued at 7 am, 30th October, 1917.

Copy No.	
1 to	C.R.A.
2	C.R.E.
3	O.C, Signals.
4/5	137th Inf: Bde.
6	138th : :
7/8	139th : :
9	178th M.G. Co.
10	D.M.G.O.
11	A.D.C. for G.O.C.
12	I Corps H.A.
13	I Corps R.A.
14/15	I Corps.
16	File.
17/18	War Diary.

S E C R E T.

Copy

G. 742/194.

Headquarters,
11th Division.

****

With reference to my Divisional Order No. 254, para. 7, sent you herewith.

Would you have any objection to your left brigade assisting 139th Infantry Brigade with Stokes Mortars during their raid about November 1st.

I would suggest that G.O.C., 139th Infantry Brigade arranges details for Stokes Mortar co-operation direct with your left brigade, if you agree. Likewise our D.M.G.O could arrange with yours Machine gun assistance required.

G.B. Sandeman Capt.
f.
Major-General,
Commanding 46th Division.

24th October, 1917.

SECRET.

46th. DIVISION ORDER No. 254.

Ref.Maps:- CITE ST.AUGUSTE(B) and
Secret Trench Maps 1/10,000 -

24th.Oct. 1917.

1. The 139th. Infantry Brigade will raid the enemy's trenches within the points H.32.d.75.50 - H.32.d.80.95 - H.33.c.05.68.

The raid will take place about November 1sr. the exact date will be notified later.

2. The object of the raid will be to obtain identifications and do damage.

Special parties will be told off to obtain ~~information~~. identifications.

3. Wire cutting will be carried out by 4.5 Howitzers and 6" Trench Mortars from now until Z Day.

4. The artillery programme will be drawn up by the C.R.A. to include co-operation by I Corps H.A.

5. O.C., No. 4 Special Company R.E., will arrange direct with 139th. Infantry Brigade for a party to fire a Thermito Bomb signal from advanced Battalion Headquarters.

6. The D.M.G.O. will arrange machine gun barrages during the raid as required by 139th. Infantry Brigade.

7. Arrangements will be made with the Division on our right to co-operate with machine guns and Stokes Mortars during the raid.

8. Watches will be synchronised at 139th. Infantry Brigade Headquarters four hours previous to Zero on Z. Day. O.C., No. 4 Special Coy. R.E., will send a representative to 139th. Infantry Brigade Headquarters at this time.

9. ACKNOWLEDGE.

(Sd).G.R. SANDMAN., Captain,

General Staff, 46th. Division.

SECRET.

G. 742/194.

Headquarters,

11th. Division.

****

With reference to my Divisional Order No. 254 para.7 sent you herewith.

Would you have any objection to your Left Brigade assisting the 139th. Infantry Brigade with Stokes Mortars during their raid about November 1st.

I would suggest that G.O.C. 139th. Infantry Brigade arranges details for Stokes Mortar co-operation direct with your left Brigade, if you agree. Likewise our D.M.G.O. could arrange with yours Machine gun assistance required.

(Sd). G.R.SANDMAN., Captain,
for Major General,
Commanding 46th. Division.

24th. October 1917.

SECRET 46th: DIVISIONAL ARTILLERY COPY NO:..4...
ORDER No: 235.

****

REFERENCE - CITE ST AUGUSTE (3) 25th: OCTOBER, 1917.
1/10.000

(1) The 6th: Battalion Sherwood Foresters will carry out a Raid on the enemy Trenches within the points H.32.d.75.50. - H.32.d.80.95. - H.33.c.05.60. during the Night 1st:/2nd: November, remaining in the enemy Trenches approximately 30 Minutes.

(2) Wirecutting will be carried out by 6 inch Trench Mortars and 4.5" Howitzers, under the orders of LOOS GROUP.

(3) 5th: Canadian Divisional Artillery will co-operate as follows:-

(a) 4 - 18 Pdrs:, 61st: Battery C.F.A. will Enfilade the German Front Line N.2.b.6.7. to H.32.d.94.00. throughout the operation.

(b) 4 - 4.5" Hows: will engage targets, to be selected by LOOS GROUP, throughout the operation.

(4) The assistance to be given by I Corps H.A. will be notified later.

(5) 10th: Battery, HULLUCH GROUP will be at the disposal of LOOS GROUP for Flank Barrage on the North of the Raid.

(6) Details of 18 Pdr: Barrages and 4.5" How: tasks, other than for 61st: Battery, Canadian Divisional Artillery, and employment of Trench Mortars during the Raid, will be settled by LOOS GROUP.

(7) ACKNOWLEDGE BY WIRE.

Major R.A.
Brigade Major.
46th: Divisional Artillery.

Headquarters R.A.

ISSUED AT 8 p.m.

COPIES NO:

1	LOOS GROUP.	
2	HULLUCH GROUP.	
3	ST ELIE GROUP.	For Information.
4	46th: Division.	For Information.
5	I Corps R.A.	For Information.
6	I Corps H.A.	For Information.
7	C.B. S.O.	For Information.
8	5th: Canadian Divisional Arty:	For Information.
9	139th: Infantry Brigade.	For Information.
10	137th. Infantry Brigade.	For Information.
11-12	War Diary.	
13	File.	

G.O.C. Force.

S e c r e t.　　　　　　G.742/198.

139th Inf. Bde
D.M.G.O.

Reference 46th Division Order No. 254, - para., 7.

139th Infantry Brigade to arrange details for Stokes Mortar co-operation direct with 33rd Infantry Brigade.

D.M.G.O., to arrange M.G. co-operation with D.M.G.O., 11th Division.

Captain,
General Staff, 46th Division.

25/10/17.

SECRET.

11th. Division No. G.S. 242.

33rd. Inf. Bde.
D.M.G.O.

Reference attached Order No. 254, para. 7, please arrange details for Stokes Mortar co-operation direct with G.O.C., 139th. Infantry Brigade.

D.M.G.O. will arrange co-operation of Machine guns direct with D.M.G.O., 46th. Division.

A.J. Bourne. Major G.S.
for Lieut.colonel,

25th. October 1917. General Staff, 11th. Division.

Copies to: 32nd. Inf. Bde.
46th. Division.

S E C R E T.

G. 742/217.

With reference to 46th Division Order No. 254, para. 1 and this office No. G. 742/196 dated 25th October, 1917.

This raid will now be carried out on night 4th/5th November and not on night 1st/2nd November as stated therein.

ACKNOWLEDGE.

G. Dowling

Lieut-Colonel,
General Staff, 46th Division.

Issued at 8 pm, 31st October, 1917, to all recipients of D.O. 254.

SECRET

Headquarters,
I Corps R.A.
I Corps H.A.)
C.B. S.O.) For
LOOS GROUP.) Information.
46th: Division.)

REFERENCE - ST AUGUSTE (3) 1/10.000 16/9/17
+ Aeroplane Photographs.

(1) The 139th: Infantry Brigade intend to carry out a Raid on the German Trenches about H.32.b.6.4. - N.2.b.6.7. on Night November 1st:/2nd:.
The Raiding Party will assemble in the QUARRY H.32.d., and will form up within 150 yards of enemy Front Line, and North of HUNT Trench. They will remain in enemy Trenches approximately 30 Minutes.

(2) Can the following co-operation from I Corps H.A. be arranged:-

(a) 6 inch Hows: to engage the following points during the Raid.

H.33.a.75.15. H.32.b.94.67.
H.33.a.35.35. N.3.a.6.4.

(b) Counter Battery work during the operation.

(c) Bombardment of the following points previous to the Raid.
Fortified Houses at :-

H.33.a.02.00. H.33.c.17.60. H.33.c.20.82.

(3) Estimates of requirements in ammunition are as follows:-

For 2 (a) 120 rounds 6 inch.

For 2 (c) According to calibre of ~~guns~~ Hows used. It is desired to render these houses untenable if possible.

H McCampbell
Brigadier General.
C.R.A. 46th; Division.

Headquarters R.A.
25/10/17

46TH DIVISION,
GENERAL STAFF.
No. G.742/204
Date 27.X.17

SECRET

O.C. LOOS GROUP.
Headquarters,
46th: Division.

Reference this office 583/3.

(1) I Corps H.A. will co-operate as detailed therein.

(2) The following special allotment of ammunition for Heavy Artillery for all purposes is made.

6" Hows:	380 rounds.
8" Hows:	200 rounds.
60 Pdr:	160 rounds.

V.B. Rowe
Major R.A.
for Brigade Major.
46th: Divisional Artillery.

Headquarters R.A.
27/10/17

SECRET

31st: OCTOBER, 1917.

O.C.
LOOS GROUP.
HULLUCH GROUP.

Headquarters, 46th: Division. I Corps R.A. I Corps H.A. 5th: Canadian Divisional Artillery. 11th: Divisional Artillery. 25th: Divisional Artillery. ST ELIE GROUP. 139th: Infantry Brigade.	For Information.

(1) The proposed Raid by 139th: Infantry Brigade on HERCULES Trench has been postponed until the Night of 4th:/5th: November.

(2) Personnel of A. and B. Batteries, 277th: Army Brigade R.F.A. will remain in action until Noon of the day following the Raid.

(3) A/231 Battery R.F.A. will move out to support 138th: Infantry Brigade Raid as already arranged: the task allotted to it by LOOS GROUP will be carried out by B/277 Battery R.F.A. from 10th: Battery/present position.
O.C. HULLUCH GROUP will arrange for this Battery to receive all necessary details.

(4) A/277 Battery will carry out the task allotted to 68th: Battery R.F.A.

(5) ACKNOWLEDGE BY WIRE.

V.B. Rae
Major R.A.
A/Brigade Major.
46th: Divisional Artillery.

Headquarters R.A.

46TH DIVISION,
GENERAL STAFF.
No. G742/216
Date 31.X.17

S E C R E T
* * * * * * *

Copy No. 9

139th INFANTRY BRIGADE ORDER No. 148.

Ref :- Map LOOS. 36.c.N.W.3. 1/10,000
Intelligence Map CITE ST. AUGUSTE (3)

Oct. 31st, 1917.

1. The 1/6th Battalion Sherwood Foresters will raid the enemy trenches within the points H.32.d.75.50 - H.32.d.80.95 - H.33.c.05.68., on night of ~~1st/2nd~~ 4/5 Novr. ZERO will be notified later.

2. The object of the raid will be to obtain identifications and do damage, special parties being told off to obtain identifications.

3. The raiding party will consist of 4 Officers and about 100 other ranks.

4. The raiding party will collect in the QUARRY H.32.d., and will assemble on a tape line approximately 150 yards in front of enemy new trench in H.32.d.

5. Artillery and Machine Gun programmes have been issued to all concerned.

6. 139 Trench Mortar Battery will with two guns barrage HERCULES TRENCH between H.32.b.6.4 and H.32.b.55.60., and with one gun fire on enemy sap at H.32.d.90.00.

   Rates of fire :-

ZERO to ZERO plus 6'	INTENSE
ZERO plus 6' to ZERO plus 30'	SLOW
ZERO plus 30' to ZERO plus 35'	RAPID

7. The withdrawal and direction signal will consist of one or more Thermite Bombs and golden spray rockets fired horizontally from about H.31.d.95.45., or either.

8. The 32nd Infantry Brigade are withdrawing all Posts in NOGGIN TRENCH east of N.2.b.20.55., from ZERO - 5' to ZERO plus 60'

9. Watches will be synchronised at Support Battalion Headquarters G.36.a.8.8 at ZERO - 5 hours. The Units concerned will send representatives.

Captain.

Brigade Major, 139th Inf.Bde.

Distribution over.

Issued at 2pm to :-

Copy No.	1.	5th Battalion Sherwood Foresters
	2.	6th Battalion Sherwood Foresters
	3.	7th Battalion Sherwood Foresters
	4.	8th Battalion Sherwood Foresters
	5.	139 M.G.Company.
	6.	139 T.M.Battery.
	7.	LOOS GROUP R.A.
	8.	465 Field Company R.E.
	9.	46th Division. ✓
	10.	32 Infantry Brigade.
	11.	137 Infantry Brigade.
	12.	Staff Captain.
	13.	Brigade Signal Office.
	14.	Brigade Pioneer Company.
	15.	"A" Company 1st Monmouths.
	16.	"B" Company 1st Monmouths.

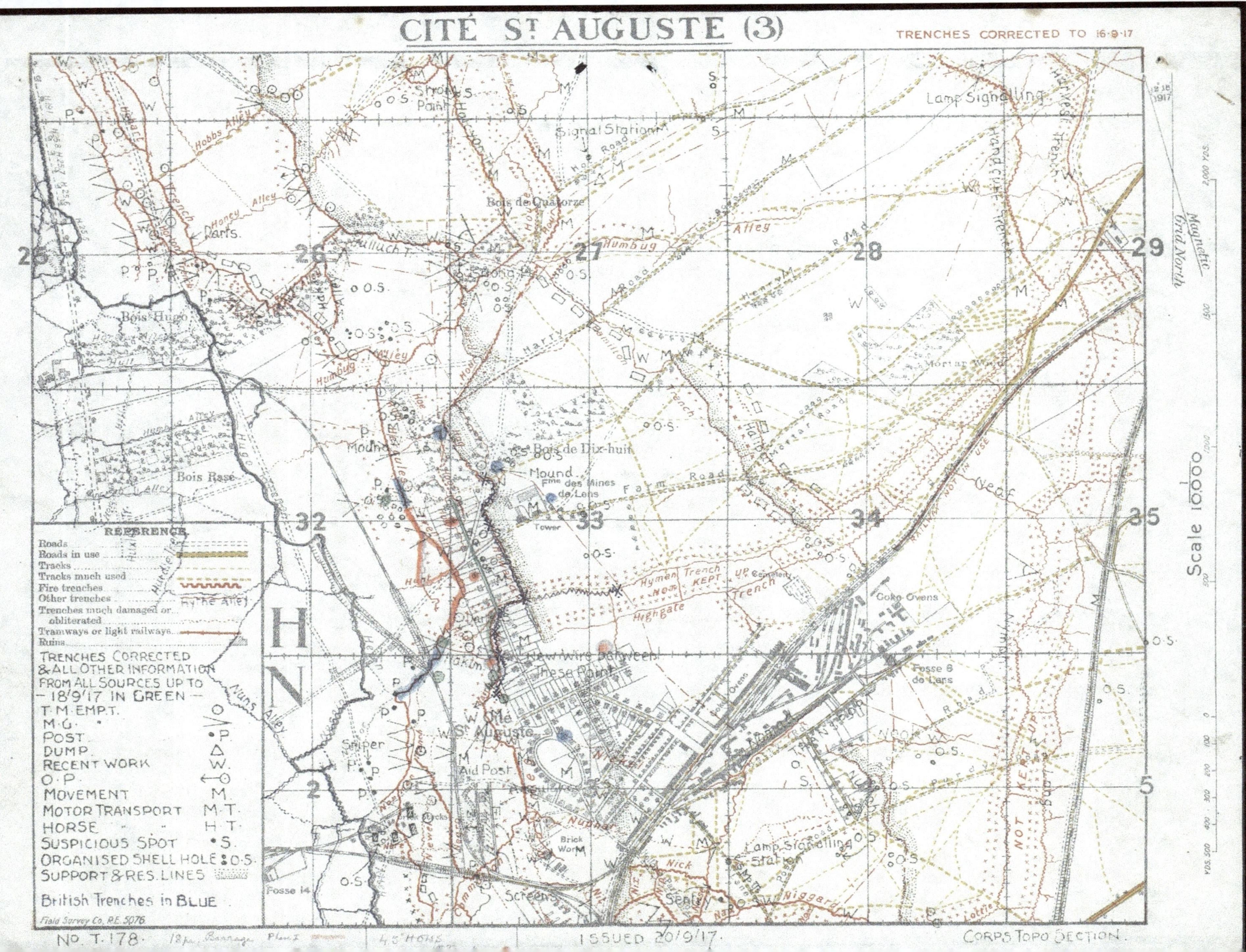

CITÉ ST AUGUSTE (3)
TRENCHES CORRECTED TO 16·9·17
Magnetic
Grid North
Scale 1/10,000
REFERENCE
Roads
Roads in use
Tracks
Tracks much used
Fire trenches
Other trenches
Trenches much damaged or obliterated
Tramways or light railways
Ruins
TRENCHES CORRECTED & ALL OTHER INFORMATION FROM ALL SOURCES UP TO – 18/9/17 IN GREEN –
T.M. EMP.T.
M.G.
POST
DUMP
RECENT WORK
O.P.
MOVEMENT M.
MOTOR TRANSPORT M.T.
HORSE H.T.
SUSPICIOUS SPOT •S.
ORGANISED SHELL HOLE O.S.
SUPPORT & RES. LINES
British Trenches in BLUE
Field Survey Co. R.E. 5076
No. T.178.
ISSUED 20/9/17.
CORPS TOPO SECTION.
Lamp Signalling
Signal Station
Bois de Quatorze
Bois Hugo
Bois Rasé
Bois de Dix-huit
Mound
Fme des Mines de Lens
Tower
Hymen Trench
NOT KEPT UP
Highgate
Coke Ovens
Fosse 8 de Lens
New Wire Between These Points
St Auguste
Aid Post
Sniper
Brick Works
Lamp Signalling Station
Fosse 14
Nuns Alley
Hobbs Alley
Honey Alley
Humbug Alley
Mortar Wood
Farm Road
Handcuff Trench
Harvest Trench
H
N

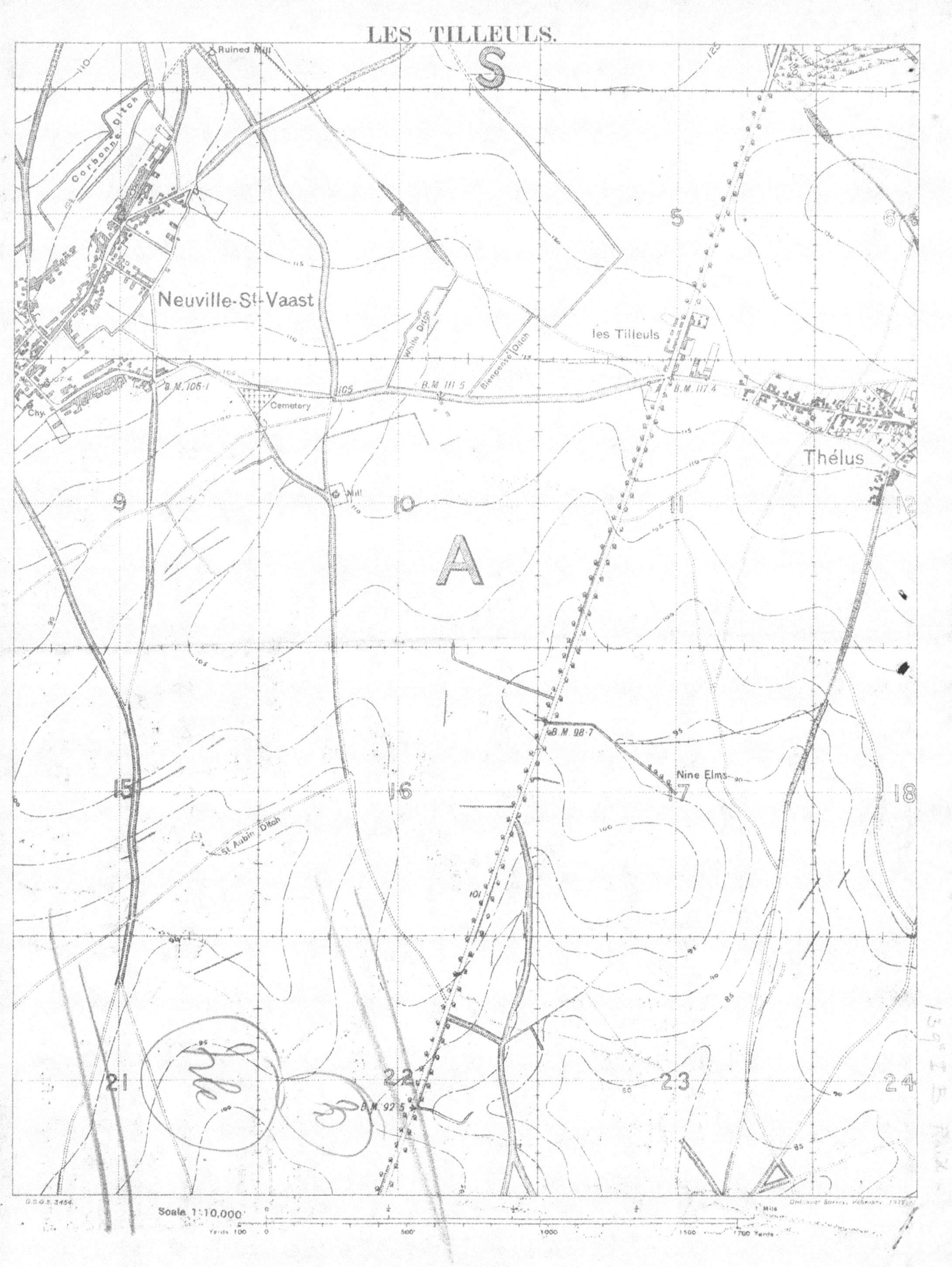
LES TILLEULS.
S
Ruined Mill
Corbonne Ditch
Neuville-St-Vaast
White Ditch
Bienoense Ditch
les Tilleuls
B.M. 106·1
B.M. 111·5
B.M. 117·4
Cemetery
Chy.
Thélus
Mill
A
B.M. 98·7
Nine Elms
St Aubin Ditch
B.M. 92·5
Scale 1:10,000
Yards
1 Mile
1700 Yards

Instructions regarding War Diaries and Intelligence Summaries are contained in F. S. Regs., Part II. and the Staff Manual respectively. Title pages will be prepared in manuscript.

WAR DIARY or ~~INTELLIGENCE SUMMARY~~.

1/6 Bn The Sherwood Foresters

(Erase heading not required.)

Army Form C. 2118.

Vol 33

Hour, Date, Place	Summary of Events and Information	Remarks and references to Appendices
4-10-17.	Major W SEATON admitted to Hospital.	B.W.V.
4-10-17. HILL 70	Battalion relieved 1/5 Battn in Front line.	B.W.V.
5-10-17	Major V.O ROBINSON, M.C., rejoined Battn from attachment to 1/5 Battn	B.W.V.
9-10-17.	Major W SEATON proceeded to England for transfer to R.F.C.	B.W.V.
10-10-17 HILL 70	Battn relieved by 1/5 Battn, & proceeded into Support.	B.W.V.
16-10-17. HILL 70	Battn. relieved 1/5 Battn. in the Line.	B.W.V.
16-10-17.	LONDON GAZETTE. Second Lieuts. to be Lieuts as from 1.7.17 — R. EVANS (D. of W.), T. GREAVES, K.H. BOND, M.C., F.W. HIPKINS, V.T.G. HORE, W.A. LYTLE, M.C., E. KERSHAW, M.C., W.T. STEPHENS, F.S. ROWLAND, M.C., W.L. COOPER. Second Lieut to be Lieut as from 26.7.17. A.F. BRIGGS	B.W.V.
19-10-17. HILL 70.	Capt. J. TOLSON wounded whilst examining his wire in front of the QUARRY. Lieut F.S. ROWLAND took over Command of the 'B' Coy	B.W.V.
21-10-17	Lt. Col. B.W. VANN, M.C., proceeded on Special leave to England. Major V.O. ROBINSON, M.C., assumed Tempy. Command of the Battalion.	B.W.V.
22-10-17. HILL 70.	Battn. relieved by 1/5 S.F. & moved into RESERVE in MAZINGARBE.	B.W.V.
24-10-17	Capt. E.S. WOOD proceeded to join R.F.C., as Observer on probation. Lieut T. GREAVES to Command "A" Coy.	B.W.V.
27-10-17.	Lt. Col. B.W. VANN, M.C., rejoined from Leave & resumed Command of Battn.	B.W.V.
28-10-17 HILL 70	Relieved 1/5 Battn in the Line.	B.W.V.
28-10-17.	Capt. J TOLSON died of wounds.	B.W.V.
31-10-17.	2/Lts. T.A. LAKE & C.F. BARHAM joined Battn. for duty.	B.W.V.
31-10-17 HILL 70.	During the month, the Front line of the HILL 70 Sector has been wired. The German wire in front of the Battn. Sector has been destroyed in liaison with the Artillery. The enemy wire has been regularly patrolled, twenty five patrols having been carried out. In no case were the enemy found in front of his wire.	B.W.V.

B. W. Vann Lieut Colonel.
Cdg. 1/6 Battn. Sherwood Foresters.

53

(9 29 6) W 3332—1107 100,000 10/13 H W V Forms/C. 2118/10.

35807. W16879/M1879 500,000 3/17 R.T. (1074) Forms W3091/3

Army Form W.3091.

19

Cover for Documents.

Raids

Nature of Enclosures.

6th Sherwood Fors

4/5 . 11 . 17

Notes, or Letters written.

Instructions regarding War Diaries and Intelligence Summaries are contained in F. S. Regs., Part II. and the Staff Manual respectively. Title pages will be prepared in manuscript.

WAR DIARY
or
INTELLIGENCE SUMMARY.
(Erase heading not required.)

Army Form C. 2118.

1/6 Notts & Derby
V1 34

Hour, Date, Place		Summary of Events and Information	Remarks and references to Appendices
3. 11. 17	HILL 70.	Bn relieved by 5th Sherwood Foresters & moved into Bde Support.	WOR
4/5. 11 17.	HILL 70	4 Officers & 125. OR. of the Bn raided the enemy trenches, capturing 3 prisoners & inflicting severe casualties on the enemy. Military Medals were awarded to CPL SIMMONDS, SGT HELLIWELL & PTE MADIN in connection with the operation.	appendices 1 & 2. WOR
9. 11. 17.	HILL 70.	Bn relieved 5th Bn in the line (H. 32. a. 6. 4 to H. 32. d. 4. 4).	WOR
15. 11. 17.	do	Bn relieved by 4th LINCS & moved into Support. (3 Coys in O.G. 2 1 Coy in O.B. 1. HQ in TOSH ALLEY)	WOR
16. 11. 17	Support	Bn moved to NOYELLES.	WOR
17. 11. 17.	NOYELLES	Bn moved to FOUQUIERES (Divl Reserve).	WOR
20. 11. 17	FOUQUIERES	2/Lt BUCKLOW G W rejoined from Sick leave.	WOR
21. 11. 17	do	2/Lt GRUNDY. W A joined Bn.	WOR
22. 11 17	do	Bn relieved 5th SF in ST ELIE SECTOR (G 12. d. 7. 1 to G. 12. c. 1. 9)	WOR
28. 11. 17	ST ELIE SECTOR	Relieved by 5th SF & moved into Bde Support (HQ & 2 Coys in PHILOSOPHE, 2 Coys in close support to Right & left Bns in trenches).	WOR
29. 11. 17.	-	C in C's list No 162 of 19th Nov. 17. Capt V. O. ROBINSON M C to be Actg Major whilst employed as Second in Command. 11. 10. 17.	WOR

V O Robinson Major
Comdg 1/6th Bn Sherwood Foresters

3HS

(9 29 6) W 3332—1107 100,000 10/13 H W V Forms/C. 2118/10.

Appendix D 3/17

SECRET. **Operation Order No. 13.** Copy No. 9.

by

Lieut. Colonel [illegible], D.S.O.

Commanding, The [illegible]

In the Field

2nd November 1917.

---

1. The [illegible] will relieve [illegible] the [illegible] [illegible] [illegible] [illegible] [illegible] [illegible] Nov. 2nd/3rd.

2. 'B' Coy. [illegible] will relieve 'D' Coy. [illegible] on the right.
'C' [illegible] 'C' [illegible] [illegible] in the centre.
'D' [illegible] 'B' [illegible] on the left.
'A' [illegible] 'A' [illegible] in support.

3. 'D' & 'C' Coys. will move off from their present positions at 6.45 pm. 'B' Coy. at 6 pm. 'A' Coy. at 6.15 pm.

4. Relief Complete will be sent in B.A.B. Code.

5. Detail:– (a) [illegible] Parties will [illegible] [illegible] at 3 pm.
(b) [illegible] [illegible] [illegible] [illegible] will be sent to [illegible] [illegible] 12 noon on the 4th inst.
(c) Support Coy. will carry [illegible] [illegible] [illegible] [illegible] [illegible] [illegible] [illegible] [illegible] [illegible] [illegible] with the [illegible] [illegible].

C W Lloyd

Capt. & Adjt.

([illegible]) for the [illegible] [illegible]

Issued at [illegible] :–

1. Commanding Officer.
2. [illegible] and [illegible]
3. O.C. 'A' Coy.
4. " 'B' "
5. " 'C' "
6. " 'D' "
7. [illegible] Officer & Quartermaster.
8/9. War Diary.
10. File.

Instructions regarding War Diaries and Intelligence Summaries are contained in F. S. Regs., Part II. and the Staff Manual respectively. Title pages will be prepared in manuscript.

WAR DIARY
or
INTELLIGENCE SUMMARY.

(Erase heading not required.)

Army Form C. 2118.

Place	Date	Hour	Summary of Events and Information	Remarks and references to Appendices
			O.O. NO 13	
			Lieut KING	

A5834 Wt. W4973/M687 750,000 8/16 D. D. & L. Ltd. Forms/C.2118/13.

Bm. 303

Headquarters

46 Division.

I should like
Zero if possible
to be at 8.40
pm. to-morrow.

[signature] Capt.
for BGC
Comdg 139. I. B.

3/11/17

S E C R E T
* * * * * *

Headquarters,

46th Division.

Reference 46th Division Order No. 258, para. 4, I should like the rate of fire altering to :-

ZERO plus 4' to ZERO plus 6'	RAPID
ZERO plus 6' to ZERO plus 8'	NORMAL
ZERO plus 8' to ZERO plus 30'	Intermittent bursts of fire on enfilade targets only.
ZERO plus 30' to ZERO plus 35'	NORMAL.

The feeling of the Officer Commanding the Battalion on this point is that we nearly always start our Machine Guns fiuring at the same time that the Infantry move forward, and the fact that both Artillery and Machine Gunsopen intense fire, proves more or less conclusively that we are about to raid, whereas an Artillery Barrage alone does not necessarily imply this.

G M S Lacey

Brig - General

3/11/17. Commanding 139th Infantry Brigade

SECRET.

I. CORPS COUNTER-BATTERY ORDER NO 51.

1. Reference (46th.Div.Order No 254.
(do. do No 251.
(I.Corps H.A. O.O.No 170.

Hostile Batteries will be neutralized as under.

Raid A. by 1/6 Sherwood Foresters.

Group.	Calibre.	Hostile Batteries.
67th.	1 9.2" how on	HZ92.
	2 6" hows on each.	HZ78. HZ87.
	1 6" ,, ,, ,,	H.11.a.50.15. HZ96.
89th.	1 9.2" how on each.	HX38. HZ77.
	1 8" ,, ,, ,,	HX6. HX9. HZ4. HZ17.
	2 6" ,, ,, ,,	HY1. HZ14. HZ95. NX60. NX90.
	1 6" ,, ,, ,,	(HX12. O.1.a.10.65. H.29.d.80.40.
		(HZ9. HZ18 (todays C.B.Report).
	3 60.pdrs. ,, ,,	H.12.c.50.20. HZ75.

2. RATE OF FIRE.

Zero to Zero plus 5 min. RAPID.
Zero plus 5 min. to Zero plus 15 min. NORMAL.
,, ,, 15 ,, ,, ,, ,, 20 ,, SLOW.
,, ,, 20 ,, ,, ,, ,, 25 ,, RAPID.
,, ,, 25 ,, ,, ,, ,, 30 ,, SLOW.

60.pdrs will fire Gas shell during the RAPID & NORMAL periods only. D & DX. during the SLOW.

3. Code word "Suitable for Gas shell" = STEWARD.
"Unsuitable for Gas shell" = BOATSWAIN.

4. ZERO HOUR for this raid will be 8.40pm. 4th.November.

5. Raid B. by 4th Batt'n Lincoln Regiment.
"STAND BY" on following Batteries.

Group.	Calibre.	Hostile Batteries.
67th.	1 6" how on each.	HX30. HX31. HX34.
	2 60.pdrs. on	HX33.
	3 60.pdrs. on each.	HW2. HW3.

On Signal to open fire:
10 minutes RAPID. followed by SLOW till further orders.

XX— ZERO HOUR for this Raid will be 9.5pm. 4th. November. —XX
Code for Gas shell as above.

6. PLEASE ACKNOWLEDGE.

Copies to:-

Hdqrs R.A. I.Corps. (1)
,, H.A. do. (1)
,, 46th. Div. (1)
,, 46th. D.A. (1)
,, 138th. I.B. (1)
,, 139th. I.B. (1)
C.B.S.O. V.Corps (1)
do. XI. do. (1)
Hdqrs 67th H.A.G. (2)
,, 89th. ,, (2)
File. (2)

4/11/17.

O C Du Port.
Lt.Col.R.A.,
C. B. S. O. I. Corps.

S e c r e t.   G.742/228.

1. With reference to 46th DIVISION ORDER No. 254 and G.742/217.

Zero hour for 6th Bn. Sherwood Foresters, 139th Infantry Brigade, Raid will be 8.40 pm., 4th November, 1917.

2. With reference to 46th DIVISION ORDER No. 251 dated 17th October and G.742/195.

Zero hour for 4th Bn. Lincolnshire Regiment, 138th Inf. Bde, Raid will be 9.5 pm., 4th November, /'17.

3. ACKNOWLEDGE.

G.R. Goodman. Capt.

for: Lieut-Colonel,
General Staff, 46th Division.

Issued at 7 a.m., 4th November, 1917
to all recipients of D.O's No. 254 and
No. 251.

S e c r e t.   G.742/227.

With reference to 46th DIVISION ORDER No. 258, dated 29th October, 1917.

Cancel para. 4 and substitute the following :-

4.	Zero plus 4' to Zero plus 6'	RAPID.
	Zero plus 6' to Zero plus 8'	NORMAL.
	Zero plus 8' to Zero plus 30'	Intermittont bursts of firo on enfilado targots only.
	Zero plus 30' to Zero plus 35'	NORMAL.

G.A. Trueman Capt.
for Lieut-Colonel,
General Staff, 46th Division.

Issued at 7 a.m., 4th November, 1917 to all recipients of D.O.258.

S E C R E T
* * * * * *

No. G.859.

46 Division

Reference 139th Infantry Brigade Order No. 148 para. 1 :-

ZERO hour will be 8.40 p.m.

ACKNOWLEDGE.

Captain.

4/11/17. Brigade Major, 139th Inf.Bde.

To :- All recipients of Order No. 148.

S E C R E T.

REPORT ON RAID CARRIED OUT BY 1/6th BATTALION

SHERWOOD FORESTERS on NIGHT NOVEMBER 4th 1917.

Ref :- Map, CITE ST AUGUSTE (3).

The area raided was NEW TRENCH H.32.d.85.45 to H.32.d.80.93., HERCULES TRENCH H.32.d.80.93 to H.33.c.05.65., HUNT TRENCH H.33.c.05.65 to H.32.d.80.50.

The object of the raid was :-
(a) To obtain identifications.
(b) To kill enemy.

1. WIRE CUTTING.
Wire cutting was commenced 10 days prior to the raid and was carried out by 4.5" Howitzers and 3" Trench Mortars. Maps showing state of enemy wire, compiled from information sent in by Lovat Scouts, Battalion and Brigade Observers and Patrols, were drawn up daily. Arrangements were made to prevent the enemy repairing his wire, by means of patrols and machine guns.

2. PREPARATIONS.
The raiding party rehearsed the operation on a flagged course which had been marked out at MAZINGARBE.

It was decided to carry out the raid with approximately 4 officers and 124 other ranks, which were subdivided into 3 parties known as "A", "B" and "C".

Mobile charges were to be taken over by the raiding party for the purpose of demolishing dug-outs.

Officers were dressed in mens' tunics and all ranks had blacked hands and faces; all identification marks were removed.

The Artillery plan was drawn up in consultation with LOOS GROUP Commander.

Machine gun barrages on the flanks of the raid were arranged by the Divisional Machine Gun Officer.

Stokes Mortars were detailed to barrage enemy front line on the north side of the raid.

3. THE RAID.
The raiding parties (under Capt: G.K.K. MAUGHAN) assembled in the QUARRY in H.32.d., by 6.15 pm., and after being checked were put in dug-outs in the QUARRY until 7.30 pm., when they moved out to their assembly positions in front of our wire about 150 yards from the German trenches.

The assembly positions had been marked out with tapes and notice boards were put up to show each party their exact position on the tape line.

The raiding parties were in position by 8.15 pm.

The assembly was done very quietly and no flares were sent up. It was not observed by the enemy.

At 8.40 pm., the artillery barrage commenced and all parties moved forward, keeping well together.

The whole party crept close up to the barrage, in fact a few men were wounded by getting too close.

There was some rifle fire on the right but no machine gun fire.

The first artillery lift took place at Zero plus 3', the second lift at Zero plus 6'.

Party

Party "A" under Lieut. C. RADFORD, went through and over the concertina wire in front of the new trench and into the trench. Finding no occupants there they proceeded as previously arranged over the top towards HERCULES TRENCH keeping just on the north side of HUNT TRENCH.

They entered HERCULES TRENCH about H.33.c.02.68.

There was a dug-out at about H.32.d.98.75 from which 2 Germans were taken. Two more emerged from the dug-out - one was shot and killed, the other escaped down HERCULES TRENCH; a mobile charge was thrown down the dug-out but failed to explode.

Near the junction of HUNT and HERCULES, probably in the latter, was another dug-out; one German was shot at the top but fell down the entrance - another was wounded but got down the dug-out; bombs were thrown after them.

One other prisoner was taken near the junction of HUNT and HERCULES, but on account of him proving awkward on the return journey was killed in the German wire.

Lieut: RADFORD, though wounded by a bullet in the abdomen before reaching the German wire, remained in command of his party and took his final objective in the German man line. He captured 4 prisoners - 2 of whom were killed on the way home on account of their reluctance to pass through their own barrage. In addition to this, he helped to get his Platoon Sergeant's body back to our lines and returned with his whole party.

The Centre Party, Party "B" under Lieut: W.LL COOPER, entered the new trench about H 32 d 8.7. They found no one here and proceeded down the new trench to its junction with HERCULES. In HERCULES just North of the junction was a dug-out. Near the dug-out was a German Post from which one prisoner was taken.

The Left Party, Party "C" under 2/Lieut: H.S. PINK, instead of entering HERCULES South of the junction NEW Trench and HERCULES Trench, went through a gap a little north of the junction about H 32 d.75.96. They reached HERCULES Trench and owing to its bad condition mistook it for the NEW Trench. They therefore crossed it and pushed on. They later found themselves amongst houses in CITE ST AUGUSTE where they naturally encountered our own barrage. Here they had several casualties and it is thought that possibly the missing men may have penetrated the barrage further than the others and possibly may have been killed. On finding out their mistake they joined Party "B" in HERCULES Trench.

At Zero plus 30' the Recall Signal which consisted of two Thermite Bombs and two golden rain rockets, were fired from our Reserve Line and the party at once commenced the withdrawal.

The bodies of 2 other ranks who had been killed were brought back.

4. CONDITION OF TRENCHES.

The NEW Trench proved to be 5' to 6' deep with well-sloped sides. It was not revetted, floorboarded or fire-stepped. The trench was dry and no signs of enemy were seen.

HUNT Trench was very similar; there were a few floorboards, probably over sump-holes.

HERCULES Trench was found to be in a bad condition. There were a few floorboards in it but it was not wide.

The wire proved to be well cut and our parties had little difficulty in getting into the trenches.

Our barrage appeared to be very good and entirely stopped any serious action by enemy machine guns or rifles.

The German barrage was slow in coming down, in fact it did not really open until about Zero plus 10'. Most of the German shelling was west of the QUARRY, on our Reserve Line and C.Ts.

Very

Very few shells fell in NO Mans Land.

5. CONCLUSION&

The enemy were apparently taken completely by surprise and apparently did not notice that their wire had been cut.

It is unfortunate that Party "C" mistook their gap by about 20 yards as this was no doubt the cause of the missing men. The night however was dark which would account for the slight error in striking the required position.

Altogether 3 prisoners were brought back alive: 12 Germans were definitely known to have been killed and it is estimated that the enemy suffered at least 20 other casualties.

Our casualties were :-

1 officer wounded.
2 other ranks killed.
14 : : wounded.
5 : : missing.

The prisoners taken were from 3 separate posts and all belonged to the 98th Res: Regt, 207th Division.

The general bearing of the Raiding Party was excellent and the men showed considerable dash. Their confidence in our own barrage has been considerably increased.

--- *** ---

G. 742/238.

Headquarters,

I Corps.

****

I forward herewith report on Raid carried out by 1/6th Batt: Sherwood Foresters on the night 4th Nov: 1917.

(Sgd) W.R.

Major-General,

General Staff, 46th Division..

8th November, 1917.

SECRET

REPORT ON ARTILLERY ARRANGEMENTS FOR RAID OF 139th: INFANTRY BRIGADE ON 4th: NOVEMBER, 1917.

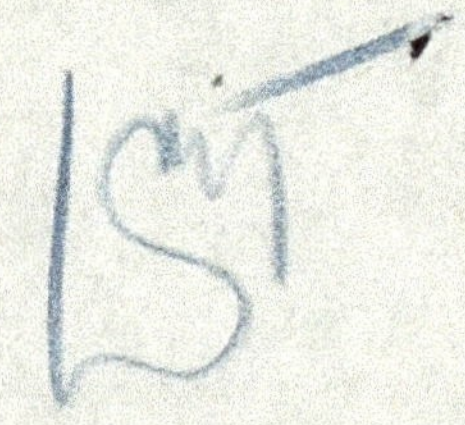

(1) Wirecutting on the Raid Front, and at numerous points N. and S. of it, was carried out mainly by Trench Mortars for several days previous to the Raid.

(2) At Zero an 18 Pdr: Barrage was placed on the whole triangle of trenches to be raided, also on the front for 250 yards N. and S. of raided front.

(3) At plus 3 Minutes the barrage on the trenches to be raided, and on the trenches for 100 yards on either side of area to be raided, moved forward on to the Main Street running through N. suburb of CITE ST AUGUSTE.

At plus 6 minutes this barrage lifted to 125 yards further E. to the E. side of the suburb: at the same time enfilade fire was placed on W. end of HYMAN Trench.

(4) A standing barrage was kept on Front Line for 150 yards N. and 300 yards S. of flanks of moving barrage, and also on 300 yards of 2nd: Line trench on the Southern flank.

(5) 4.5" Hows: engaged:-

(a) Trench Mortar and Machine Gun Emplacements on Right flank of Raid.

(b) Organised shell holes on left flank of Raid.

(c) 2 fortified houses close behind trench to be raided. (At plus 3 minutes fire lifted off these on to selected points further E.).

(6) Heavy Artillery engaged selected strong points - one in CITE ST AUGUSTE, the others near the FMe des MINES and vicinity.

Arrangements for Counter Battery work on numerous Hostile Batteries were prepared.

(7) Operations proceeded as planned, and Infantry reached all objectives.

As the Raid took place in the dark, no observation was possible.

STOP FIRING was received about plus 50 minutes.

(8) Enemy retaliation was late and fell mostly to N. of Raid front.

None of our Batteries were fired upon.

xxxxxxxxxxxxxxx

46TH DIVISION.
GENERAL STAFF.
No. G 742/238
Date 7.11.17

S E C R E T
* * * * * *

Copies to Corps

Headquarters,

46th Division.

I beg to forward herewith, Report on Operations carried out by the 1/6th Battalion, The Sherwood Foresters, on night November 4th, 1917.

Brig - General.

7/11/17. Commanding 139th Infantry Brigade.

G.S.O.1
G.O.C.

9/10

S.C. [illegible] — Operations Orders No. 10. — Copy No. 9

by

Lieut. Col. [illegible] U.S.A.

Commanding [illegible]

In the Field,

November 8th, 1917.

[illegible]

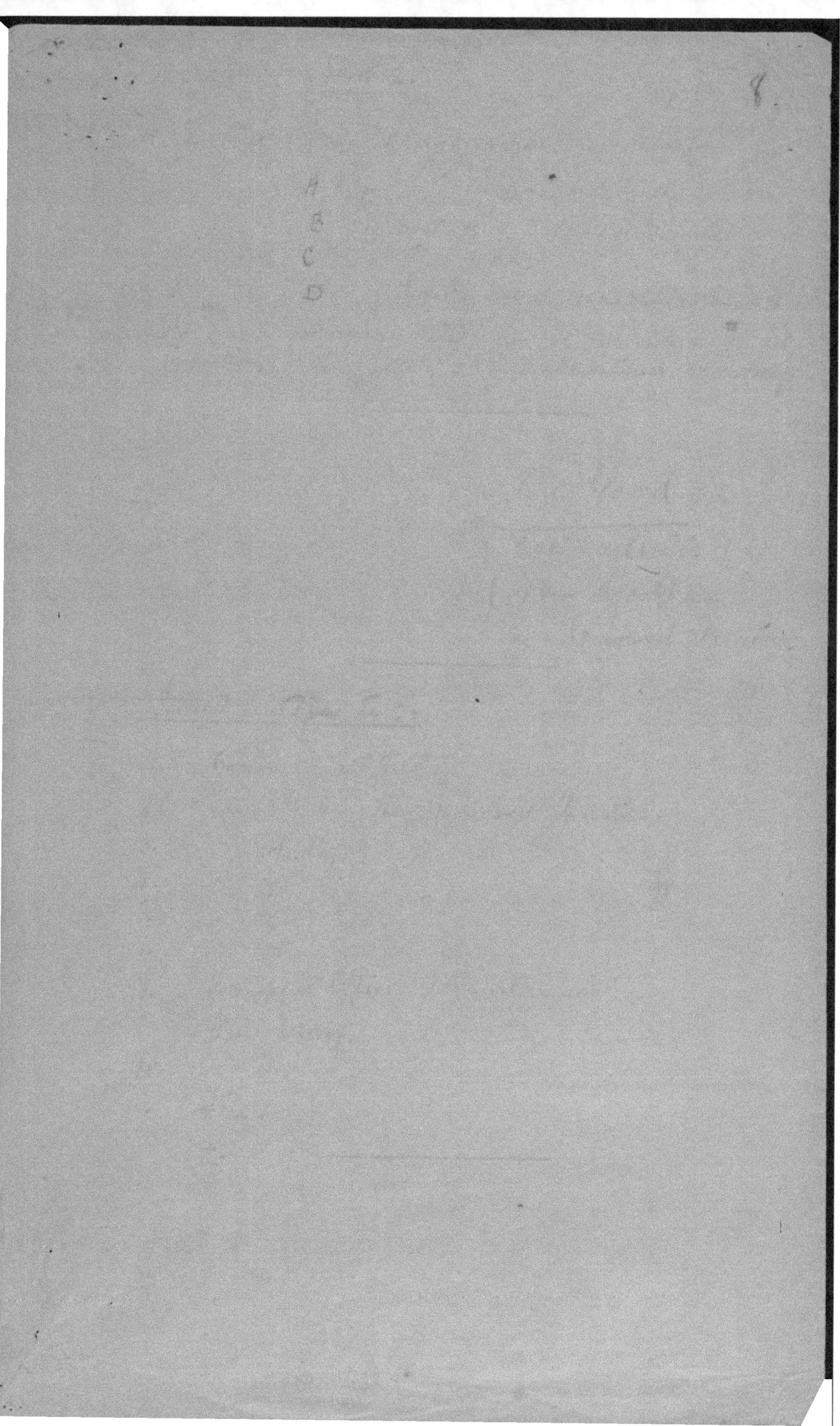

I.O.

SECRET.

46th Division.

No. 153 (G.O). 10th November, 1917.

The Corps Commander makes the following comments on the raid carried out by the 1/6th Bn: Sherwood Foresters on the night November 4th/5th, 1917 :-

"A good raid. The point which strikes me with regard to the Left Party (C) is that the objective given to this party was one which was likely to lead to the very mistake which did occur. At night an error of 20 yards in direction is one which may easily happen, consequently it would have been better if party "C" had been given a definite objective in HERCULES Trench well N. of its junction with HUNT Trench with orders that on reaching HERCULES Trench they were to work South and meet party "B" at the junction of HERCULES and HUNT Trenches. This plan would have had the further advantage of intercepting any Germans who were escaping northward along HERCULES Trench.

I notice that the whole of "C" Party overshot their objective and got into CITE ST. AUGUSTE. This being so the O.C.Party should have been able to withdraw them all when he discovered his mistake. The fact that he lost 5 men, about whom we have no certain information as to whether they were taken prisoners or became casualties, points to control being somewhat lacking in this party at a critical moment."

G. V. Horden

Brig: General,

General Staff, I Corps.

139 I.B.

For infn ~~and~~ ~~in~~ ~~contn~~ and commn to all concerned

(sgd) F.a.D.

10.11.17.

15/16

SECRET. Copy No. 10

OPERATION ORDER No. 16.
by
Lieut-Col. W.C.N. Toller, D.S.O.,
Commanding, The Robin Hoods,
In the field.
November 15th. 1917.

1. The Robin Hoods will relieve the 4th. Battalion Leicestershire Regiment in the ST. ELIE Left Subsection on the night of the 15/16th. November 1917.

2. Dispositions in the line will be as follows :- "D" Coy. right: "A" Coy. centre: "B" Coy. left: "C" Coy. in Support.

3. "B" and "C" Coys. will leave PHILOSOPHE at ~~4.15~~ 4.15. p.m. and will be met by guides at Left Battalion Headquarters STANSFIELD ROAD at 5 p.m.
Guides for "A" and "D" Coys. will be at the forward support Coy. Headquarters at 4 p.m.

4. Relief complete will be sent in B.A.B. code.

5. List of stores taken over and Garrison States to reach the Orderly Room by 7.30 a.m. 16th. inst.

6. Detail for 2 Coys. in PHILOSOPHE.

(a) Blankets and packs will be collected at 1 p.m.
(b) Officers' valises and spare mess boxes will be collected at 1 p.m.
(c) Signalling equipment, mess boxes, medical stores, Lewis Guns and ammunition for trenches will be collected at 2.30 p.m.

7. Two Coys. at PHILOSOPHE will collect Lewis Guns at MANSION HOUSE dump on the way up, and each Coy. will carry two sets of pouches: The remainder of the ammunition will be fetched from EXETER CASTLE dump as soon as possible after relief.

Signed C.W.GOOD Captain & A/Adjt.
7th. (Robin Hood) Bn. The Sherwood Foresters.

Issued at 12 noon to :-
1. Officer Commanding.
2. O.C. 4th. Leicestershire Regt.
3. O.C. "A" Coy.
4. O.C. "B" Coy.
5. O.C. "C" Coy.
6. O. C."D" Coy.
7. Transport Officer.
8. Quartermaster.
9. War Diary.
10. War Diary.
11. File.

22/23

S E C R E T.
- - - - - -

Copy No. 9.

OPERATION ORDER No. 17.
by
Lieut-Col. W.S.N. Toller, D.S.O.,
Commanding, The Robin Hoods,
In the field.
21st. November 1917.

1. The Robin Hoods will be relieved in the ST. ELIE LEFT Subsection by the 8th. Battalion Sherwood Foresters, on the night of the 22/23rd. inst.

2. On relief the Battalion will be in Brigade Support with Headquarters, "A" and "B" Coys. in PHILOSOPHE, "D" Coy. CHAPEL ALLEY, and "C" Coy. in CURLY CRESCENT.

3. Completion of moves will be sent to Battalion Headquarters in the case of forward Coys. by B.A.B. Code, and in the case of "A" and "B" Coys. by runner.

4. Dispositions of the 8th. Battalion Sherwood Foresters in the line will be :-

"A" Coy. on the Right. "D" Coy. in Support.
"C" " " " Left. "B" " " Reserve.

5. Advance parties will reach their destination by 2.30 p.m.

6. Officers Commanding "C" and "D" Coys. will send a responsible N.C.O. to Support Coy. Headquarters to take over Stores, at 2.30 p.m. on day of relief.

7. "B" and "D" Coys. 8th. Bn. Sherwood Foresters will leave close Support position, to commence relief, at 3.45 p.m. Coys. in PHILOSOPHE are leaving at 4 p.m. There will be a regimental policeman at junction O.B.1 and STANSFIELD ROAD to control traffic. He will allow none of outgoing Battalion to pass until all Coys. 8th. Bn. Sherwood Foresters have passed that point.

8. DETAIL.
(a) Lewis Guns and ammunition of "C" and "D" Coys. will be carried.
(b) Lewis Guns and ammunition of "A" and "B" Coys. will be taken to EXETER CASTLE as soon as possible after relief. From this dump they will be pushed on trucks to MANSION HOUSE dump and thence by limber to PHILOSOPHE. Each of these Coys. will detail 1 N.C.O. and one man to load and push; they will remain with the guns until they are stored at PHILOSOPHE.
(c) Mess kits, etc. of "C" and "D" Coys. will be carried.
(d) Stores for PHILOSOPHE (Mess boxes, Medical stores, Signalling equipment, Reserve Lewis Gun Ammunition, etc.) will be taken to EXETER CASTLE dump by 4.30 pm
(e) Transport Officer will have sufficient limbers at MANSION HOUSE dump at 7 p.m.

9. Headquarter Details, "A" and "B" Coys. will bathe on the day following relief.

10. Acknowledge.

(Sd) C.W.GOOD Capt. & A/Adjt.
7th. (Robin Hood) Bn. The Sher. Fors.

SECRET.

Copy No. 10.

OPERATION ORDER NO. 18
by
Lieut-Col. W.S.N. Toller, D.S.O.,
Commanding, The Robin Hoods,

In the field.
November 24th. 1917.

1. On the night of the 25/26th. "A" and "B" Coys. will relieve "C" and "D" Coys. in Forward Support. "C" and "D" Coys. will take over billets occupied by "A" and "B" Coys. respectively.

2. "A" Coy. will leave PHILOSOPHE at 4 p.m. and will relieve "C" Coy. in CURLY CRESCENT. "B" Coy. will leave at 4.15 p.m. and will relieve "D" Coy. in CHAPEL ALLEY. All movement will be by platoons at 200 yards interval.

3. Lewis Guns and Ammunition, mess kits, etc. will be sent by truck, and will be ready for collection at 3.30 p.m. Transport Officer will detail transport. Lewis Gun N.C.O. and 1 man of each Coy. will load trucks.

4. Advance Parties (1 Officer per Coy., 1 N.C.O. per platoon, Coy. Gas N.C.O.) will reach their destination by 2.30 p.m.

5. "A" and "B" Coys. will wire relief complete to this office in B.A.B. Code. "C" and "D" Coys. will send a runner to Battalion Headquarters when Coys. are all present in billets.

6. Lewis Guns, mess kits, etc. of "C" and "D" Coys. will be carried on returning trucks. Transport Officer will arrange transport from MANSION HOUSE dump.

7. Blankets of "A" and "B" Coys. will be rolled in bundles of 10 and taken to Advanced Stores by 12 noon.

8. Officers Commanding "A" and "B" Coys. will take over standing working parties.

9. Officers Commanding Coys., Quartermaster, and Transport Officer to acknowledge.

Signed C.W. GOOD Captain & A/Adjt.
7th. (Robin Hood) Bn. The Sherwood Foresters.

Issued at 1 p.m. to :-

1. Commanding Officer.
2. O.C. 8th. Bn. Sher. Fors.
3. O.C. "A" Coy.
4. O.C. "B" Coy.
5. O.C. "C" Coy.
6. O.C. "D" Coy.
7. Transport Officer.
8. Quartermaster.
9. War Diary.
10. War Diary.
11. File.

Intelligence
Officer.

(2 Copies O.O. 18.
for War Diary)

appendix E

OPERATION
ORDERS

SECRET. Copy No ---- 9

OPERATION ORDER No. 19
by
Lieut-Col. W.S.N. Toller, D.S.O.,
Commanding, The Robin Hoods,
In the Field.
Nov. 27th. 1917.

1. The Robin Hoods will relieve the 8th. Battalion The Sherwood Foresters in the ST. ELIE LEFT Section on the night of the 28/29th. Inst.

2. "C" Coy. Robin Hoods will relieve "A" Coy. 8th. Sherwood Foresters on the right.
"D" " " " " " "C" " 8th. Sherwood Foresters on the left.
"A" " " " " " "D" " 8th. Sherwood Foresters. in Support.
"B" " " " " " "B" " 8th. Sherwood Foresters. in Reserve.

3. "A" and "B" Coys. will leave Forward Support positions at 3.45 p.m. "D" and "C" Coys. and Headquarters Details will leave PHILOSOPHE in that order, commencing at 4 p.m., by platoons at 200 yards interval.

4. Relief complete will be sent in B.A.B. Code.

5. Advance parties will reach their destination by 2.30 p.m.

6. Detail:-
(a) Forward Coys. will carry Mess kits, Lewis Guns, Ammunition, etc. to the line.
(b) Lewis Guns and ammunition of "C" and "D" Coys. will be taken by limber to MANSION HOUSE Dump, where it will be picked up by Coys. and caried to the line.
(c) Lewis Guns and Ammunition will be collected at 3 p.m.
(d) Mess kits, (Headquarters, "C" & "D" Coys.), Signalling Equipment, Medical Stores, etc. for the line will be collected at 3 p.m.
(e) All blankets will be rolled in bundles of 10 and taken to Advanced Stores by 10 a.m.
(f) Officers' valises, and Spare mess kit will be collect ed at 2 p.m.

7. List of Stores taken over will reach the Orderly Room by 12 noon on the day following relief.

8. Officers Commanding Companies, Quartermaster, and Transport Officer, to acknowledge.

Signed C.W.GOOD Captain & A/Adjt.
7th. (Robin Hood) Bn. The Sherwood Foresters.

Issued at 8 p.m. to :-

1. Commanding Officer.
2. O.C. 8th. Bn. Sher.F.
3. O. C. "A" Coy.
4. O. C. "B" Coy.
5. O. C. "C" Coy.
6. O. C. "D" Coy.
7. Transport Officer.
8. Quartermaster.
9. War Diary.
10. War Diary.
11. File.

S E C R E T
* * * * * *

REPORT ON RAID CARRIED OUT BY

1/6th BATTALION SHERWOOD FORESTERS, ON NIGHT

NOVEMBER 4th, 1917.

****

Ref :- Map CITE ST.AUGUSTE (3)

The area raided was NEW TRENCH H.32.d.85.45 to H.32.d.80.93., HERCULES TRENCH H.32.d.80.93 to H.33.c.05.65., HUNT TRENCH H.33.c.05.65 to H.32.d.80.50.

The object of the raid was :-
(a) To obtain identifications
(b) To kill enemy.

1. WIRE CUTTING.

Wire cutting was commenced 10 days prior to the raid and was carried out by 4.5" Howitzers and 3" Trench Mortars. Maps shewing state of enemy wire, compiled from information sent in by Lovat Scouts, Battalion and Brigade Observers and Patrols, were drawn up daily. Arrangements were made to prevent the enemy repairing his wire, by means of Patrols and Machine Guns.

2 PREPARATIONS.

The Raiding Party rehearsed the operation on a flagged course which had been marked out at MAZINGARBE.
It was decided to carry out the raid with approximately 4 Officers and 124 other ranks, which were subdivided into 3 parties known as "A" "B" & "C"
Mobile charges wre to be taken over by the Raiding Party for the purpose of demolishing dugouts.
Officers were dressed in mens' tunics and all ranks had blacked hands and faces; all identification marks were removed.

The Artillery Plan was drawn up in consultation with LOOS GROUP Commander.

Machine Gun Barrages on the flanks of the Raid were arranged by the Divisional Machine Gun Officer.

Stokes Mortars were detailed to barrage enemy front line on the North side of the raid.

3. THE RAID. (under Capt G.R.N. MAUGHAN)

The Raiding Parties assembled in the QUARRY in H.32.d., by 6.15 p.m., and after being checked were put in dugouts in the QUARRY until 7.30 p.m., when they moved out to their assembly positions in front of our wire about 150 yards from the German trenches.

The assembly positions had been marked out with tapes and notice boards were put up to show each party their exact position on the tape line.

The Raiding Parties were in position by 8.15 p.m.

The assembly was done very quietly and no flares were sent up. It was not observed by the enemy.

At

At 8.40 p.m., the Artillery barrage commenced and all parties moved forward, keeping well together.
The whole party crept close up to the barrage, in fact a few men were wounded by getting too close.

There was some rifle fire on the right but no Machine Gun fire.

The first Artillery lift took place at ZERO plus 3', the second lift at ZERO plus 6'.

Party "A" under Lieut.C.RADFORD, went through and over the concertina wire in front of the New Trench andinto the Trench. Finding no occupants there they proceeded as previously arranged over the top towards HERCULES TRENCH keeping just on the North side of HUNT TRENCH.

They entered HERCULES TRENCH about H.33.c.02.68.

There was a dugout at about H.32.d.98.75 from which 2 Germans were taken. Two more emerged from the dugout - one was shot and killed, the other escaped down HERCULES TRENCH; a mobile charge was thrown down the dugout but failed to explode.

Near the junction of HUNT and HERCULES, probably in the latter, was another digout; one German was shot at the top but fell down the entrance - another was wounded but got down the digout; Bombs were thrown after them.

One other prisoner was taken near the junction of HUNT and HERCULES but on account of him proving awkward on the return journey was killed in the German wire.

Lieut.RADFORD though wounded by a bullet in the abdomen ~~which remained in~~ before reaching the German wire, remained in command of his party and took his final objective in the German main line. He captured 4 prisoners - 2 of whom were killed on the way home on account of their reluctance to pass through their own barrage. In addition to this, he helped to get his Platoon Sergeant's body back to our lines and returned with his whole party.

The Centre Party, Party "B" under Lieut.W.L.COOPER, entered the New Trench about H.32.d.8.7. They foundno one here and proceeded down the new trench to its junction with HERCULES. In HERCULES just North of the junction was a dugout. Near the dugout was a German Post from which one prisoner was taken.

The Left Party, Party "C" under 2/Lieut.H.S.PINK, instead of entering HERCULES South of the junction NEW TRENCH and HERCULES TRENCH, went through a gap a little North of the junction about H.32.d.75.96. They reached HERCULES TRENCH andowing to its bad condition mistook it for the NEW TRENCH. They therefore crossed it and pushed on. They later found themselves amongst Houses in CITE ST.AUGUSTE where they naturally encountered our own barrage. Here they had several casualties and it is thought that possibly the missing men may have penetrated the barrage furtherthan the others and possibly may have been killed. On finding out their mistake they joined Party "B" in HERCULES TRENCH.

At ZERO plus 30' the Recall Signal which consisted of two Thermite Bombs and two golden rain rockets, were fired from our Reserve Line andthe party at once commenced the withdrawal.

The bodies of 2 other ranks who had been killed were brought back.

4. CONDITION OF TRENCHES.

The NEW TRENCH proved to be 5 to 6' deep with wellmsloped sides. It was not revetted, floorboarded or fire-stepped. The Trench was dry and no signs of enemy were seen.

HUNT TRENCH was very similar; there were a few floorboards, probably over sump holes.

HERCULES

HERCULES TRENCH was found to be in bad condition. There were a few floor boards in it but it was not wide.

The wire proved to be well cut and our parties had little difficulty in getting into the Trenches.
Our barrage appeared to be very good and entirely stopped any serious action by enemy Machine Guns or rifles.

The German barrage was slow in coming down, in fact it did not really open until about ZERO plus 10'. Most of the German shelling was West of the QUARRY, on our Reserve line and C.Ts. Very few shells fell in 'No Man's Land'

6. CONCLUSION.

The enemy were apparently taken completely by surprise and apparently did not notice that their wire had been cut.

It is unfortunate that Party "C" mistook their gap by about 20 yards as this was no doubt the cause of the missing men. The night however was dark which would account for the slight error in strking the required position.

Altogether 3 prisoners were brought back alive.; 12 Germans were definitely known to have been killed and it is estimated that the enemy suffered at least 20 other casualties.

Our casualties were :-

1 Officer wounded.
2 other ranks killed.
14 " " wounded
5 " " missing.

The prisoners taken were from 3 separate posts and all belonged to the 98th Regiment, 207th Division.

The general bearing of the Raiding party was excellent and the men shewed considerable dash. Their confidence in our own barrage has been considerably increased.

-------oOo------

SECRET

REPORT ON ARTILLERY ARRANGEMENTS FOR RAID OF 139th: INFANTRY BRIGADE ON 4th: NOVEMBER, 1917.

(1) Wirecutting on the Raid Front, and at numerous points N. and S. of it, was carried out mainly by Trench Mortars for several days previous to the Raid.

(2) At Zero an 18 Pdr: Barrage was placed on the whole triangle of trenches to be raided, also on the front for 250 yards N. and S. of raided front.

(3) At plus 3 Minutes the barrage on the trenches to be raided, and on the trenches for 100 yards on either side of area to be raided, moved forward on to the Main Street running through N. suburb of CITE ST AUGUSTE.

At plus 6 minutes this barrage lifted to 125 yards further E. to the E. side of the suburb: at the same time enfilade fire was placed on W. end of HYMAN Trench.

(4) A standing barrage was kept on Front Line for 150 yards N. and 300 yards S. of flanks of moving barrage, and also on 300 yards of 2nd: Line trench on the Southern flank.

(5) 4.5" Hows: engaged:-

(a) Trench Mortar and Machine Gun Emplacements on Right flank of Raid.

(b) Organised shell holes on left flank of Raid.

(c) 2 fortified houses close behind trench to be raided. (At plus 3 minutes fire lifted off these on to selected points further E.).

(6) Heavy Artillery engaged selected strong points - one in CITE ST AUGUSTE, the others near the FMe des MINES and vicinity.

Arrangements for Counter Battery work on numerous Hostile Batteries were prepared.

(7) Operations proceeded as planned, and Infantry reached all objectives.

As the Raid took place in the dark, no observation was possible.

STOP FIRING was received about plus 50 minutes.

(8) Enemy retaliation was late and fell mostly to N. of Raid front.

None of our Batteries were fired upon.

xxxxxxxxxxxxxx

Instructions regarding War Diaries and Intelligence Summaries are contained in F. S. Regs., Part II. and the Staff Manual respectively. Title pages will be prepared in manuscript.

WAR DIARY
of 1/6th Bn Sherwood Foresters
~~INTELLIGENCE~~ SUMMARY.
(Erase heading not required.)

Army Form C. 2118.

Vol 35

Hour, Date, Place		Summary of Events and Information	Remarks and references to Appendices
3. 12. 17	PHILOSOPHE	Lt Col B.W. VANN M.C, proceeded on leave to England & Major T.O. ROBINSON M.C. assumed temporary command of the Battalion.	BWV
4. 12. 17	ST ELIE RIGHT	Bn relieved 5th Sherwood Foresters in the line (G.12.d.7.1 to G12.c.1.9)	BWV
10. 12. 17	do	Relieved by 5th S.F. & moved into Divisional Reserve at YERQUIN. 2/Lieuts C. W. KIRK; S.G. JOHNS & P.A. TOMPKINSON joined the Battn.	BWV
11. 12. 17	YERQUIN	LIEUT C.G. RADFORD awarded the military cross in connection with the raid on the night 14/15 Nov. 1917.	BWV
16. 12. 17	YERQUIN	The Battn relieved 5th S.F. in ST ELIE RIGHT SECTOR	BWV
17. 12. 17		LONDON GAZETTE. The following were mentioned in the Despatches of the Field Marshal Commanding in Chief for Gallantry & devotion to duty:- 2/Lieut (A/Capt) B.E. JOHNSON. Capt (A/Lt Col) C.B. JOHNSON. 2/Lieut J. TAYLOR. 240562 SERGT. G. P. BAGSHAW.	BWV
BWV 17. 12. 17	ST ELIE RIGHT.	Lt Col B.W. VANN M.C. rejoined from leave & resumed command of the Battalion.	BWV
22. 12. 17	do.	Relieved by 5th S.F. & moved to Brigade Support. (2 Companies & H.Q in PHILOSOPHE & 2 Coys in close support.	BWV
28. 12. 17	BDE RESERVE	Battn relieved 5th S.F. in St ELIE RIGHT Sector.	BWV

B.W. Vann Lieut Col
Comdg 1/6 Sherwood Foresters.

355

(9 29 6) W 3332—1107 100,000 10/13 H W V Forms/C. 2118/10.

To Headquarters,
30th Infantry Bde.

Report on Hostile Bombardment on night of 30 Nov/1st Decr.

At about 12.20 am the enemy again put down a Heavy Artillery & Trench Mortar Barrage, chiefly on BORDER and HAIRPINS and in rear.

At about 12.45 am a party of about 6 of the enemy were seen at NORTHERN CRATER. They approached the Tunnel Entrance and threw bombs and explosive charges at the shelter. Fire was opened from the Lewis Gun and by rifles from under the shelter, where some of the men had been withdrawn to. The enemy were driven off, but no identification was obtained. Slight damage was done to the trench bottom and two of the sentry post were blown down, but no damage was done to the Tunnel Entrance.

Damage to Reserve Line is now fairly considerable. GORDON ALLEY in three places, each of about 50 yards, is now nothing but a series of Trench Mortar Craters.

The junction of O.B.x and GORDON ALLEY is completely blown in.

as is also R.55. Machine Gun Emplacement. It would not take long to get O.B.4. repaired; O.B.I, is not badly damaged. GORDON ALLEY forward of O.B.I will require about 20 men for two or three nights.

(Signed)

W. Y. N. Toller. D.S.O.
Lieut Colonel.

7th (Robin Hood) Bn., The Sherwood Foresters.

1/12/17.

SECRET.

O.C. "A" Coy. O.C. "C" Coy. Batt. Intell Off. Medical Officer.
O.C. "B" Coy. O.C. "D" Coy. O.C. H.Q. Coy.

8th December. 1917.

1. A gas operation will be carried out by No. 4 Special Coy. R.E. on the HULLUCH and ST. ELIE fronts on 9th December.
This operation will consist of a rehearsal of the smoke screen to be used in connection with a forthcoming raid.

2. Targets. (1) for smoke:-

H.19.a.6.6 - H.13.c.6.3. Southern dummy screen.

G.5.c.7.1. - G.5.c.2.3. Northern dummy screen.
If wind is between W & N.W., bombs will be dropped 200 yards N.E. of targets named.

H.13.c.5.8 - H.13.a.3.3. Real raid front. Southern Smoke barrage.
If wind is between S.W. and S bombs will be dropped 200 yds E of targets named.

G.12.d.7.8 - G.12.b.2.1. Real raid front. Northern Smoke barrage.

Targets (2) for Gas.
Southern Dummy smoke screen.
Smoke screen, real raid - Southern barrage.
Raid area.
Smoke screen, real raid - Northern barrage.
Northern dummy smoke screen.

3. All ranks (with the exception of Batt. H.Q.) will wear box respirators and all gas doors will be closed from ZERO - 5 till "All Clear" is given.

4. Alternative ZERO hours have been arranged as follows:-
First ZERO 10 A.M.
Second ZERO 1.30 P.M.

5. The following code words will be used:-

Operations will take place at First Zero — FIRST SHELL.
Operation will take place at Second Zero — SECOND SHELL.
Operation completed "All clear" — BURST.
Operation cancelled for the day — BLIND.

Captain & Adjutant.
1/6th Bn. Sherwood Foresters

SECRET.

Relief Orders

by Major V. O. Robinson. M. C., Cmdg. 1/6th Bn. Sherwood Foresters.

15th December. 1917.

1. The Battalion will relieve the 1/5th Battn. Sherwood Foresters in the line tomorrow evening. Relief complete to be reported to Battn. H.Qrs. by the code words "MINCE PIE".

2. Dispositions of Companies will be as under:-

Lr. "A" Coy 6th S.F. will relieve Lr. "C" Coy. 5th S.F. on the RIGHT.
Lr. "B" Coy 6th S.F. will relieve Lr. "B" Coy. 5th S.F. in the CENTRE.
Lr. "D" Coy 6th S.F. will relieve Lr. "D" Coy 5th S.F. on the LEFT.
Lr. "C" Coy 6th S.F. will relieve Lr. "A" Coy. 5th S.F. in SUPPORT.

3. The Battalion will leave the present area at 1.0 p.m., march by Coys. at 100 yards interval as far as SAILLY LABOURSE, & thence by platoons at 200 yards interval to NOYELLES.

Order of March "D". "A". "B". "C". "H.Qrs."
Head of Column: On road 200 yards S.E. of Batt. H.Qrs.
Dress:- Fighting Order. Greatcoats rolled round the haversack & kept in position by entrenching tool shaft.

4. Lewis Guns & Ammunition will go by limber to MANSION HOUSE DUMP & by trolley to the Battn. Dump in the line. Platoons to pick them up as they pass.
The Transport Officer to detail necessary transport. Coy L.G. N.C.O's & 1 man per L.G. Team to accompany limbers which will follow behind Lr. "D" Coy on the march.

5. An Advance Party composed as under will parade at Batt. H.Q. at 11.0 A.M.

1 Officer per Company.
R.S.M.
1 N.C.O. per Platoon.
2 Signallers per Coy & Battn. H.Qrs
2 Runners.

Haversack Rations to be taken by this party.

6. Stand to will be at 6.15 A.M. and 4.0 P.M.

7. ACKNOWLEDGE.

E. Kershaw.
Captain & Adjutant
1/6th Battalion The Sherwood Foresters

Lewis Gun NCO.

SECRET

O.O./G./1.

O.C. 'A' 'B' & 'D' Coys. O.C. 'C' Coy. O.C. HQrs. Coy.
Battn. Intelligence Officer. " Medical Officer (for information)

17th December. 1917.

1. On the night 17th/18th December No 4 Special Coy. R.E. will bombard selected points in HAMLET and FOSSE ALLEY.

2. Targets:- (1) HAMLET TRENCH from SCHOOLHOUSE to HOMER ALLEY.
(2) HAMLET TRENCH from HAGGARD ALLEY to GAMBIT ALLEY.
(3) FOSSE ALLEY from GIPSY ALLEY to G.6.a.0.2.

3. Codes:-

Gas will be fired at first Zero	FIRST ALPHA.
First Zero cancelled; Gas will be fired at Second Zero	SECOND ALPHA.
Operation cancelled for the night	IBED.
Operation complete "ALL CLEAR"	OMEGA.

4. Precautions:- All ranks except the Support Coy. & Battn. HQrs will wear box respirators and all gas blankets will be down from ZERO - 5 till "ALL CLEAR".

5. Zeros:-

1st Zero	9.0 p.m. 17/12/17.
2nd Zero	12.0 midnight. 17/18/12/17.

Capt & Adjutant.
1/6th Battn. The Sherwood Foresters.

SECRET
To. O. C. Companies. Battn. Intelligence Officer.

Artillery arrangements in connection with Defence Schemes.

(i) The S.O.S. Signal will only be sent in the event of a hostile attack developing.
This will be sent
(a) By Telephone
(b) By Rockets or VERY Light.
The S.O.S. Signal is at present RED.
On receipt of S.O.S. Signal, Batteries will open on their S.O.S. barrage lines. The Signal must be confirmed by message as soon as possible.
Message to be sent is
"S.O.S. ELIE SOUTH"

(ii) In the event of a large enemy raid or a heavy hostile bombardment of our trenches the message to be sent is
"ATTACK ELIE SOUTH"

(iii) The original "ATTACK" Schemes e.g. ATTACK LANCER will be used as before to deal with an enemy attack on a small scale such as a Raid.
For these the call "ATTACK" is to be abolished and the word "RAID" is to be substituted.
The message to be sent therefore is
RAID LANCER
or RAID ROAD

(iv) The present S.O.S. Calls for an Attack on a small scale remain unaltered.
The message to be sent is
S.O.S. LANCER
or S.O.S. ROAD.

(v) The messages to be sent in case of Cloud Gas, Shell Gas or Tanks are respectively
G.A.S. ELIE SOUTH
POISON ELIE SOUTH
S.O.S. TANK ELIE SOUTH.

(P.T.O)

The S.O.S. and ATTACK calls for the Left Battalion of the Brigade are

S.O.S. ELIE NORTH.

ATTACK. ELIE NORTH etc.

The General difference between S.O.S. and ATTACK calls is that in the former the barrage falls in NO MAN'S LAND; in the latter on the enemy front line.

15/1/18.

Captain & Adjutant.
1/6th Battn. Sherwood Foresters

SECRET To be handed over on relief.

List of Hostile Trench Mortars Active on ST. ELIE Front (139 Inf. Brigade) and Code Names.

MINNIE ROAD (SOUTH)
(Right Company Right Subsector)

H.7.a.05.15.	=	RUM.
H.7.a.80.10.	=	MILK.
H.7.d.20.40.	=	WHISKEY.
G.12.b.49.19.	=	SODA.
G.12.a.85.30.	=	BEER.
H.7.a.30.34.	=	SKITTLES.
H.13.a.99.60.	=	BILLIARDS.

MINNIE ROAD (NORTH)
(Centre Company Right Subsector)

G.12.b.49.19.	=	SODA.
G.12.a.85.30.	=	COFFEE.
G.12.a.42.28.	=	COCOA.
H.7.a.30.34.	=	SKITTLES.
H.7.a.59.11.	=	PEPPER.
H.7.c.04.47.	=	SALT.
G.12.a.80.20	=	MUSTARD.

MINNIE LANCER
(Left Company Right Subsector)

H.7.d.20.40.	=	WHISKY.

MINNIE QUARRIES.
(Right Company Left Subsector)

G.6.c.35.90.	=	BLIND.
G.5.d.80.20.	=	MICE.
G.5.d.45.90.	=	FARMER.

MINNIE BORDER.
(Left Company Left Subsector)

G.5.d.80.20.	=	MICE.
G.5.b.70.40.	=	TAIL.
G.5.d.10.80.	=	CARVING.
G.5.b.00.10.	=	KNIFE.
G.5.d.70.60.	=	SIGHT.
G.5.d.45.90.	=	FARMER.

MINNIE GORDON.
(RUSSIAN SAP. Left Subsector)

G.5.d.10.80	=	CARVING.
G.5.b.00.10.	=	KNIFE.
G.5.d.70.60.	=	SIGHT.

P.T.O.

If a Company is being seriously bombed by several T.Ms their code word is sent through i.e. "MINNIE LANCER" or "MINNIE BORDER" and as many T.Ms. as possible are at once engaged.
In the case of one T.M. causing considerable annoyance the separate code word is sent through i.e. "BEER" or "TEA" and it is engaged.
In addition to sending the call through to the Group. R.A. Companies will inform all 3" & 6" T.M. personnel in their area, so that fire can at once be opened by them.

THIS LIST CANCELS PREVIOUS LISTS. 14.12.17.

SECRET.

To O^s. C. Companies.

It has now been definitely ascertained that the enemy has recently employed a method of discharging gas, which is similar in principle to our Projector attacks, several hundred gas bombs being fired simultaneously into a comparatively small area. A "blind" containing Phosgene has been found.

Reports show that adequate warning of this attack can be obtained from the flash and noise of discharge. A sheet of flame appeared to run along the German trenches accompanied by an explosion which was loud enough to rouse men who were asleep. The bombs were seen in the air in large numbers and made a loud whizzing noise. They burst with a loud detonation, producing a thick, white cloud of gas.

Where the alarm was given and respirators adjusted immediately, practically no casualties occurred. At one point five bombs burst in a trench without harming the occupants. The Box Respirator affords protection against very high concentrations of Phosgene which pass at once through the German respirator.

All ranks must be warned to expect discharges of this kind and must be informed of the signs by which the discharge can be recognised. Sentries must give the alarm without the slightest delay and lower the blankets of the entrances of protected dugouts.

As the gas cloud produced by the simultaneous discharge of a number of gas bombs may be effective at a considerable distance from where they burst, the above measures of protection must be adopted wherever the flash or explosion is detected, not only in the vicinity of the place where the bombs burst, but throughout the area likely to become dangerous from gas according to the direction of the wind.

Particular care is to be taken that this information is passed at once to all ranks and necessary precautions taken.

Captain & Adjutant.
1/6th Battalion The Sherwood Foresters.

20/12/17.

SECRET. Relief Orders O.O./A/1.
by Lt. Colonel. B.W. Vann. M.C., Cmdg. 1/6th Bn. The Sherwood Foresters
21st December. 1917.

1. The Battalion will be relieved by the 5th Bn Sherwood Foresters in the line tomorrow evening.

2. Companies will be relieved as under:-
Lr. 'A' Company. 6th S.F. by Lr. 'C' Company 5th S.F. on the RIGHT.
Lr. 'B' Company. 6th S.F. by. Lr. 'B' Company 5th S.F. in the CENTRE.
Lr. 'D' Company. 6th S.F. by. Lr. 'A' Company 5th S.F. on the LEFT.
Lr. 'C' Company 6th S.F. by. Lr. 'D' Company 5th S.F. in SUPPORT.

3. Relief complete to be reported to Battn. H.Qrs. by the code word "TURKEY."

4. On relief the Battalion will move into Brigade Support and will be distributed as follows:-

Battalion H.Qrs. / Lrs. 'A' & 'B' Companies	PHILOSOPHE.
Lr. 'C' Company	In SUPPORT to RIGHT Battalion.
Lr. 'D' Company	In SUPPORT to LEFT Battalion.

Lrs. 'C' & 'D' Companies will come under the orders of O's. C. Right and Left Battalions respectively for tactical purposes. Both Companies to "Stand to" the morning after relief.

5. 1 Officer & 1 N.C.O. per platoon of each of Lrs. 'C' & 'D' Coys. will report to the Adjutant at 11 AM. and proceed to their new Sectors to take over.
An Advance Party composed as under will parade at Battn H.Qrs at 1.30 p.m. under Capt. Greaves and proceed to PHILOSOPHE.
2 N.C.O's per Lrs. 'A', 'B' & H.Qrs. Coys.
Provost Sergeant.
2 Batmen per Lrs. 'A', 'B' & H.Qrs. Coys.
2 Battalion Signallers.
2 Battalion Runners.

6. <u>Headquarters & Lrs. 'A' & 'B' Coys.</u> Lewis Guns to be carried out by L.G. Sections. Lewis Gun Ammunition to be handed to Sgt. Reece at the Dump as platoons pass.
Officers Mess Kit, Cooking Dixies, Medical & Signalling Kit, O.R. Boxes, Canteen Stores & Surplus Battn. Trench Stores to be handed to the R.S.M. at the Dump by 4 p.m.
<u>Lrs. 'C' & 'D' Companies</u> will make their own arrangements for carrying out Lewis Guns, L.G. Ammunition, Officers Mess Kit, Cooking Dixies etc.

7. The Transport Officer will detail 2 limbers to be at MANSION HOUSE DUMP at 4 p.m. to convey Kit & Stores to PHILOSOPHE.

8. ACKNOWLEDGE.

Capt. & Adjutant.
1/6th Battn. The Sherwood Foresters

SECRET. Relief Orders O.O./A/2.

by Lieut.-Colonel B. W. Vann, M.C., Cmdg. 1/6th Bn. Sherwood Foresters.

24th December, 1917.

1. The following inter Company relief will take place tomorrow.
   No. "A" Coy. will relieve No. "C" Coy. in SUPPORT to the RIGHT Battalion.
   No. "B" Coy. will relieve No. "D" Coy. in SUPPORT to the LEFT Battalion.

2. Relief complete to be reported to Battn. Headquarters of RIGHT and LEFT Battalions respectively.

3. Movement from PHILOSOPHE to be by platoons at 200 yards interval. No. "A" Coy. No. 1 Platoon to move off at 4 p.m.

4. Arrangements for taking over L.G. Ammunition, Cooking Dixies, etc. to be made between Company Commanders concerned.

5. 1 Limber will be at the disposal of Companies for conveying kit, stores, etc. to and from MANSION HOUSE. All such Kit of Nos. "A" & "B" Companies to be stacked outside Battalion Headquarters by 3 p.m.

6. On relief, Nos. "A" & "B" Companies will come under the orders of O.C. Right and Left Battalions respectively for tactical purposes and work.

   Nos. "C" & "D" Companies will take over billets in PHILOSOPHE vacated by Nos. "A" and "B" Companies.

7. ACKNOWLEDGE.

[illegible signature]

Captain & Adjutant.

1/6th Battalion Sherwood Foresters.

(ii). REPORT on PATROL carried out by 2/Lt: C.F.BARHAM and 2/Lt:A. LAKE of 6th SHERWOOD FORESTERS on 22nd December, 1917.

Task.	Time & Place of departure.	Time & Place of return.
To confirm the report of former daylight patrol of same Unit as to the existence of an enemy Post on LOOKOUT CRATER.	10.50 a.m. G.12.c.56.75.	12.15 p.m. G.12.c.50.75.

2/Lt: LAKE and myself proceeded from No.7 LOOKOUT round outer edge of LOOKOUT CRATER to a point G.12.c.52.82. when we entered enemy's trench. After examining the right sap we returned and crawled over block in enemy trench on the left of point of entry and crawled along the trench running in the direction of QUARRIES, at a point about 15 yards along we found enemy trench was in good condition and good repair, also a latrine recently used. Following trench to the right we suddenly came on German dug-out, the entrance facing his own line, and a sentry was emerging from dug-out at the moment of our arrival. He turned suddenly and saw us (we were then at a distance of 3 yards from him) and he put up his hands in token of surrender, but apparently altering his mind, he suddenly reached for his rifle which had bayonet fixed, and attempted to turn on us. We fired at very close range with our revolvers, the German being apparently hit low, twice in the stomach, and the second time we fired he fell with a hit in the left cheek and fell headlong down dug-out steps. Immediately after our opening fire two shots were fired at us from the left by enemy behind barricade in trench with wire in front of it, followed by rapid rifle fire and we consequently were unable to follow up our advantage as the shots were very close, we were obliged to retreat hastily, being in a very exposed position and managed to jump into crater and return quickly to our own lines.

Immediately after our shooting the German, there were shouts on stairway of dug-out which apparently contained a good number of the enemy.

We found that trench at point G.12.c.51.86 was completely blocked with barbed wire and sandbags, the wire crossing the trench - this was the point the enemy opened fire on us and obliged us to return - his distance from us being about 20 to 25 yards. The sap facing LANCER is apparently not used and is in bad condition. We were unable to obtain any information as to identity as we were already heavily fired at.

The German was in full equipment as if moving, mess tin strapped to his back with other things.

Corps Commander's remarks:-

"I think this was a most enterprising patrol and would like both Officers congratulated for me on their bold and useful work".

G.V. Horden.

Brigadier General,
General Staff, I Corps.

1st January, 1918.

Distributed
3 Bns. 5 each
CRA 1
CRE 1

I CORPS

Monthly Record of Patrol work of exceptional merit

DECEMBER 1917.

---

(1). REPORT on DAYLIGHT PATROL carried out by 2/Lieut: WINT and 10 O.R. of 1/5th N.STAFFORDSHIRE Regt. on 21/12/17.

At 8.5 a.m. on the 21st inst. a party of 1 Officer (2/Lt: WINT) and 10 O.R. having crept out to the old front line at H.19.c.98.30 made a sudden dash to the enemy line at H.19.d.10.45. The enemy wire was crossed without difficulty and the party reached the trench and jumped in. Immediately on the right was a hostile party of at least 20 men.. Rifle and revolver shots and bombs were exchanged, and the officer seeing that his party was outnumbered, ordered them to withdraw. He himself was the last to leave the trench and at least 3 of the enemy were shot dead and probably others were wounded by bombs. While the party was returning to our lines, heavy rifle fire was opened on them and several were hit. The officer and a Corporal were caught in the enemy wire but managed to escape, and as many bombs were being thrown at them, they dropped into a shell-hole close to the wire. Here the Corporal bound up the wounds on the Officer's hand and knee.

A party of 10 of the enemy then left their line and coming near the shell-hole shouted "hands up, we know where you are". At the same moment rifle and Lewis gun fire from our front line knocked out four of the enemy and the remainder retired, while the officer and corporal made a dash for a ditch and ultimately succeeded in getting back to our trenches. While they were getting in, three more of the enemy were hit by our snipers. Also at the moment when the party commenced to withdraw our snipers accounted for three of the enemy who got out of their trench.

Two of our men were wounded near our own line and after two men had been hit in going to help them, a third man was killed.

Gaps were then cut in our own wire in a disused trench and the two men were brought in, one of whom died immediately. Two of the patrol are at present missing.

The enemy suffered at least 13 casualties and probably more.

The enemy were wearing dark grey uniform, pork-pie caps with a red band and a small grenade badge, similar to our Royal Fusiliers' but light in colour.

One man stated that the collars of the tunics were red.

Sd/H.POCHIN, Major,
21/12/17. Commanding 1/5th Bn:N.Staffs. Regt.

Corps Commander's remarks:-

"I consider this a very/fine bit of work, and wish 2/Lt: WINT and the members of his patrol congratulated for me on their dash and enterprise. It is by individual and collective acts of gallantry such as was shown by this patrol that we establish our superiority over the enemy".

P.T.O.

Instructions regarding War Diaries and Intelligence Summaries are contained in F. S. Regs., Part II. and the Staff Manual respectively. Title pages will be prepared in manuscript.

WAR DIARY
of 1/6th Sherwood Foresters
INTELLIGENCE SUMMARY.
(Erase heading not required.)

Army Form C. 2118.

Vol 36

Hour, Date, Place	Summary of Events and Information	Remarks and references to Appendices
Night 2/3. Jan. 18 ST ELIE SECTOR	The enemy attempted to raid our trenches but was completely repulsed. For good work on this occasion 2/Lieut C.F. BARHAM was awarded the M.C & 240244 L/Cpl E.H WHITE, 240436 Pte A. KNOWLES & 240205 W. THOMPSON were awarded the M.M.	See appendices I. II & III. WR
1. Jan 18. HONOURS & AWARDS.	The following were included in the New Years Honours List:- MILITARY CROSS Capt (A/Major) W. SEATON. D.C.M. 240029 Coy Sgt Maj T.W. SLATER. MENTIONED IN DESPATCHES. Capt (A/Lt Col) C.B JOHNSON. Lt (A/Capt) B.E. JOHNSON. Lieutenant J. TAYLOR. 240552 Sgt G.P. BAGSHAW.	WR
3 Jan 18.	Battn was relieved by 5th S. For in front line & moved into Divl Reserve at VERQUIN. 2/Lt C.W. KIRK wounded in Action.	WR
9. Jan 18.	Bn relieved 5th S.F. in ST ELIE SECTOR. (H.32.a.6.4 – H.32.d.4.4).	WR
14. Jan 18.	Lt N.H.G. LAWLESS (R.S.C.) 2/Lt R.A. FRITH & 2/Lt F.A. MYCOCK joined the Battn	WR
17. Jan 18.	Bn relieved by 5th S.F. & moved into Bde Support (HQ & 2 Coys in PHILOSOPHE, 2 Coys in close support.	WR
21 Jan 18	Bn relieved by 9th LANCASHIRE FUSILIERS & moved to NOEUX LES MINES.	WR
22. Jan 18.	Bn moved into billets at LAPUGNOY.	
23 Jan 18	2Lt W.T. STEPHENS authorised to wear badges of rank of CAPTAIN	WR
24 Jan 18	2Lt H.D. VAUGHAN (2/1 SHERWOOD RANGERS) posted to Bn & joined for duty.	WR
29. Jan 18.	10 Officers & 185 O.R. posted from 1/7th Sherwood Foresters and joined the Bn.	WR WR
30. Jan 18.	The Battn provided a party of 12 Officers & 450 O.R. to strengthen the reserve line in the LE RUTOIRE & VERMELLES SECTION	WR

W Robinson Major for Lt Col.
Comdg 1/6 Sherwood Foresters

365

(9 29 6) W 3332—1107 100,000 10/13 H W V Forms/C. 2118/10

JAN 18
DEC 17

S E C R E T.
* * * * * *

No. G.1070.

Headquarters,

46th Division.

REPORT ON ENEMY RAID EVENING OF 2.1.1918.

About Midday yesterday Battalion observers noticed that the enemy had removed his wire at G.12.c.45.95.

Suspecting a hostile Raid Officer Commanding, 6th Sherwood Foresters took precautionary measures by strengthening Posts at BRESLAU and at LOOKOUT.

The 8th Battalion, Sherwood Foresters on the Left were also informed of this and they made special arrangements to co-operate by rearranging their Lewis Guns to cover No Mans Land in the threatened area.

At 5.45 pm. the 6th Battalion Sherwood Foresters sent out a Fighting Patrol of 2 Officers and 25 O.Ranks from LOOKOUT POST to investigate the enemy gap, enter the hostile trenches and obtain prisoners.

Special arrangements were made with the Artillery in connection with this.

Owing to watchfulness on the part of the enemy it took some time to reach the enemy wire.

A party of the enemy was located in front of his wire opposite BRESLAU who fired and bombed our men before they had time to rush them. The enemy was driven off by Rifle & Lewis Gun fire.

A few of our men succeeded in entering the enemy trenches and engaged his Posts with rifle fire and bombs but were unable to obtain a prisoner and withdrew.

We had a few men wounded and all were back in our Trenches by 8 pm.

At 9.20 pm. a very heavy bombardment was opened by the enemy from South of HULLUCH ROAD to North of HAIRPIN CRATERS, this extended later further North and eventually covered practically the whole of the Brigade Front.

Parties of the enemy were seen approaching LOOKOUT & BRESLAU Posts and "S. O.S. LANCER" was sent through.

Our Machine guns and Artillery and Trench Mortars opened out rapidly and it is thought they must have inflicted heavy casualties on the enemy.

At the time all our Posts were standing to and opened heavy Lewis Gun and Rifle fire, particularly across the North side of LOOKOUT Post, where large numbers of the enemy were seen.

The whole of No Mans Land between HAIRPIN CRATERS & LANCER was plastered with Lewis Gun and Rifle fire.

On the 6th Battalion S. F. front the enemy attempted in strength to approach our Posts at LANCER via LANCER Craters, but were driven off with bombs and rifle fire; at the same time another party also in strength attempted to enter BRESLAU Post but were driven off by Lewis Gun and Rifle fire.

None of our Posts were at any time entered.

(It is

It is thought that the enemy sustained heavy casualties in these attempts. Owing to the difficulty in communicating with the Company in HAIRPIN CRATERS and arranging for them to cease fire, some time elapsed before patrols could be sent out to search for enemy dead, this unfortunately gave tne enemy time to remove his casualties.

Our casualties in this Battalion were 2 killed, and 9 wounded all of which were the result of the enemy barrage.

On the 8th Battalion, S.F. front owing to "S.O.S. LANCER" practically covering HAIRPIN CRATERS the Company Commander did not consider it necessary to send "ATTACK QUARRIES"

Between 9.35 & 9.45 pm. various enemy groups approached ~~the~~ Post to the rear ~~Right~~ and Left ~~Posts~~ of HAIRPIN i.e. STUDIO II and RAT CREEK. The groups appeared to consist of 8 - 12 men. All groups seemed quite confused and our men had no difficulty in driving them off with Rifle and Lewis gun fire.

One of the enemy parties on being challenged replied "FREUND" and another "SECHSISCH"

Smoke bombs fell in HAIRPIN CRATERS which made some men think there was gas.

Two of the enemy were seen approaching a Post South of HAIRPIN, our men rushed out and took them prisoners.

When barrage died down at about 10 pm. patrols were sent out and one dead German was found about 40 yards from STUDIO II Post.

No further trace could be found of any of the enemy.

The casualties in this Battalion were 1 Officer and 7 O.Ranks wounded (none serious)

In both Battalions we were ready for the Raid and all ranks shewed considerable coolness.

The keenness and action of Lewis Gun teams was very marked.

It is difficult to estimate the exact strength of the raiding party but it is estimated at between 150 and 200 men.

J.C.Blackwell

3.1.1918.

Lieut - Colonel.
Commanding, 139th Infantry Brigade.

SECRET Relief Orders O.O./A/4.

by Lieut. Colonel B.W. Vann. M.C., Cmdg. 1/6th Bn. Sherwood Foresters.

2nd January. 1918.

1. The Battalion will be relieved by the 1/5th Battalion Sherwood Foresters on the evening of the 3rd inst.

2. Companies will be relieved as under:-

Lr 'B' Company. 6th S.F. by Lr 'D' Coy. 5th S.F. on the RIGHT.
Lr 'C' Company. 6th S.F. by Lr 'B' Coy. 5th S.F. in the CENTRE.
Lr 'D' Company 6th S.F. by Lr 'A' Coy. 5th S.F. on the LEFT.
Lr 'A' Company 6th S.F. by Lr 'C' Coy. 5th S.F. in SUPPORT.

3. Relief complete to be reported to Bn. H.Qrs. by the code words SHORT LEAVE.

4. On relief the Battalion will move into Brigade Reserve at VERQUIN.

5. The Light Railway from PHILOSOPHE to LABOURSE will be at the disposal of Companies, trains leaving PHILOSOPHE (G.13.C.50.05.) at the following times:-

7.15 p.m. 7.45 p.m. 8.30 p.m.

Capt. Greaves to report at Brigade H.Qrs at 6.30 p.m. and superintend entraining. Companies will march independently from LABOURSE to VERQUIN at intervals of at least 200 yards interval between Companies.

6. Lewis Guns and L.G. Ammunition to be handed to Sgt. Reece at the Dump as platoons pass.

The undermentioned Stores and Kit to be stacked at the Dump by 4 p.m., One N.C.O and 2 men per Company and Company Cooks to report to R.S.M. at same time.

1. Officer's Mess Kit. 2. Cooking Dixies
3. Signalling & Medical Stores. 4. Orderly Room & Canteen Boxes.
5. Surplus Battalion Trench Stores.

The Transport Officer to detail sufficient limbers to be at MANSION HOUSE DUMP at 7 p.m. to convey the above mentioned Lewis Guns & Ammunition, stores & kit to VERQUIN.

7. An Advance Party composed as under will report at Battn. H.Qrs. at 1.30 p.m. and march to VERQUIN, to take over billets and act as guides to the Battalion:-

1. 2 N.C.O's per Company & Battn. H.Qrs.
2. 2 Officer's Servants per Company & Battn. H.Qrs.
3. Provost Sergeant.
4. 2 Battalion Signallers.
5. 2 Battalion Runners.

8. Officer's chargers will be on the PHILOSOPHE - BETHUNE RD. 400 yards W of PHILOSOPHE cross roads by 8 p.m.

9. ACKNOWLEDGE.

Captain & Adjutant.
1/6th Battalion The Sherwood Foresters

SECRET. Relief Orders O.O./A./5.

by Lieut. Colonel. B. W. Vann. M.C., Cmdg. 1/6th Bn Sherwood Foresters.

8th January. 1918.

1. The Battalion will relieve the 5th Battalion Sherwood Foresters in the line tomorrow evening.

2. Companies will relieve as under:-

Lr. 'A' Company 6th S.F. will relieve Lr. 'D' Company 5th S.F. on the RIGHT.
Lr. 'B' Company 6th S.F. will relieve Lr. 'B' Company 5th S.F. in the CENTRE.
Lr. 'C' Company 6th S.F. will relieve Lr. 'A' Company 5th S.F. on the LEFT.
Lr. 'D' Company 6th S.F. will relieve Lr. 'C' Company 5th S.F. in SUPPORT.

3. Relief complete to be reported to Battn. H.Qrs. by the code words BULLY BEEF.

4. Lewis Guns and L.G. Ammunition will be taken by light railway to Battalion Dump and picked up by Platoons as they pass.

5. Stand to will be at 6.15 A.M and 4.15 P.M.

6. An Advance Party composed as under will parade at Battalion Headquarters at 11 A.M. under the R.S.M.

1. 2 N.C.O's. per Company.
2. Sergt. Drummer Bunting.
3. Corpl. Vanes.
4. 2 Signallers per Company & Battn. H.Qrs.
5. 2 Battalion Runners.

Dress:- Fighting Order. Haversack Rations to be taken.

7. ACKNOWLEDGE.

Capt. & Adjutant.
1/6th Battalion Sherwood Foresters.

WARNING ORDER No. 1 Copy No. 8.

by

Lieut-Col. W.S.N. Toller, D.S.O.,
Commanding, The Robin Hoods,

In the field,
January 14th. 1918.

1. The Robin Hoods will leave the present area by Route March about mid-day on Wednesday the 16th. inst. on being relieved by the 11th. Battalion, The Manchester Regiment.

2. Advance Party of 1 N.C.O. per Coy. and Sergt. Macklin from Headquarters will parade at Orderly Room at 9 a.m. in Full Marching Order, and will proceed to new billeting area under Captain J.C. Warren, M.C. Two days' rations will be carried.
This party will remain in the new area until the arrival of the Battalion.

3. Transport Officer will arrange to remove all stores possible on the 15th. inst.

C W Good.
.... Captain & Adjt.
7th. (Robin Hood) Bn. The Sherwood Foresters.

Issued at 11 a.m. to :-

1. Commanding Officer.
2. Officer Commanding "A" Coy.
3. Officer Commanding "B" Coy.
4. Officer Commanding "C" Coy.
5. Officer Commanding "D" Coy.
6. Transport Officer.
7. R.Q.M.S.
8. War Diary.
9. War Diary.
10. File.

SECRET.

O.O./A/6.

Battalion Warning Order
by Lieut. Colonel. B.W. Vann. M.C., Cmdg. 1/6th Bn. Sherwood Foresters
" 15th January. 1918.

1. The Battalion will be relieved on the night of the 17th/18th by the 9th Battalion Lancashire Fusiliers.
On relief the Battalion will march to billets at LABOURSE and SAILLY LABOURSE.

2. Advance Parties will proceed to SAILLY LABOURSE in the early afternoon of the 17th to take over billets.

3. On the 18th inst. the Battalion will march to LAPUGNOY and occupy billets there.
Advance Parties have already been sent.

4. 1 Officer per Company and 1 N.C.O. per platoon (3 platoons per Company) of the 9th Lancashire Fusiliers will be attached to the Battalion from midday 16th inst.

5. ACKNOWLEDGE and DESTROY.

Captain & Adjutant.
1/6th Battn. Sherwood Foresters..

SECRET. Relief Orders O.O/A/7.
by Lieut Colonel B. W. Vann. M. C., Cmdg. 1/6th Bn. Sherwood Foresters.

16th January 1918

1. The Battalion will be relieved in the line by the 5th Bn. Sherwood Foresters on the evening of the 17th/18th.

2. Relief complete to be wired to Battalion H.Qrs. in B.A.B. Code.

3. Companies will be relieved as under:-
Ltr. "A" Coy. 6th S.F. by Ltr. "D" Company 5th S.F. on the RIGHT.
Ltr. "B" Coy. 6th S.F. by. Ltr. "B" Company 5th S.F. in the CENTRE.
Ltr. "C" Coy. 6th S.F. by. Ltr. "A" Company 5th S.F. on the LEFT.
Ltr. "D" Coy. 6th S.F. by. Ltr. "C" Company 5th S.F. in SUPPORT.

4. On relief the Battalion will move into Brigade Support. Dispositions as under:-

Battalion Headquarters } Ltrs "C" & "D" Companies }	PHILOSOPHE.
Letter "A" Company	In Support to Right Battalion.
Letter "B" Company	In Support to Left Battalion.

5. Lewis Guns and Ammunition of Ltrs "C" & "D" Companies to be handed to Corporal Vanes at the Dump as platoons pass. Officers Mess Kit and Cooking Dixies of H.Qrs and Ltrs "C" & "D" Companies to be stacked at the Dump by 4 P.M.; also Orderly Room & Canteen Boxes, Signalling & Medical Kit and Surplus Battalion Trench Stores.
Lewis Guns & Ammunition, Kit and Stores of Ltrs "A" & "B" Companies to be carried out under Company arrangements.

6. A complete list of Trench Stores to be handed over will be sent to Battalion H.Qrs. by 6 A.M. tomorrow.

7. O's C. Ltrs. "A" & "B" Companies will report personally to O's C. Right and Left Battalions respectively as soon as their Companies are in the support dug-outs.

8. The Transport Officer will detail 2 limbers to be at MANSION HOUSE DUMP at 7·30 P.M. to convey Lewis Guns, Ammunition, Kit and Stores to PHILOSOPHE.

9. ACKNOWLEDGE.

Captain & Adjutant
1/6th Battalion The Sherwood Foresters.

SECRET. O.O/A./8.

Relief Orders

by Lieut. Colonel. B. W. Vann. M.C., Cmdg 1/6th Sherwood Foresters.

18th January 1918

1. Letters "C" and "D" Companies will relieve Letters "A" and "B" Companies in the Right and Left Forward Support tomorrow evening.

2. Relief complete to be reported in B.A.B. Code to Battalion Headquarters of the Right and Left Battalions in the line.

3. 1 Limber will be at the disposal of Companies at PHILOSOPHE for conveying kit and stores to MANSION HOUSE DUMP.
All such kit to be stacked outside Battalion Headquarters by 3 P.M.

4. Lewis Gun Ammunition and Cooking Dixies will be handed over. Lewis Gun Ammunition of Letters "C" and "D" Companies to be handed in at Battalion H.Qrs and drawn by Letters "A" and "B" Companies on arrival at PHILOSOPHE.

5. All details regarding working parties found by Companies in Support must be carefully handed over.

6. Companies to acknowledge.

Captain & Adjutant.
1/6th Battalion Sherwood Foresters.

SECRET. **Relief Orders** O.O/A/9.

by Lieut. Col. B. W. Vann. M.C., Cmdg. 1/6 Bn. Sherwood Foresters

19th January 1918.

Ref Map. BETHUNE combined Sheet
FRANCE 36.B

1. The Battalion will be relieved by the 9th Bn. Lancashire Fusiliers in Brigade Support on the evening of the 21st inst.

2. Guides will be required. Number, time and place to be notified later.

3. Relief complete to be reported to Battalion Headquarters
Nos "A" and "B" Companies by runner.
Nos "C" and "D" Companies in B.A.B. Code.
Nos "C" and "D" Companies will report Relief complete to O.C. Right and Left Battalions in the line respectively.

4. On relief the Battalion will march to billets at BRACQUEMONT, NOEUX LES MINES.
Headquarters, Nos "A" & "B" Coys as one party. Nos "C" & "D" Coys independently.
Route PHILOSOPHE – MAZINGARBE – L.22. Central – L.21.C. – NOEUX LES MINES.

5. Two guides for each of Nos "C" and "D" Companies will be picked up on the PHILOSOPHE – MAZINGARBE RD 100 yards S.W. of PHILOSOPHE cross roads.

6. Headquarters Nos "A" & "B" Companies.
Lewis Guns and Ammunition will be handed to Sgt. Reece at Battn. H.Qrs at 4 p.m.
Officer's Valises and Mess Kit, Signalling and Medical Kit, O.R. and Canteen boxes to be stacked outside Battn. H.Qrs. by 5 P.M.
Letters "C" and "D" Companies.
Lewis Guns, Ammunition and Mess Kit to be handed to Sgt. [illegible] Bunting at MANSION HOUSE DUMP as platoons pass.

7. The Transport Officer will detail 3 limbers to be at Battalion H.Qrs. at 5 P.M.; and 1 limber to be at MANSION HOUSE DUMP at 6 P.M. to convey the above mentioned baggage to NOEUX LES MINES.

8. ACKNOWLEDGE.

Captain & Adjutant
1/6th Battalion Sherwood Foresters

SECRET.

Reference [illegible] para 2.

4 guides per company and 1 for Battalion H.Qrs will report at Battalion H.Qrs at 4.30 P.M. for further instructions.

[illegible signature]

Captain & Adjutant.

1/6th Battn. Sherwood Foresters

Battalion H.Qrs. will consist of the following:-

Commanding Officer
Capt. Greaves.
2/Lt. Coates.
Medical Officer.
Aid Post Staff.
1 Orderly Room Clerk.

4. A Muster Parade of the Battalion under the Adjutant will be held at 8 A.M. on the Football Ground for Selecting N.C.O's & men for "X" & "Y" Parties.
Dress:- Clean Fatigue.

5. Bn.H.Qrs. "X" & "Y" Parties will parade in Main Street LAPUGNOY at 10 A.M.
Head of Column opposite "D" Coy. Mess facing the Church.
Dress:- Fighting Order. Great coats rolled round the haversack & secured in position by Entrenching Tool Shaft. Steel Helmets.
The parties will then embus for their respective areas.

6. An Advance Party under 2/Lt. Coates & composed as under will parade outside Bn. Orderly Room at 9 A.M. prompt and proceed by lorry to new areas

4 C.Q.M. Sergeants.
4 Bn. Runners of "Y" Party.

Dress:- As for 10 A.M. parade.

7. The following Time Table will be strictly observed for handing in Kit, Stores etc.

8.45 A.M. Packs at C.Q.M. Sgts. billets.
H.Q. Packs at Tailors Shop.

9.0 A.M. Officers Valises to be outside respective Coy. Messes.
2 Lewis Guns per Coy. & 24 magazines per gun to be outside Bn. Orderly Room.

9.15 A.M. Blankets in bundles of 10 to be at Q.M. Stores; also Trench Medical Kit.

9.30 A.M. Officers Mess Kit to be outside Coy. Messes.

8. Rear Bn. H.Qrs. & Q.M. Stores will remain at LAPUGNOY.
The Transport Officer will meet the Staff Captain at the Church LABOURSE at 3 P.M. & will be allotted Transport lines there.

SECRET. Operation Order No. 20. Copy No. 5..

By Lieut. Col. B. W. Vann. M.C., Cmdg. 1/6th Bn. Sherwood Foresters.

" 30th January. 1918.

Ref. Map. BETHUNE combined sheet Edition. 6.

1. The Battalion, less a proportion of all ranks ~~[illegible]~~ ~~[illegible]~~ will proceed to the VERMELLES AREA today to work on the defences of that locality.

2. "X" Party {Hrs "A" & "B" Coys. under Capt. Stephens will work on the LE RUTOIRE Section, and will be billeted in NOYELLES.

"Y" Party {Hrs "C" & "D" Coys. will work on the VERMELLES Section and will be billeted in ANNEQUIN.

Battalion H.Qrs. will be at ANNEQUIN.

3. "X" and "Y" Parties will be composed as under:-

"X" Party.
Capt. Stephens
Lt. Briggs.
2/Lt. Shenton.
2/Lt. Mackay.
2/Lt. Johns
2/Lt. Frith.
2 C.S.M's.
8 Sergeants
200 O.R. (including ~~24 O.R. of H.Qrs Coy. also~~ 4 Stretcher Bearers.
3 Company Runners
1 Officer's Mess Cook & 2 Officers Servants.
3 Company Cooks.
2 Sanitary men.

"Y" Party.
Capt. Hipkins.
2/Lt. Lake
2/Lt. Parkinson.
2/Lt. Moore.
2/Lt. Bucklow
2/Lt. Fouch.
2 C.S.M's.
8 Sergeants.
200 O.R. (including 24. O.R. of H.Q. Coy. 4 Stretcher Bearers)
1 Officers Mess Cook & 3 Officers Servants.
3 Company Cooks.
2 Sanitary men.
6 Battalion Runners (with 2 cycles)

9. Details with regard to Training for the portions of the Battalion not proceeding to the forward area will be issued later; also particulars as to billets, cookhouses, etc.

10. ACKNOWLEDGE.

E. Wenham.
Captain & Adjt.
1/6th Bn. Sherwood Foresters.

Issued at 5·30 A.M. by runner.

Copies to:-

Copy. No. 1. O.C. "A" Coy.
" " 2. O.C. "B" Coy.
" " 3. O.C. "C" Coy.
" " 4. O.C. "D" Coy.
" " 5. O.C. H.Q. Coy.
" " 6. Adjt. for Commanding Officer.
" " 7. Quartermaster.
" " 8. Transport Officer.
" " 9. File.
" " 10. War Diary.

Report on Enemy Raid on

APPENDIX I
WAR DIARY
JAN. 18

About mid-day yesterday, we found out that the enemy
had removed his wire at G.12.c.43.90 AAA. During previous 24 hours, he
had sent quite a number of T.M's round BRESLAU, + had damaged our
wire there – also at DEVON DUMP AAA Special dispositions were made
with L.G's at BRESLAU + LOOKOUT. Both these posts were strengthened
+ damaged wire was repaired AAA. A fighting patrol which had
been detailed to attack enemy post at G.12.c.50.90 was ordered to
be ready at dusk to try to anticipate the enemy – investigate the
gap – enter the hostile trenches + get prisoners AAA Flank
Battalions, Brigade + Artillery Group were warned, + special
arrangements made AAA The C.O., with F.O.O. established advanced
HQ. at LOOKOUT POST with through communication to Battery + Battn
HQ. AAA. The fighting patrol of 2 Offrs. 25 O.R. went out from
LOOKOUT at 5.40, but it took them a long time to reach enemy's
wire owing to watchfulness of enemy AAA. The men were very
cold + ground was slippery AAA The enemy bombed them
heavily before they could rush him, + met them with rifle fire
AAA. They had several casualties + only a few penetrated enemy's
trenches, though his posts were engaged with rifle fire + bombs.
AAA. Party withdrew without prisoners, + all were back by
about 8 p.m. At 9.20, a very heavy bombardment was opened
from South of HULLUCH ROAD, + seemed to extend to HAIRPIN AAA
The S.O.S. LANCER was sent through, as the enemy were seen to be
trying to get in to LOOKOUT + BRESLAU AAA All our posts were standing
to, + opened heavy L.G. + rifle fire, particularly across front to
left of LOOKOUT, where large numbers of enemy were seen AAA
The whole front, + wire across to left battalion was swept with
a stream of bullets AAA Numbers of enemy who tried to enter
over CRATER between LANCER + LOOKOUT were soon bombed away
Very large numbers who attacked BRESLAU were driven off to
the left, + none of our posts were entered AAA All our men
remained at their posts in spite of the very heavy bombardment
which was very severe round BRESLAU + LOOKOUT. 700 T.M's fell
in DEVON DUMP + caused six casualties. QUARRY BAY, ST GEORGE'S
TRENCH + DEVON LANE were also heavily shelled, Our barrage
came down at once + I consider that very heavy casualties
were inflicted on enemy by our fire. It was some time before
we could have patrols out round BRESLAU, as it took some time
to communicate with right Coy. of left Battn, + so the enemy
had time to take in his casualties AAA. T.M's contributed
largely to making our barrage good AAA Our casualties were
15 + posts + trenches were damaged in several places

(sd) B. W. Vann, Lt Col.,
O.C. Garnet

APPENDIX II WAR DIARY

Remarks by Corps Commander on action taken against enemy raids on night 2/3rd inst in the ST ELIE SECTOR.

"This was a good defence. Both Battalions "are to be congratulated on their preliminary "arrangements all of which seem to have "worked out well. Special praise is due to "the Battn observers who detected indications "of an attack early in the day. Their "alertness contributed in no small way to the "successful defence. I am pleased to notice "the use of the rifle & the keenness of the "L.G. Teams & also the promptitude with "which patrols were sent out after the "enemy had been repulsed. I also note "with pleasure the offensive spirit "displayed by the despatch of the fighting "patrol early in the afternoon. This might "have had great results.

——— " ———

APPENDIX III
WAR DIARY
JAN. 1918.

Copy.

First Army No G.S. 969.
I Corps No. 596 (G.b)
46th Division G. 727/500.

I Corps.

Ref: your 344 (G.O) dated 7-1-18.

The Army Commander has made the following remarks -

"I agree with G.O.C., I Corps. The arrangements for the reception of the raids appear to have been well thought out, organized and carried out by the troops. I feel especially ready to commend the dispatch of the strong fighting patrol as soon as it was dusk. This shows a fine offensive spirit and it is at the same time a very excellent precaution against surprise. I congratulate all concerned"

(Sgd) W. H. Anderson.
Major. General.
General Staff, First Army.

First Army.
10th January. 1918.

(2)

139th. Infantry Brigade (3)

The above is forwarded with reference to the two enemy raids attempted by the enemy on the night 2nd/3rd January, 1918, report of which was forwarded under your No. G.1040 of 3/1/18.

(Sd) G. R. Sandman. Capt
for Lieut Col.
General Staff, 46th Division

11-1-18

Instructions regarding War Diaries and Intelligence Summaries are contained in F. S. Regs., Part II. and the Staff Manual respectively. Title pages will be prepared in manuscript.

WAR DIARY of 1/6th Bn Sherwood Foresters. INTELLIGENCE SUMMARY.

(*Erase heading not required.*)

Army Form C. 2118.

Vol 37

Hour, Date, Place		Summary of Events and Information	Remarks and References to Appendices
5. 2. 18		CAPT G.K.K. MAUGHAN and 240018 C.S.M. BENNETT awarded the BELGIAN CROIX DE GUERRE.	BWV.
6. 2. 18	LAPUGNOY	Detachment left at LAPUGNOY (less transport) moved to BURBURE.	
7. 2. 18		Battn moved back from forward area (ANNEQUIN & NOYELLES) to BURBURE.	BWV.
9. 2. 18	BURBURE	The Bn marched into Billets at LAIRES the move of the Battn being carried out as part of a Divisional Tactical Scheme.	BWV.
10. 2. 18	LAIRES	Lieut F.S. ROWLAND M.C. rejoined the Bn from England.	BWV.
16. 2. 18	LAIRES	Lieut C.K.H.C. BLACKNALL rejoined Bn from I Corps School	BWV.
		2/Lieut W. BLOOD joined from England	BWV.
10. 2. 18 to 28. 2. 18	LAIRES.	This period has been devoted to general training including:-	
		1 MUSKETRY (a) A.R.A Competitions. (b) Divisional classification	BWV.
		2 DRILL.	
		3 TACTICAL EXERCISES. (a) The attack. (b) The counter attack	
		4 LECTURES	
		5 SPORTS.	
23. 2. 18	LAIRES	Annual Officers' Sergeants' [illegible] at which were present MAJ. GENL THWAITES C.B. & [illegible] S. CAREY C.B.	BWV.

(9 29 6) W 3332—1107 100,000 10/13 H W V Forms/C. 2118/10.

57 Bn Sherwood Foresters Lieut-Colonel c/o 1/6 Sherwood Foresters

1/6 Notts & Derby

March 1918

20th Division

12th K.R.R.C.

Vol: 3

Sept. 15

Instructions regarding War Diaries and Intelligence Summaries are contained in F. S. Regs., Part II. and the Staff Manual respectively. Title pages will be prepared in manuscript.

WAR DIARY
or
INTELLIGENCE SUMMARY.
(Erase heading not required.)

Army Form C. 2118.

1/6 Notts + Derby

Vol 38

Hour, Date, Place		Summary of Events and Information	Remarks and references to Appendices
1-3-18	LAIRES.	Lieut G S RIVINGTON to I Corps Gas School	WR
2-3-18	"	2/Lieut H. T. WOOD on leave.	WR
4-3-18	"	Lieut C V H C BLACKWALL on leave	WR
6-3-18	"	Battalion marched to AUCHY AU BOIS and there embussed for BEUVRY. Transport Lines at LE QUESNOY.	WR
11-3-18	BEUVRY	2/Lieut. C F BARHAM on leave	
14-3-18	"	Battalion moved into Brigade Support of CAMBRIN SECTOR.	WR
		Battalion H.Qrs. "C" and "D" Companies at BEUVRY. "A" Company in WIMPOLE ST. LA BASSEE 36C N.W.1. 1/10,000 A.26 b 50 50. "B" Company in FACTORY DUGOUTS. A.26 d. 20 30	WR
14-3-18	"	Captain E.F WINSER attached to 465 Field Coy R.E. 2/Lt. J.F DENNIS on leave	WR
15-3-18	"	2/Lieut. R.W OAKLEY from Hospital (South of France)	WR
18-3-18	"	Lt Col B.W VANN M.C. proceeded on leave. Major V O ROBINSON M.C. took over temporary command of the Battalion.	WR
19-3-18	"	Lieut. W.T. STEPHENS rejoined from First Army Infantry School & took over command of "D" Coy	WR
19-3-18	LONDON GAZETTE	MILITARY MEDAL awarded to Cpl WHITE E.H, Pte KNOWLES R & L/Corp. THOMPSON W, all "D" Coy, for conspicuous Gallantry during enemy raid near HULLUCH on Jan 2nd 1917.	WR
20-3-18	BEUVRY	Battalion relieved 1/8th Sherwood Foresters in the ANNEQUIN LOCALITY. Bn H.Q. "C" & "D" Coys in ANNEQUIN; "A" & "B" Coys in SAILLY LABOURSE	WR
22-3-18	ANNEQUIN.	Capt. T. GREAVES rejoined from 1st Army Musketry School 2/Lieut. S.N DEURANCE rejoined from Hospital Enemy raided the 1/8th Bn. The Battn. "Stood to" in Billets	WR
24-3-18	"	Battalion relieved by 1/5th Sherwood Foresters in ANNEQUIN LOCALITY & relieved 1/8th Sherwood Foresters in the CAMBRIN SECTOR, A.28 c 50.30 to A.21 d. 70.50. Dispositions reorganised for expected enemy attack 25.3.18. Front line lightly held. Reserve line strengthened. Battalion H.Q. moved to FACTORY TRENCH from No 1 SIDING. 1/8th Bn Sherwood Foresters held in close support.	
27-3-18	CAMBRIN SECTOR	Battalion relieved by 1/5th South Lancs & 6th York & Lanc Regt (32 Inf Brigade) and moved to billets in SAILLY LABOURSE.	WR

385

(9 29 6) W 3332-1107 100,000 10/13 H W V Forms/C. 2118/10.

Instructions regarding War Diaries and Intelligence Summaries are contained in F. S. Regs., Part II. and the Staff Manual respectively. Title pages will be prepared in manuscript.

WAR DIARY ~~6td~~ or INTELLIGENCE SUMMARY.

(*Erase heading not required.*)

Army Form C. 2118.

Hour, Date, Place		Summary of Events and Information	Remarks and references to Appendices
28 3 · 18	SAILLY LABOURSE	Battalion embussed for BULLY GRENAY, from whence at dusk they marched to CITE' ST PIERRE and relieved the 1/5th Battalion Sherwood Foresters in BRIGADE SUPPORT to ST. EMILE SECTOR LENS 36.C S.W.1 N.13. b 60.10 to N 2 d 40.85.	WR
31 3 18	BRIGADE SUPPORT CITE' ST PIERRE	Battalion relieved 1/8th Battalion Sherwood Foresters in the RIGHT SUB SECTOR of the ST. EMILE SECTOR, N 13 b 60.10 to N 8 d 10.80.	WR.
31 · 3 · 18	"	2/Lieut J.F DENNIS. M.C returned from leave.	WR.

W Robinson Major.
Commanding 1/6th Bn The Sherwood Foresters

(9 29 6) W 3332—1107 100,000 10/13 H W V Forms/C. 2118/10

SECRET   COPY NO. 11..

OPERATION ORDER NO 28.

BY LIEUT. COL. A.V.VANN M.C., COMMANDING 1/6TH SHERWOOD FORESTERS.

REF. MAP.CORNS 1/20,000.   8th March,1916.

1. The Battalion will relieve the 1/4th Batt.Lincoln Regt. in the Left Subsector of the CAMBRIN Sector tomorrow. Relief to be complete by 1 P.M.

2. The dispositions of the Battalion will be as follows:-

Battalion Headquarters. G.2.a.9.2.
Right "C" Coy. Right Front Sector. ("C" Coy. 4th.Lincs.)
Left "A" Coy. Left Front Sector. ("A" Coy. 4th.Lincs.)
Support "D" Coy. Support. [illegible] TRENCH- ("B" Coy. 4th.Lincs.)
Reserve "B" Coy. Reserve -FACTORY DUGOUTS-("D" Coy. 4th.Lincs.)
M.G. Post. near Battalion Headquarters.

3. Movement from BEUVRY to ANNEQUIN will be by platoons at 200 yards interval in the following order "C" "A" "D" "B" "H.Qrs" First platoon of "C" Company to move off at 8-30 am. Platoons to march on the side of the road under the trees.

4. 2 guides per Company and 1 for Battn.Headquarters will be met at the ANNEQUIN cross roads F.30.a.15.75.

5. Lewis Guns & Ammunition will be carried by limbers as far as the track leading to RAILWAY ALLEY,F.30.b.3.2.and picked up by platoons as they pass this point.

6. "Stand to" will be at the following times:-
[illegible] A.M.   6-30 P.M.

7. Cooking will be carried out under Coy arrangements. The water supply is obtained from the tanks in [illegible] PARADE.

8. Relief complete will be reported to Battalion Headquarters [illegible].

9. ACKNOWLEDGE.

Captain & Adjutant.
1/6th Battalion Sherwood Foresters.

(P.T.O.)

Issued at 8 p.m. by runner

Copies to :-

Copy No.1. - O.C."A" Coy.
" " 2. O.C."B"Coy.
" " 3. O.C."C" Coy.
" " 4. O.C."D" Coy.
" " 5. O.C."H.Qrs" Coy.
" " 6. Adjutant for Commanding Officer.
" " 7. Quartermaster.
" " 8. Transport Officer.
" " 9. Medical Officer.
" " 10. O.C. 1/5th Lincoln Regiment.
" " 11. File.
" " 12. War Diary.

SECRET

COPY No. 10

OPERATION ORDER NO. [illegible]

BY LIEUT-COLONEL [illegible] COMMANDING 1/6TH BATTALION SHERWOOD FORESTERS.

[illegible] 1/20,000. 19th March, 19[illegible]

1. The Battalion will move into Brigade Support of the [illegible] SECTOR [illegible] and will be distributed as follows:-
Battalion Headquarters } at [illegible].
[illegible] "C" & "D" Coys. }
"A" Company in Support in [illegible] at present occupied by [illegible] North Staffords.
"B" Company in [illegible] DUGOUTS at present occupied by [illegible] Company of [illegible].
[illegible] Battalion Scouts, 4 Battalion Runners and 1 N.C.O. and 3 [illegible] will be attached to [illegible] "B" Company.
"A" Company will come under the orders of the O.C. [illegible] [illegible] otherwise ordered.
"B" Company will be under the direct orders of Major [illegible].

2. Movement of [illegible] "A" & "B" Companies from [illegible] will be by platoons at [illegible] interval, first platoon of "A" Company to leave at [illegible] A.M. [illegible] platoon of "B" Company to leave at [illegible] A.M.
DRESS: Fighting Order, [illegible] Water bottles filled and [illegible] to be carried.

3. [illegible] "A" Company will be met at cross roads [illegible] at [illegible] A.M.
[illegible] "B" Company will be met at the [illegible] cross roads [illegible] at [illegible] A.M.

4. Lewis Guns and Ammunition will be carried up by [illegible] following in rear of the first platoons of Nos. "A" & "B" Companies [illegible] as far as the [illegible] cross roads at [illegible] and in the case of No. "B" Coy. as far as the [illegible] cross roads at [illegible].
[illegible] Company to march with [illegible] and hand over [illegible] and Ammunition to platoons as they pass.

5. [illegible] will be carried out under Company arrangements.

6. The [illegible] for Nos. "A" & "B" Companies will be at [illegible] to which [illegible] will be [illegible] at [illegible] P.M.

7. [illegible] to be reported to Battalion Headquarters [illegible] "B" Company will, in addition, report to the Headquarters of the [illegible]

8. [illegible] at [illegible] the Battalion will [illegible] that they [illegible] must reach Battalion Orderly Room [illegible]

[illegible]

[Signature]. [illegible]
[illegible]

Issued at 4.45 pm [illegible]

Copy No.		Copy No.	
1.	O.C. "A" Coy.	[illegible]	O.C. "B" Coy.
2.	O.C. "C" Coy.	[illegible]	O.C. "D" [illegible]
3.	Adjt. [illegible]	[illegible]	[illegible]
4.	Transport Officer.	[illegible]	Medical Officer.
9.	O.C. [illegible] Sherwood Foresters.		
10. ✓	File.	[illegible]	[illegible] File.
11.	O.C. [illegible] Coy.		

SECRET. [illegible] 15

Operation Order No. [illegible]

by Lt. Col. V. O. Robinson M.C. [illegible] 6th Foresters

23rd March. 1918

Ref. Map LA BASSEE [illegible]

1. The Battalion will relieve the 8th Bn. Sherwood Foresters in the CAMBRIN Sector tomorrow. The 8th Bn. Sherwood Foresters will take over billets vacated by the Battalion in the ANNEQUIN LOCALITY.

2. The Battalion will be distributed as under:

Battalion Headquarters	NO. 1. SIDING.
Lr. "C" Company 6th S.F. will relieve Lr. "A" Coy. 8th S.F. on the RIGHT.	
Lr. "A" Company, 6th S.F. will relieve Lr. "B" Coy. 8th S.F. in the CENTRE.	
Lr. "D" Company, 6th S.F. will relieve Lr. "C" Coy. 8th S.F. on the LEFT.	
Lr. "B" Company, 6th S.F. will relieve Lr. "D" Coy. 8th S.F. in SUPPORT.	
Battalion Aid Post	ROBERTSON ALLEY.

3. Movement from SAILLY LABOURSE and ANNEQUIN will be by platoons at intervals of 200 yards – the first platoons of "A" and "C" companies to move at 4.30 am.
Headquarters company to follow in rear of Lr. "D" company.
Dress:- Fighting Order, Great coats rolled. Water bottles filled.

4. 5 Guides per Company and 1 for Battn. H.Q.rs will be met at road junction A.20.c.1.2. Routes for respective Companies from this point will be as follows:-

Lr. "C" Company	via	RAILWAY ALLEY.
Lr. "A" Company	via	MAISON ROUGE.
Lr. "D" Company	via	THE LANE.
Lr. "B" Company		2 platoons via RAILWAY ALLEY 2 platoons via MAISON ROUGE.
Battalion H.Q.rs.	via	BURBURE TRENCH.

5. Lewis Guns & Ammunition will be carried as far as road junction A.20.c.1.2. by limber & picked up by platoons as they pass this point.

6. Cooking will be carried out under Coy. arrangements. The water supply is obtained from tanks in the Tunnels.
Rations will be brought up by limber to CAMBRIN dump each evening & from there by trolley to Coy. dumps. O.C. Coys. will arrange for Coy. dumps to be reconnoitred and a sentry posted at the respective dumps at 8 p.m. to await the arrival of ration trucks.

7. Defence Schemes, Artillery Support Schemes, Aeroplane Photos, Intelligence Maps & trench stores will be taken over on relief.

8. Particular care must be taken by all Officers that SECRET Intelligence maps showing routes up to the trenches & marking tracks & trenches behind Coy. Sectors are not taken into the trenches. This includes the GORRE Map 1/20,000.

9. Relief complete to be reported to Bn. H.Qrs. in B.A.B. Code.

PART. II.

1. Dumps:- The Dumps & Times for handing in Kit & Stores, &c. in the present area are as follows:-

Lrs. "A" & "B" Companies:- opposite Lr. "B" Coy. Huts.
Lrs. "C" "D" & H.Q.rs Coys:- at Lr. "D" Coy. H.Q.rs.

8.0 AM.	Officers Valises. Blankets rolled in bundles of ten.
8.15 AM.	Packs.
8.30 AM.	Lewis Guns & Ammunition. Medical & Signalling Kit. Orderly Room & Canteen boxes.
9.0 AM.	Officers Mess Kit for the trenches & surplus Officers Mess Kit.

2. The Transport Officer will detail 2 L.G. limbers to be at SAILLY LABOURSE and 2 at ANNEQUIN at 9.0 AM. These will be loaded & proceed to road junction at A.20.c.1.2. at 9.15 AM.
Separate orders for removing remainder of Kit & Stores are issued to the Transport Officer direct.

3. ACKNOWLEDGE.

E. [illegible]
Captain & Adjutant
6th Battn. The Sherwood Foresters

Issued at 10 pm by runner.
Copies to:-

Copy No. 1. O.C. "A" Company.
" " 2. O.C. "B" Company.
" " 3. O.C. "C" Company.
" " 4. O.C. "D" Company.
" " 5. O.C. "H.Q." Company.
" " 6. Adjutant for C.O.
" " 7. Quartermaster.
" " 8. Transport Officer.
" " 9. Lewis Gun Officer.
" " 10. Medical Officer.
" " 11. R.S.M.
" " 12. Signalling Sergeant.
" " 13. O.C. 8th Sherwood Foresters
" " 14. O.C. 5th Sherwood Foresters
" " 15. ✓ File.
" " 16. War Diary.

<u>SECRET</u> Relief Orders

by Major. V. O. Robinson M. C., Cmdg 6th Sherwood Foresters

27th March 1918

Ref MAP. LA BASSEE 1/10,000.

1. The Battalion will be relieved in the CAMBRIN Sector today by the 1/5th South Lancs, 166 Inf. Brigade, and a Battalion of the 32nd Inf Brigade to be notified later.

2. The Boundary between the 1/5th South Lancs + 32nd Inf. Brigade will be A.27.b.45.35 – A.27.a.70.00 – LEWIS KEEP (inclusive to 166 Inf. Bgde) – CHURCH WEST KEEP (inclusive to 166 Inf Bgde).

3. Relief will be carried out as under

Lr. 'D' Coy. 6th S.F. will be relieved by Lr 'B' Coy. 1/5th South Staffs.
Lr. 'A' Coy. 6th S.F. will be relieved by Lr. "D" Coy. 1/5th South Staffs
Lrs. 'C' + 'B' Coys. 6th S.F. by Coys. of the Battalion of the 32nd Brigade

4. Relief of Lrs "D" + 'A' Coys. to be complete by 3 P.M.
Relief of Lrs. 'C' + "B" Coys. by 12 midnight 27th/28th.
Report relief complete to Bn H.Qrs in B.A.B. Code.

5. On relief Lr "D" Coy. will proceed to billets at SAILLY · LABOURSE.
Lr "A" Coy. to dugouts in VILLAGE LINE near present Bn. H.Qrs. until relief of Lrs "C" & "B" Coys. – then to SAILLY LABOURSE.
Lrs. "C" & "B" Coys to billets at SAILLY LABOURSE

6. An Advance Party of 1 Officer & 1 N.C.O. per Coy. to report at Bn. H.Qrs. as soon as possible after receipt of these orders.

7. Transport Arrangements re Lewis Guns etc. will be notified later.

8. ACKNOWLEDGE

Capt & Adjt.
1/6th Sherwood Foresters

SECRET.

Relief Orders

by Major. V. O. Robinson. M. C., Cmdg. 1/6th Bn. Sherwood Foresters.

30th March. 1918.

Ref. Map. LENS 36 c. S.W. 1/10,000.

1. The Battalion will relieve the 8th Bn. Sherwood Foresters in the RIGHT SUB SECTOR of the ST. EMILE SECTOR tomorrow evening.

2. Distribution of Battalion will be as under:-

Battalion Headquarters HOSPITAL. M. 12. d. 99. 74.

Lr. "A" Coy. 6th S.F. will relieve Lr. "B" Coy. 8th S.F. on the RIGHT. Company H.Qrs. N. 13. b. 60. 45.

Lr. "B" Coy. 6th S.F. will relieve Lr. "C" Coy. 8th S.F. on the LEFT. Company H.Qrs. N. 8. b. 1. 3.

Lr. "C" Coy. 6th S.F. will relieve Lr. "A" Coy. 8th S.F. in the RIGHT SUPPORT. Company. H.Qrs. N. 7. d. 32. 02.

Lr. "D" Coy. 6th S.F. will relieve Lr. "D" Coy. 8th S.F. in the LEFT SUPPORT. Company H.Qrs. N. 8. c. 12. 99.

Battalion Aid Post N. 7. c. 1. 7.

Battalion Dump. M. 12. b. 2. 4 COLONY SIDING.

3. 4 Guides for each of Lrs. "A" & "C" Coys. will be at Battn. H.Qrs. in the line at 8.0 P.M.

Lrs. "B" & "D" Coys. will each send two runners to Battn. H.Qrs. in the line at 7.0 P.M. These runners to conduct guides to present Coy. H.Qrs.

4. Coys. will not vacate present position until after dusk and not before 7.45 P.M.

5. Lewis Guns & Ammunition will be carried in to the line under Coy. arrangements.

6. Advance Parties from each Coy. will be sent up tomorrow afternoon independently.

2 Runners per Coy. will report at Bn. H.Qrs. of 8th S.F. at 3.0 P.M. to act as guides for the Advance Parties of the 8th S.F.

7. The The Cookhouse for all Coys. is situate at N. 7. c. 1. 7. Lrs. "C" & "D" Coys. will each provide two parties, each of 8 O.R. to carry meals to Coys. in the line and to their own Companies.

8. Water tanks are situate at the following positions:-

N. 7. C. 1. 6. N. 7. C. 9. 2.

The supply of petrol tins is limited.

9. Defence Schemes, Artillery arrangements, Trench Stores etc. will be taken over on relief. Complete lists of above to be forwarded to Battn. H.Qrs. by 7.0 A.M. April 1st

10. Relief complete to be reported to Battn. H.Qrs. in B.A.B. Code.

11. ACKNOWLEDGE.

PART. II.

1. Blankets will not be taken in to the line but dumped in bundles of 10 at COLONY SIDING after dusk & not later than 8.15 p.m. All Kit & Stores for the trenches, also Cooking Dixies will be dumped at COLONY SIDING after dusk.

2. Cellars, latrines, etc., will be left in a clean and sanitary condition.

Captain & Adjutant.
1/6th Bn. Sherwood Foresters....

SECRET. O.O./G/1

To O's. C. "A", "B", "C", "D", "HQ" Companies
Battn. Intelligence Officer. Medical Officer.

31st March 1918.

1. On the night 31st March/1st April, or if conditions are unfavourable, on the first favourable night "B" Special Coy. R.E. will discharge gas projectors on enemy trenches [illegible] ST. EMILE SECTION from position in N.7.d.

2. At the same time if conditions are favourable, "O" Special Coy. R.E. will project gas from LENS SECTION and "M" Special Coy. R.E. will project gas from HILL 70 SECTION.

3. Precautions. Mrs "B" and "D" Companies will wear box respirators and take cover, from Zero minus 5 until "ALL CLEAR" is received from Battn. H.Qrs.
Men of Mr "C" Company N. of N.7.d.8.1. will wear box respirators during the same period.

4. Zero hour will be 3 A.M.

5. The following code words will be used:-
Operation will take place tonight = CANADA.
Operation will not take place tonight = AUSTRALIA.
The Code word will be followed by O.C. Special Coy's name:-

"B" Special Company	SUMNER.
"M" " "	WILSON.
"O" " "	HADLEY.

Thus "AUSTRALIA HADLEY" will mean Operation will not take place tonight by "O" Special Coy. R.E.

6. Coy. Gas. N.C.O's will examine their Sectors immediately after the projection has taken place and report the result to Battn. H.Qrs. Box Respirators however will not be taken off until the "ALL CLEAR" is received from Battalion Headquarters.

7. ACKNOWLEDGE.

Captain & Adjutant.
16th Bn. Sherwood Foresters.

139th Brigade.

46th Division.

1/6th BATTALION

SHERWOOD FORESTERS

APRIL 1918.

Instructions regarding War Diaries and Intelligence Summaries are contained in F. S. Regs., Part II. and the Staff Manual respectively. Title pages will be prepared in manuscript.

WAR DIARY

~~or~~ 1/6th Bn Sherwood Foresters.

~~INTELLIGENCE SUMMARY.~~

(*Erase heading not required.*)

Army Form C. 2118.

Vol 39

Hour, Date, Place		Summary of Events and Information	Remarks and references to Appendices
3.4.18		Lt Col B.W. VANN M.C. rejoined from leave and resumed command of Battn	BWV.
5.4.18	CITÉ ST PIERRE SECTOR	Battn relieved by 1/5 SHERWOOD FORESTERS & moved into Bde Support in CITÉ ST PIERRE.	BWV
9.4.18	ST EMILE SECTOR	Battn relieved 1/8th SHERWOOD FORESTERS in LEFT SUBSECTOR.	BWV
9.4.18		C in C's LIST No 182. Lt F.S. ROWLAND M.C. to be A/Capt whilst comdg a Coy.	BWV
11.4.18	ST EMILE SECTOR.	Relieved by 58th CANADIANS (3rd CAN. DIV) moved back to billets at PETIT SAINS.	BWV
12.4.18	PETIT SAINS.	Bn marched into Huts at HOUCHIN.	BWV
18.4.18	HOUCHIN	Battn (less reserve details) moved to Billets at VAUDRICOURT	BWV
20.4.18	VAUDRICOURT	Battn moved back to HOUCHIN.	BWV
23.4.18	HOUCHIN	Bn (less details) moved to BETHUNE, details & transport to FOUQUIERES	BWV.
23.4.18	FOUQUIERES	CAPT & QM. W.D. JAMIESON wounded by shell.	BWV.
24.4.18		Battn relieved 4th Bn KINGS SHROPSHIRE L.I. in line, on right of LOCON ESSARS SECTOR	BWV.
28.4.18		Bn relieved by 1/5th LINCOLN REGt & moved into Divl Reserve at VERQUIN.	BWV.
30.4.18	VERQUIN.	LIEUT Y.F.G. HORE rejoined ~~[illegible]~~ from England after 6 months tour of duty at home	BWV.

B.W. Vann Lieut Colonel
Comdg 1/6 Sherwood Foresters

395

SECRET. Operation Order No 26 Copy No.....

by Lieut. Col. B. W. Vann, M.C., Cmdg. 1/6th Bn. Sherwood Foresters

9th April 1918.

Ref. Map. LENS 36. c. S.W. 1/10,000.

1. The Battalion will relieve the 8th Bn. Sherwood Foresters in the LEFT SUBSECTOR of the ST. EMILE SECTOR this evening.

2. Distribution of Battalion will be as follows:-

Battalion Headquarters N.7.b. 75.02.

"B" Coy. 6th S.F. will relieve "A" Coy. 8th S.F. on the RIGHT. Coy. H.Qrs. N.8.a.95.25.

"C" Coy. 6th S.F. will relieve "B" Coy. 8th S.F. in the CENTRE. Coy. H.Qrs. N.8.a.50.95.

"D" Coy. 6th S.F. will relieve "D" Coy. 8th S.F. on the LEFT. Coy. H.Qrs. N.7.b.60.86

"A" Coy. 6th S.F. will relieve "C" Coy. 8th S.F. in SUPPORT. Coy. H.Qrs. N.7.b.12.68.

Battalion Aid Post N.7.b.90.05.

Battalion Dump N.7.a.2.5. EDDY DUMP.

3. 4 Guides from the 8th S.F. for each of "A", "B", "C" & "D" Coys. will report at respective Company H.Qrs. in CITE ST PIERRE at 7.30 p.m. 1 Guide for H.Qrs. Coy. will report at Bn. H.Qrs. at 7 p.m.

4. Companies will not vacate present positions until 8 p.m. & will move off in the following order "D", "C", "B", "A", "H.Q." by Platoons at 2 minutes intervals.

5. Lewis Guns & Ammunition, Mess Kit, Medical, Canteen & other stores etc. will be carried in to the line under Coy. arrangements.

6. Advance Parties consisting of 1 Officer per Coy. & 1 N.C.O. per platoon will be sent up this afternoon independently.

7. The Cookhouse for all Coys. is situate at N.7.a.2.5 (EDDY DUMP) & all Coys. will arrange to have their dixies at COLONY SIDINGS at 7.30 p.m. Coys. will provide their own carrying parties for meals.

8. The Water Tanks are situate at N.7.a.2.5 (EDDY DUMP)

9. Defence Schemes, Artillery arrangements, Trench Stores &c will be taken over on relief. Complete list of above to be forwarded to Battn. H.Q. by 9 a.m. April 10th.

10. Relief complete to be reported by Fullerphone to Bn. H.Qrs. by code word "GIN". Companies will also report Relief complete by Runner.

11. ACKNOWLEDGE.

PART. II.

1. Officers Valises, Sgt. Tailors & Sgt. Shoemakers Kit & Blankets rolled in bundles of 10 will be dumped at either COLONY SIDINGS or OPERA SPUR DUMP after dusk but not later than 8 p.m.

2. All cellars, latrines &c. will be left in a clean & sanitary condition. O.C. Coys. will render a Certificate to this effect, & that the same were inspected by an Officer to Bn. H.Qrs. by 9 a.m. Apr. 10th.

T. Greaves

Capt. & Adjutant

1/6th Bn. Sherwood Foresters

P.T.O.

[Is]sued by runner at 7 am. 9/6/18

Copies to:-

Copy No. 1 O.C. A. Coy.
" " 2 O.C. B. Coy.
" " 3 O.C. C. Coy.
" " 4. O.C. D. Coy.
" " 5. O.C. H.Qrs Coy.
" " 6. Adjutant for C.O.
" " 7. Medical Officer.
" " 8. Signalling Officer & Intelligence Officer
" " 9 Quartermaster.
" " 10. Transport Officer.
" " 11. O.C. 5th Sherwood Foresters.
" " 12 O.C. Left Flank Bn.
" " 13 War Diary.
" " 14. File.

SECRET. Copy No. 11

Operation Order No 27.

by Lieut. Col. B. W. Vann. M. C., Cmdg. 1/6th Sherwood Foresters.

Ref. Map. LENS. 36. c S.W. 1. 1/10,000. 11th April. 1918.

1. The Battalion will be relieved by the 58th Canadian Infantry Battalion (9th Canadian Infantry Brigade) in the line this evening.

2. Companies will be relieved as under:–

"B" Coy. 6th S.F. by "A" Coy. 58th Canadians on the RIGHT.
"C" Coy. 6th S.F. by "D" Coy. 58th Canadians in the CENTRE.
"D" Coy. 6th S.F. by "B" Coy. 58th Canadians on the LEFT.
"A" Coy. 6th S.F. by "C" Coy. 58th Canadians in SUPPORT.

3. 2 Guides per platoon & 1 per Coy. H.Qrs (9 per Coy) and 2 Guides for Bn. H.Qrs. will report at Bn. H.Qrs. at 7 P.M.

4. On relief the Battalion will move into billets at FOSSE 10. One Guide per platoon and 2 Guides per Battn. H.Qrs. from details in rest will meet platoons at the SQUARE, BULLY GRENAY and guide them to billets at FOSSE 10. Company Commanders horses will be at M. 8. d. 35. 90 at 12 midnight.

5. Lewis Guns & Ammunition, Mess Kit, Trench Stores, Medical Canteen & other stores and Cooking Dixies to be carried out under Company arrangements to EDDY DUMP (N. 7 a. 2. 5.). Coy. Lewis Gun N.C.O's will remain at EDDY DUMP in charge of their guns and come down on the train with them.

6. No advance parties will be sent. These will be found by the details resting at BULLY GRENAY.

7. Trench Maps, Aeroplane Photos, Defence Schemes, Trench Stores &c will be handed over on relief.

8. Relief complete to be reported to Bn. H.Qrs. by code word "BRANDY". Coys. will also report to Bn. H.Qrs. at FOSSE. 10. by runner when they are all in billets.

9. ACKNOWLEDGE by wire.

PART. II.

1. All cellars, dugouts, latrines &c will be left in a clean and sanitary condition. O.C. Coys. will render a certificate to this effect & that the same have been inspected by an Officer to Bn. H.Qrs. by 9 am. 12/4/18.

[illegible signature]
Captain & A/Adjutant
1/6th Battn. Sherwood Foresters

(P.T.O.)

Issued at 2.30pm by runner.
Copies to:-

Copy No. 1. O.C. A. Company
" " 2 " B "
" " 3 " C "
" " 4 " D "
" " 5. " H.Q. "
" " 6 Transport Officer.
" " 7 Quartermaster.
" " 8. Medical Officer.
" " 9. Adjutant for C.O.
" " 10. Signal Officer & Intelligence Officer
" " 11. O.C. 58th Can. Inf. B[illegible]
" " 12. O.C. Right Flank Battn.
" " 13. O.C. Left Flank Battn.
" " 14 War Diary ✓
File.

SECRET. Operation Order No 28 by
Lieut Col B.W. Vann M.C.
Commanding 1/6th Bn Sherwood Foresters.

12th Apl 1918.

REF MAP LENS. 11.

1. The Battalion will march to DIEVAL today.
2. Battn Parade at 12:30 P.M on road leading past Bn H.Q
Head of Column opposite H.Q. mess & facing S.W.
Order of March:- Band "C" - "D" - Drums - "A" - "B" - H.Q. -
Transport in rear of H.Q. Coy.
Coys to march at intervals of 100 yards
Dress:- Full marching Order. Steel helmets.
3. Lewis Guns & Ammunition will be carried on L.G. Limbers.
Each O.C. Coy to detail a party of 1 NCO & 5 men to report
to Q.M. at once to pack L.G. Ammunition in tins and load
on transport.
4. Officers' Valises, blankets rolled in bundles of 10, medical
& Signalling Kit and O.R. Boxes to be stacked at Q.M. Stores
on main Road near L[?] "A" & "B" Coys at 11 am. Officers mess
Kit to be outside respective messes by 11.45 am.
5. An advance party composed as under to report at Bn
O.R. at 11 am ready to move off:- 2/Lt MYCOCK, 1 NCO.
from Q.M. Stores, 1 N.C.O Transport (MOUNTED), 1 NCO per Coy
including H.Q. Coy. (NCO's to be detailed from those
at BULLY GRENAY.) yesterday
6. Billets to be left in a clean & sanitary condition &
a report to this effect rendered to O.R. by 12 noon.
7. Sick Parade will be at 11 am at AID POST (Billet 666,
Near Bn H.Q.
8. ACKNOWLEDGE.

[signature]
Capt & Adjt.
1/6th Bn Sherwood Foresters.

SECRET. Operation Order No. 31. Copy No 14

By Lieut Col. B. W. Vann M. C., Commanding 1/6th Bn. Sherwood Foresters

Ref. Maps GORRE } 1/20,000. 2nd April. 1918
LACOUTURE }

1.

1. The Battalion will relieve the 4th Bn. Kings Shropshire Light Infantry Regiment in the line tonight.

2. The Battalion Boundaries are approximately as follows:-

Left. Canal running through X. 8. b & c with extreme Left Post about X. 8 C. 4. 1.

Right. Line running from X. 15. Central through X. 20. b. 55. 80.

8th Bn. Sherwood Foresters on the Right of Battalion.

18th Kings. 9th Brigade on the Left of Battalion.

3. The Battalion will be distributed as follows:-

Battalion H.Qrs. X. 20 a. 1. 6.

'D' Company will relieve 'D' Coy. 4th K.S.L.I. on the RIGHT.
Coy. H.Qrs. about X. 14. d. 60. 60.

'C' Company will relieve 'B' Coy. 4th K.S.L.I. on the LEFT.
Coy. H.Qrs. about X. 14. b. 00. 35.

'A' Company will relieve 'C' Coy. 4th K.S.L.I. in SUPPORT.
Coy. H.Qrs. about X. 20. b. 40. 40.

'B' Company will relieve 'A' Coy. 4th K.S.L.I. in RESERVE.
Coy. H.Qrs. about X. 20. c. 25. 95.

Battalion Aid Post X. 20. d. 40. 80.

Battalion Dumps at Bn. H.Qrs. & near Support Coy. H.Qrs

4. Movement from BETHUNE will be by platoons at 200 yards' interval in the following order:- "D" "C" "A" "B" "H.Qrs"
First platoon of "D" Company to move off at 8-30 P.M.

Dress:- Fighting Order. Greatcoats rolled. Waterbottles filled. Each N. C. O & man to carry 170 rounds S.A.A.

Route:- Road from E. 11. a. 80. 50 - cross roads E. 6. a. 25. 99 - main ESSARS RD.

5. 1 Guide per platoon, 1 per Coy H.Qrs & 2 per Bn. H.Qrs. will be at Road junction X. 20. c. 5. 3. at 9. 0 p.m.

A Battalion Scout will be attached to each platoon before leaving BETHUNE.

6. Lewis Gun Limbers will march in rear of first platoon of each Coy as far as Road junction X. 20. c. 5. 3.

Coys. to draw 4 Guns & 24 magazines per gun. A further 10 magazines per gun to be unloaded & left in charge of 2/Lt. Hycock as a Bn. Reserve.

7. Cooking will be carried out under Coy. arrangements
3 Dixies for each of A, B, and H.Qrs Coys. will be sent to Battn. H.Qrs.
Tommy Cookers will be supplied to "C" and "D" Coys.

8. Water will be sent up in petrol tins. Coys. are responsible for returning as many petrol tins complete with stoppers as they receive.

9. Artillery arrangements, Defence Schemes, Trench Stores &c will be taken over in relief, also a reserve of S.A.A. amounting to 100 rounds a man (at Coy H.Qrs) & 2 boxes per Lewis Gun.

S.O.S. is a Green Rifle Grenade Signal.

10. Coy Commanders will see to it that all N.C.O's know their way to Coy. H.Qrs & in addition 2 men per platoon to know shortest route to the Coy. & Battn. H.Qrs.

(P.T.O.)

12. There will be no movement by day except in cases of extreme urgency.
13. Relief complete to be reported on Fullerphone by code words "GUM BOOTS".
14. ACKNOWLEDGE.

PART. II.

1. Officers Valises Blankets, Packs, Orderly Room & Canteen Boxes to be stacked at the Tobacco Factory by 6.30 P.M.
Officers mess kit to be stacked by 7.30 P.M.
2. Billets & latrines to be left in a clean and sanitary condition.

[signature] Captain & Adjutant
6th Bn. Sherwood Foresters. . . .

Issued at by runner.
Copies to:-

Copy no. 1. O.C. A. Coy.
" " 2 O.C. B. Coy.
" " 3 O.C. C. Coy.
" " 4 O.C. D. Coy.
" " 5 O.C. H.Q. Coy.
" " 6 Adjutant for C.O.
" " 7 Transport Officer.
" " 8 Quartermaster.
" " 9 Medical Officer.
" " 10 Signal Officer & L.G. Officer.
" " 11 O.C. 7th Kings Shropshire Light Infantry.
" " 12 O.C. 8th Sherwood Foresters.
" " 13. O.C. Reserve Personnel.
" " 14 War Diary.
" " 15 File.

46/139

Army Form C. 2118.

1/6 Notts & Derby

WAR DIARY
or
INTELLIGENCE SUMMARY.
(Erase heading not required.)

Instructions regarding War Diaries and Intelligence Summaries are contained in F. S. Regs., Part II. and the Staff Manual respectively. Title pages will be prepared in manuscript.

Hour, Date, Place		Summary of Events and Information	Remarks and references to Appendices
VERQUIN	2. 5. 18.	The Battalion relieved the 1/6th North Staffs Regt. in Right Subsector of the GORRE SECTOR	WR/Major
GORRE	4. 5. 18	The Battalion were relieved by the 1/8th Sherwood Foresters and moved into Brigade Support, Headquarters in LE QUESNOY	WR Major
LE QUESNOY	6. 5. 18	The Battalion relieved the 1/5th Sherwood Foresters in the Left Subsector of the GORRE SECTOR	WR Major
GORRE	8. 5. 18	2/Lieut S G JOHNS wounded in action	WR Major
"	10. 5. 18	Relieved by the 1/4th Leicesters and took over bivouacs in VAUDRICOURT PARK. Casualties during the tour:- Killed 1 Other Rank Wounded 1 Officer, 7 Other Ranks. Gassed 8 Other Ranks.	WR Major
VAUDRICOURT	12. 5. 18	The Battalion relieved the 1/6th North Staffs Regt. in Brigade Support of the ESSARS SECTOR. 2/Lieut. G.W BUCKLOW proceeded to England to join R.A.F.	WR Major
ESSARS	16. 5. 18	Battalion relieved the 1/5th Sherwood Foresters in the Left Subsector of the ESSARS SECTOR.	WR Major
"	20. 5. 18.	Battalion relieved by the 1/8th Sherwood Foresters and moved into Brigade Support of the ESSARS SECTOR	WR Major
BRUAY	23. 5. 18	Lieut Col B.W. VANN M.C and Surgeon Major A.W. SHEA to Hospital.	WR Major
ESSARS	25. 5. 18	Battalion relieved by 1/6th North Staffs Regt in the ESSARS Sector and took over Bivouacs in VAUDRICOURT PARK Casualties during tour:- Killed 7 Other Ranks Wounded 15 Other Ranks. Gassed 23 Other Ranks. The following Officers and N.C.O. were mentioned in the Despatch of the Field Marshall Commanding in Chief for gallant Service in the Field:- Surgeon Major A.W. SHEA Q.M. and Hon Capt. W.D. JAMIESON. 240469 Sgt. J.P. MIDDLETON.	WR Major
VAUDRICOURT	27. 5. 18	QM and Hon Lieut. S.B BOULTON joined the Battalion for duty	WR Major

(9 29 6) W 3332—1107 100,000 10/13 H W V Forms/C. 2118/10.

Army Form C. 2118.

Instructions regarding War Diaries and Intelligence Summaries are contained in F. S. Regs., Part II. and the Staff Manual respectively. Title pages will be prepared in manuscript.

WAR DIARY
or
INTELLIGENCE SUMMARY.

(Erase heading not required.)

Hour, Date, Place		Summary of Events and Information	Remarks and references to Appendices
VAUDRICOURT WOOD	28-5-18.	Battalion was inspected by the G.O.C. Division on the Football Ground, GOSNAY.	[illegible] Major
"	30.5.18.	Battalion relieved the 1/4th Leicesters on the Left Subsector of the GORRE SECTOR	[illegible] Major

V. O. Robinson. Major.
Commanding 1/6th Sherwood Foresters

(9 29 6) W 3332—1107 100,000 10/13 H W V Forms/C. 2118/10.

SECRET. Operation Order No. 33.
by Lt. Col. B. W. Vann. M. C., Commanding 1/6th Sherwood Foresters
4th May. 1918.

1. The Battalion will be relieved by the 1/8th Sherwood Foresters in the line this evening.

2. Companies will be relieved as under:-
B Coy 6th S.F. by C Coy. 8th S.F. LEFT.
D Coy. 6th S.F. by. B Coy. 8th S.F. RIGHT.
A Coy 6th S.F. by. A Coy. 8th S.F. SUPPORT.
C Coy. 6th S.F. by. D Coy. 8th S.F. RESERVE.

3. 5 Guides per Company will be found by H.Qrs. Coy. These guides will be at F.4.a.5.2. by 9.45 p.m. & will guide platoons as far as Coy. H.Qrs. 4 Guides per Coy. will be at Coy. H.Qrs. at 10 p.m. to guide platoons up to their positions.

4. 1 Officer per Coy. & 1 N.C.O. per platoon will remain with the 1/8th S.F. until tomorrow morning. They will report to their Coys. by 4.30 am.

5. On relief the Battalion will move into Brigade Reserve.

6. Companies will take over from the 1/8th Sherwood Foresters as follows:-
'B' Coy. 6th S.F. relieves 'D' Coy. 8th S.F. LEFT. Coy. H.Qrs. F.4.a.60.15.
'D' Coy 6th S.F. relieves 'A' Coy. 8th S.F. RIGHT. Coy. H.Qrs. F.10.a.50.96.
'A' Coy. 6th S.F. relieves 'B' Coy. 8th S.F. RIGHT SUPPORT. Coy. H.Qrs. F.3.d.45.10.
'C' Coy. 6th S.F. relieves 'C' Coy. 8th S.F. LEFT SUPPORT. Coy. H.Qrs. F.8.b.86.83
Battalion H.Qrs. F.3.c.15.10.
Dump. – KANTARA DUMP F.3.c.75.15.
Aid Post F.3.b.5.6.

7. The Left Front Coy. will have 2 platoons in LOISNE TRENCH & 2 platoons in the Southern end of GORRE WOOD.

The Right Front Coy. will have 2 platoons in positions near road from F.4.a.4.2 to F.4.b.2.2. & 2 platoons in Support in Gun pits somewhere near Coy. H.Q.

The Right Support Coy will have 2 platoons near road from F.4.c.4.0. to F.4.c.0.6. & 2 platoons on the side of Canal from F.9.b.90.90. to F.3.d.7.4.

The Left Support Coy. is in cottages near F.8.b.9.7. & stands to in case of alarm in F.2.d. N. of CANAL and EAST of ROAD.
The above dispositions are only approximate & on arrival in Support, Coy. Commanders will immediately reconnoitre their "Stand to" positions & make certain that all N.C.O's & men know these in case of alarm during the night. Coys. will "Stand to" tomorrow morning 5.4.18.

8. 1 N.C.O. & 1 man of the 1/8th S.F. & 4 N.C.O's of 1/6th S.F. who have already reconnoitred positions in Support will meet each Coy. at F.4.a.5.2. after relief & act as guides to new positions.

9. Lewis Guns & Ammn, Mess Kit, Stores, Dixies &c. will be carried out under Coy. arrangements.

10. Relief complete to be reported to Battn. H.Qrs by code word "GUM".

11. Coys. will report to Bn. H.Qrs. as soon as they are in position in Support by code word "RATS".

12. Acknowledge.

Captain & Adjutant
1/6th Bn. Sherwood Foresters

SECRET. Operation Order No. 35.
by Lieut. Colonel. B. W. Vann, M.C., Cmdg. 1/6th Bn. Sherwood Foresters.
6th May. 1918.

1. The Battalion will relieve the 1/5th Sherwood Foresters in the LEFT SUBSECTOR of the GORRE SECTOR this evening.

2. Distribution of Battalion will be as follows:-

Battalion Headquarters X. 28. a. 40. 80.

'A' Coy. 6th S.F. will relieve 'D' Coy. 5th S.F. on the LEFT. Coy. H.Qrs. X. 22. d. 20. 2[illegible]
'B' Coy. 6th S.F. will relieve 'A' Coy. 5th S.F. on the RIGHT. Coy. H.Qrs. X. 29. a. 10. [illegible]
'C' Coy. 6th S.F. will relieve 'C' Coy. 5th S.F. in SUPPORT. Coy. H.Qrs. F. 3. b. 40. 90
'D' Coy. 6th S.F. will relieve 'B' Coy. 5th S.F. in RESERVE. Coy. H.Qrs. F. 3. b. 40. 75

Battalion Aid Post X. 28. a. 7. 7.
Battalion Dump. F. 3. c. 6. 0. (KANTARA DUMP)
Battalion Forward DUMP. F. 4. a. 1. 6.

3. 5 Guides for 'B' Coy. will be at X. 28. c. 65. 65. (Bridge of ROUTE. A. over CANAL) at 9.45 P.M. to conduct to Coy. H.Q.

5 Guides for 'A' Coy. will be at X. 28. c. 10. 60 (100 yards NORTH of N.E. Corner of GORRE WOOD) at 9.45 p.m.

5 Guides for each of 'C' and 'D' Coys. will be at X. 28. c. 10. 50 (N.E. Corne[r] of GORRE WOOD) at 9.45 p.m.

4. The first platoon of 'D' Coy. will not reach N.E. Corner of GORRE WOOD till 10 P.M.

5. 1 Officer per Coy. and 1 N.C.O. per platoon will be left by each of D (Left) and A (Right) Coys. of the 5th Sherwood Foresters and will be at the disposal of A and B Companies, 6th Sherwood Foresters respectively. These Officers & N.C.O's should return to their Companies before dawn.

6. 'A' Coy. 6th S.F. will leave 1 N.C.O. & 1 man to act as guides for 'A' Coy. 5th S.F. Guides to be at X. 28. c. 65. 65. (Bridge over Canal at ROUTE. A) at 11.0 P.M.

'C' Coy. 6th S.F. will leave 1 N.C.O. & 1 man to act as guides for 'D' Coy. 5th S.F. Guides to be at F. 3. c. 90. 90. (half way between LA BASSEE CANA[L] and GORRE WOOD) at 11.0 P.M.

7. Lewis Guns & Ammunition, Mess Kit &c will be carried into the line under Coy. arrangements.

8. 'C' and 'D' Coys. will each take 3 Dixies with them into the line. The 3 Dixies of 'A' and 'B' Coys. will be left at KANTARA DUMP by 8.15 p.m. 1 Cook from each of 'A' and 'B' Coys. will report to Battn. H.Qrs. in the line by 11.0 P.M.

9. Defence Schemes, Artillery arrangements, Trench Stores &c will be taken over on relief. Complete lists of above to be forwarded to Bn. H.Qrs by 7 A.M. May 7th.

10. Relief complete to be reported to Battn. H.Qrs. by code word "BRANDY."

11. Acknowledge.

PART. II.

All cellars, billets, latrines &c. will be left in a clean & sanitary condition & a certificate to this effect & that same have been inspected by an Officer will be sent to Bn. H.Qrs by 7 A.M. 7/5/18.

Captain & Adjt.
1/6th Bn. Sherwood Foresters.

SECRET. Operation Order No 21 Copy No. 9

by Lieut Col B. W. Vann M.C. Comdg 1/6th Sherwood Foresters

8th Feby 1918.

Ref Map HAZEBROUCK 5A

1. In connection with a Divisional Tactical Scheme (detail herewith) in which the 139th Brigade forms part of the main body, the Battalion will march by the following route to an unknown destination:- BELLERY - AMETTES - NEDON - NEDONCHELLE - FONTAINE LES HERMANS - FEBVIN PALFART.

2. The Battalion will parade on the Green opposite "C" Coy mess at 9.[illegible] am

DRESS:- Mounted Officers. Full marching order less packs. Steel Helmet to be carried on the horse. Field Boots or Leggings. Spurs.

Subaltern Officers. Full marching order. Steel helmet under the supporting straps of the pack. Puttees.

Other Ranks. Full marching order. Waterproof sheet rolled round leather jerkin the whole on the top of the pack under the supporting straps. Steel helmets on the front of the pack under the supporting straps, mess tins hanging from the bottom of the pack. Box respirator on the left [illegible] P.H. Helmet on the right side. Waterbottles filled.

3. The transport will be drawn up on the [illegible] Road by 9 am. Head of the column facing N.W. clear of road junction near "C" Coy mess

4. Order of March:- DRUMS. A. B. C D H.Q. Distance between Coys 10 yds. The transport will march in [illegible]

5. A Billeting party composed as under will parade at Orderly Room at 8.30 am.

2/Lt A. COATES (mounted)

4 C.Q.M. Sgts. (with Bicycles)

1 N.C.O. for H.Q. Coy (with Bicycle)

1 N.C.O. for Q.M. Stores. (with Bicycle)

1 N.C.O. for Transport (mounted)

3 Battn Runners.

DRESS:- Full Marching Order. Rations for 9½

6\. Watches will be synchronised at Battn O.R. at 8 a.m.

7\. <u>Acknowledge</u>

[signature]

Capt & Adjutant.

1/6th Bn Sherwood Foresters

Issued at 4 p.m. to

1. Commanding Officer
2. O.C. "A" Coy.
3. " "B" Coy
4. " "C" Coy
5. " "D" Coy.
6. Quartermaster
7. Transport Officer
8. Medical Officer.
9. War Diary. ✓
10. File.

SECRET. Operation Order No. 36 by Lt. Col. B. W. Vann, M.C., Commanding 1/6th Battalion Sherwood Foresters. 10th May 1918.

Ref. maps:- LOCON (Edition 8), GORRE, 1/20,000.

1. The Bn. will be relieved by the 4th. Bn. Leicestershire Regt. in the line this evening.
2. Dispositions of relieving Bn. will be notified later.
3. 2 guides per platoon, 1 per Coy. H.Qrs., & 2 per Bn. H.Qrs will be sent to road junction X.27.c.2.6 at 9.45 p.m.
4. Secret disposition & intelligence maps, aeroplane photos & trench stores will be handed over on relief.
5. The following personnel will remain with the relieving unit for 24 hours after relief:-

    1 Officer Battn. H.Qrs.
    1 Officer of each of "A" & "B" Coys.
    1 N.C.O. per platoon of each of "A" & "B" Coys.
    1 N.C.O. per Coy. of each of "C" & "D" Coys.

6. Relief complete to be reported to Bn. H.Qrs. by code word "NUTS".
7. On relief, platoons will move off independently to VAUDRICOURT wood, and take over bivouacs vacated by 4th. Leicestershires. Guides found by Reserve personnel at BRUAY, will be at the VAUDRICOURT PARK gates on the VERQUIN – VAUDRICOURT RD. from 12.30 A.M. (10th/11th. inst.) onwards.
8. Lewis Guns & ammunition will be carried by platoons as far as Railway Crossing E.18.b.7.2 on BEUVRY–BETHUNE RD., and from thence by limbers.
9. Mess Kit, Cooking dixies, Bn. stores etc., to be dumped outside Bn. H.Qrs. by 10.30 p.m.
10. Acknowledge by wire.

Issued at 2.30 A.M. by Runner:-
Copies to:-

Copies nos. 1 to 5	- - -	O.C. Coys.
Copy no. 6	- - -	Adjt. for C.O.
" " 7.	- - -	M.O. & L.G. Officer.
" " 8.	- - -	Transport Officer.
" " 9.	- - -	Quartermaster.
" " 10.	- - -	O.C., Reserve Personnel.
" " 11.	- - -	O.C. 1/5th S.F.
" " 12.	- - -	O.C. 1/6th S. Staffs.
" " 13.	- - -	War Diary.
" " 14.	- - -	File.

Operation Order No 37. Copy No. 13.
by Lieut. Col. B. W. Vann. M.C., Cmdg. 1/6th Bn. Sherwood Foresters.
14th May. 1918

Ref. Maps BETHUNE 1/40,000
LOCON Ed. 8.

1. The Battalion will relieve the 6th North Staffs in SUPPORT of the ESSARS SECTOR tonight

2. Distribution will be as follows:-
Battalion H.Qrs. X.25.b.05.50.

'A' Coy. will relieve 'D' Coy. 6th North Staffs on the RIGHT.
Coy. H.Qrs. LA MOTTE FARM X.26.c.40.60.

'D' Coy will relieve 'C' Coy. 6th North Staffs in the CENTRE
Coy. H.Qrs X.19.d.45.5.

'C' Coy. will relieve 'A' Coy. 6th North Staffs on the LEFT.
Coy. H.Qrs. X.19.a.6.4.

'B' Coy. will relieve 'B' Coy 6th North Staffs in LE HAMEL & on relief come under the orders of O.C. Right Battn. Coy H.Qrs. X.20.d.90.35.
Battalion Aid Post at Battn. H.Qrs.
Ration Dumps. Bn H.Qrs.
Rd junction X.19.d.60.30. (for A, C & D. Coys.)

3. Movement from the Camp will be by platoons at 200 yds. interval Coys moving off in the following order:-
'B', 'D', 'C', 'A', H.Qrs.
First platoon of 'B' Coy. to move out at 7.30 P.M.
Route VERQUIN - E.24.d.3.1. - E.18.d.4.5. - along railway to E.7.b.1.4. - E.7.a.6.8. - thence by shortest route.
Dress: Fighting Order. Pack to be worn in place of haversack

4. 1 Guide per platoon, 1 per Coy H.Qrs & 2 per Bn H.Qrs. will be met in road about F.7.a.9.8.

5. Lewis Guns & Ammn. (24 magazines per gun) will be carried by limber to E.7.b.1.7. & picked up there by platoons as they pass.

6. Cooking will be carried out under Coy arrangements and at night.

7. An Advance Party composed as under will parade outside Bn. H.Qrs. at 3.0 p.m. & proceed to the line under Senior N.C.O.
1 N.C.O. per Coy
Signalling Sergeant & 2 Bn. Signallers.
Scout Corporal & 2 Bn. Scouts
4 Bn Runners
1 Runner per Coy.
Dress:- as in para 3.

8. Coys. will detail the following N.C.O's & men for duty on CANAL BRIDGES & report at Bn. H.Qrs at 4.30 p.m.:-
'A' Coy. 1 N.C.O. & 1 man.
'B' Coy. 2 men.
'C' Coy. 1 N.C.O. & 1 man.
'D' Coy. 2 men.
N.C.O's should be reliable & intelligent
Dress. as in para. 3.

(P.T.O.)

4. Relief complete to be reported to [illegible] by code "LEEKE".

5. Acknowledge by runner.

PART II

1. Officers Valises, Surplus Mess Kit, Blankets rolled in bundles of 10 and haversacks to be stacked outside Bn H.Qrs at 5-0 P.M. Mess Kit, Signalling, Orderly Room & Medical Kit & [illegible] Dixies for the line to be stacked outside Bn. H.Qrs. by [illegible]. Lewis Guns & Ammn. to be handed in to Sgt. Bellamy at [illegible] H.Qrs at 4-0 p.m.

2. Tents, Bivouacs, latrines &c. to be left in a [illegible] & sanitary condition.

[signature] Capt. & Adjt.
1/6th Bn. Sherwood Foresters.

Issued at 12 noon by runner.
Copies to:-

Copy No.	1	O.C. 'A' Coy.
" "	2	" B "
" "	3	" C "
" "	4	" D "
" "	5	" H.Q. "
" "	6	Adjt. for C.O.
" "	7	Medical Officer
" "	8	Transport Officer.
" "	9.	Quartermaster.
" "	10	O.C. 1/5th North Staffs.
" "	11.	O.C. 1/8th Sherwood Foresters
" "	12	O.C. Reserve Personnel.
" "	13. ✓	File.
" "	14.	War Diary.

SECRET.

Operation Order No. 38, by Lt.Col. B.W. Vann, M.C.
Commanding 1/6th Battn. Sherwood Foresters.

Ref. Map:- LOCON, Ed. 8. 15th May, 1918.

1. The Battn. will relieve the 5th Sherwood Foresters in the line tomorrow evening, (LEFT SUBSECTION, ESSARS SECTOR).

2. Distribution of Bn. is as follows:- Bn. H.Qrs. X.20.a.2.6.
D Coy. relieves "C" Coy. 5 S.F. on the RIGHT, ~~B Coy relieves B~~
B " " B " " in the CENTRE
C " " A " " on the LEFT.
A " " D " " in RESERVE.
Bn. Aid Post X.20.d. 50.75.

3. 4 guides per Coy. for A, C & D Coys. will be at the Shrine, X.20.c.58.35 at 9.30 pm; 4 for B Coy. at X.20.b.85.15, at the same time.

4. Movement from present positions will be by platoons at 2 minutes interval, and not before 9.15 p.m.

5. Lewis Guns & Ammunition & all other stores will be carried under Coy. arrangements.

6. Defence Schemes, Artillery arrangements, aeroplane photos & trench stores will be taken over on relief.

7. Password till "Stand-to" on the morning of the 17th will be ARCHIE

8. Relief complete to be reported to Bn. H.Qrs. by code word BEANS.

9. Acknowledge by wire.

[signature]
Capt. & Adjutant.
1/6 Bn. Sherwood Foresters.

Issued at 11.55 p.m.

Copies to:	Copy No. 1—5.	O.C. Coys.
	" " 6.	Adjt. for C.O.
	" " 7	Medical Officer
	" " 8.	Transport Officer
	" " 9	Quartermaster
	" " 10.	O.C., 1/5 S.F.
	" " 11.	O.C. 8th S.F.
	" " 12.	O.C. Reserve Personnel.
	" " 13.	File.
	" " 14.	War Diary.

SECRET   Operation Order No. 48.   Copy No. 12.
by Lieut. Col. B. W. Vann. M. C., Cmdg. 1/6th Sherwood Foresters.
19th May. 1918

Ref. Maps LOCON 1/10,000 Ed. 8.
BETHUNE 1/40,000.

1. The Battalion will be relieved by the 5th Battn. South Staffs on the night of the 19th/20th.

2. Companies will be relieved as under:-
"B" Coy. by "C" Coy. 5th South Staffs on the RIGHT.
"A" Coy. by "B" Coy. 5th South Staffs on the LEFT.
"D" Coy. by "D" Coy. 5th South Staffs in SUPPORT.
"C" Coy. by "A" Coy. 5th South Staffs in RESERVE.

3. 5 Guides per Company & 2 per Battn. H.Qrs. to report at Battn. Orderly Room at 10·30 P.M.

4. Relief complete to be reported to Battalion H.Qrs. by code word "CASH."

5. On relief platoons will march to VAUDRICOURT PARK independently and occupy bivouacs vacated by 6th North Staffs, in the same camp as before. C.Q.M.Sgts. to await platoons in the Camp and direct them to bivouacs.

6. Lewis Guns & Ammunition to be carried by platoons to level crossing at F.7.C.1.7. and carried from there by limber. All other Stores for conveyance by limber to be at Battn. H.Qrs. by 11-0 P.M.

7. Officers chargers will be at Railway Bridge E.18.C.7.1. from 12·30 A.M.

8. Arrival in camp to be reported to Battn. H.Qrs.

9. ACKNOWLEDGE.

[signature]
Captain & Adjutant.
1/6th Battn. Sherwood Foresters.

Issued at 2 A.M. by runner.
Copies to:-
Copy No. 1. O.C. A. Coy.
" " 2. O.C. B Coy.
" " 3. O.C. C Coy.
" " 4. O.C. D Coy.
" " 5. O.C. H.Q. Coy.
" " 6. Adjutant for C.O.
" " 7. Medical Officer.
" " 8. Quartermaster.
" " 9. Transport Officer.
" " 10. O.C. 1/5th South Staffs.
" " 11. O.C. Battle Details.
" " 12. War Diary & File.

SECRET. Operation Order No. 39, by Lieut. Col. B.W. Vann, M.C.
Commanding 1/6 Battalion Sherwood Foresters.

Ref. map. LOCON. Ed. 8, 1/10,000. 19th May, 1918.

1. The Bn. will be relieved by the 8th Bn. Sherwood Foresters in the line tomorrow night.

2. Coys. will be relieved as under:-

D Coy.	by	A Coy.	8 S.F.	on the Right.
B "	"	B "	—	in the Centre.
C "	"	D "	—	on the Left.
A "	"	C "	—	in Reserve.

3. 5 guides of each of A, B & C Coys. & 2 of Bn. H.Qrs. to be at the Shrine X. 20. c. 55. 35 at 10 p.m., 5 of D Coy. at Cross roads X. 20. b. 90. 15 at 10 p.m.

4. Defence Schemes, Artillery arrangements, Intelligence maps & Trench Stores to be handed over on relief.

5. On relief, the Bn. will move into Bgde. Support, Coys taking over the same positions as before.
Bn. H.Qrs. & [illegible] will be at X. 25. a. 7. 2.
C Coy. H.Qrs. will be at X. 26. b. 05. 80. (old Bn. H.Qrs.)

6. Lewis Guns & Ammunition, Officers mess kit & Cooking dixies to be carried out under Coy. arrangements.

7. Relief complete in the line to be reported by Coys to Bn. H.Qrs. by code word WHIT, & arrival in support positions by code word MONDAY.

8. Acknowledge by wire.

E. [illegible]
Capt. & Adjt.,
1/6th Bn. Sherwood Foresters.

Issued at 11.55 p.m.
Copies to :-

Copy nos.	1 – 5.	O.C. Coys.
" no.	6.	Adjt. for C.O.
" "	7.	Medical Officer.
" "	8.	Transport Officer.
" "	9.	Quartermaster.
" "	10.	O.C. 1/8 S.F.
" "	11.	O.C. 1/5 S.F.
" "	12.	O.C. Reserve Personnel.
" "	13.	File
" "	14.	War Diary.

SECRET.

Copy No. 11

Operation Order No. 41 by Major V. O. Robinson, M.C.,
Commanding 1/6th Battalion Sherwood Foresters.

Ref. Maps. LOCON, Ed. 8, 1/10,000. 25 May, 1918.
BETHUNE Combined sheet, 1/40,000.

1. The Battn. will be relieved by 1/6th Bn. N. Staffs. Regt. in Bgde. Support tonight.

2. Coys. will be relieved as under:-
B. Coy. by D. Coy. 6th N. Staffs.
D. Coy. by C — ——————
C. Coy. by A — ——————

A Coy. will not be relieved. They will not vacate present positions until 11.0 p.m.

3. 4 guides per B, C & D Coys. to be at PONT TOURNANT Bridge F.7.a.6.8 at 10 p.m.

4. Relief complete to be reported to Bn. H.Qrs. by code word STOCKS.

5. On relief, platoons will march independently to VAUDRICOURT PARK, & take over bivouacs vacated by 6th N. Staffs. Guides found by personnel at BRUAY, will be outside the Park Gates to meet them.

6. Lewis Guns & Ammunition to be handed to Sgt. Bellamy at PONT TOURNANT, on South side of CANAL, & carried from there by limbers. Officers' Mess Kit, Medical Kit + other stores to be dumped at Bn. H.Qrs. by 10 p.m.

7. Coys. to report arrival in VAUDRICOURT PARK by runner.

8. Acknowledge by wire.

E. [illegible]
Captain & Adjutant
1/6th Bn. Sherwood Foresters.

Issued at 2.0 p.m. by runner.

Copies to

Copies	Nos.	1 – 5.	O.C. Coys.
Copy	No.	6.	Adjt. for C.O.
"	"	7.	Medical Officer.
"	"	8.	T.O., + Q.M.,
"	"	9.	O.C. 1/6th N. Staffs.
"	"	10.	O.C. Reserve Personnel.
"	"	11.	File. ✓
"	"	12.	War Diary.

SECRET

Operation Order No. 42.

By Major. V. O. Robinson. M.C., Cmdg. 1/6th Battn. Sherwood Foresters

Ref. maps. BETHUNE Comb. 1/20,000 — 30th May. 1918

GORRE 1/20,000.

1. The Battalion will relieve the 1/4th Leicestershire Regt. in the Left Sub Sector of the GORRE SECTION tonight.

2. "B" Company will relieve "B" Company on the RIGHT.
"A" Company will relieve "C" Company on the LEFT.
"C" Company will relieve "D" Company in SUPPORT
"D" Company will relieve "A" Company in RESERVE.
Battalion H.Qrs. will be at LOISNE CHATEAU.
Regimental Aid Post at adjacent Farm.

3. Movement from VAUDRICOURT will be by platoons at 200 yards interval – Companies in the following order "B" "A" "C" "D" "H.Q." First platoon of "B" Company to move off at 8·15 p.m.

Route. VERQUIN – E.24.d.35.20 – E.18.d.4.6. – along railway to Midland Bridge about X.2.d.4.4.

Dress:- Fighting Order. Greatcoats rolled round haversacks. 170 rds. S.A.A.

4. Guides of 1/4th Leicesters will be at Midland Bridge from 10 P.M. onwards. First platoon of "B" Company will not cross CANAL before 10·15 P.M.

5. Lewis Guns and Ammunition will be carried by limbers as far as level crossing at F.7.b.1.7. – from thence by platoons.

6. Defence Schemes, Artillery arrangements, Aeroplane photos and Trench Stores to be taken over on relief.

7. Cooking in the line is carried out at Support Coy. H.Qrs. Water Supply is at Battalion H.Qrs.

8. Relief complete to be reported to Battn. H.Qrs by code word "GINGER."

9. An Advance Party composed as under will parade outside Orderly Room at 7·30 P.M.:-
1 N.C.O. per Company & Bn. H.Qrs. — 4 Battn. Runners.
2 Battalion Signallers. — 1 Signaller per Coy.
Dress:- as in para. 3.

10. Companies will find the following personnel for Brigade duties:-
"D" Company 1 N.C.O. & 1 man. } Brigade Guard.
"A" Company 2 men }
"C" Company 1 N.C.O. & 1 man. Brigade Storemen.
Selected N.C.O's. to report at Orderly Room at 1·30 P.M. for instructions. Party to parade at Orderly Room at 4·30 P.M.
Dress:- as in para. 3. Rations for 31st

11. Acknowledge.

PART. II.

1. Officers Valises, Surplus Mess Kit, Packs & Blankets, 50 rounds S.A.A. per man to be stacked outside Orderly Room by 3·0 P.M.

2. Lewis Guns & Ammunition, Trench Mess Kit, Medical Kit, Cooking Dixies, Signalling, Canteen & O.R. boxes at same place by 8·0 p.m.

3. A certificate that Tents, Bivouacs, latrines, etc. have been left in a clean & sanitary condition will be rendered to O.R. by 8·0 P.M.

[signature]
Captain & Adjutant.
1/6th Bn. Sherwood Foresters.

Issued at 12 noon by Runner.

Copies to :- No. 1 O.C. 'A' Coy.
" 2 O.C. B Coy.
" 3 O.C. C. Coy.
" 4 O.C. D. Coy.
" 5 O.C. H.Q. Coy.
" 6 Adjt. for C.O.
" 7 Quartermaster.
" 8 Transport Officer.
" 9 Medical Officer.
" 10 O.C. 1/4th Leicesters.
" 11 File.
" 12 War Diary.

(6339) Wt. W160/M3016 1,500,000 10/17 McA & W Ltd (E 1898) Forms W3091. Army Form W.3091.

Cover for Documents.

70.

Nature of Enclosures.

46TH DIVISION,
GENERAL STAFF.
No.
Date 7.9.18

Raid

6th Sherwoods 7th June 18

Notes, or Letters written.

Instructions regarding War Diaries and Intelligence Summaries are contained in F. S. Regs., Part II. and the Staff Manual respectively. Title pages will be prepared in manuscript.

WAR DIARY
or
INTELLIGENCE SUMMARY.
(*Erase heading not required.*)

Army Form C. 2118.

1/6 Notts + Derby

Vol 41

Place	Date	Hour	Summary of Events and Information	Remarks and references to Appendices
LONDON GAZETTE	3-6-18.		SURG-MAJOR A W SHEA awarded Distinguished Service Order.	BWV
			240017 R.Q.M. Sergt. W. BARKER awarded Distinguished Conduct Medal	BWV
LEFT SUBSECTOR GORRE SECTOR	night 6/7-6-18		A party consisting of Lieut. H. D Vaughan (in command), 2/Lieut. F TOUCH, D.C.M. and 58 other ranks raided area enclosed by X.23.c.97.80 – X.23.c.85.60 – X.23.d.00.50 – X.23.d.10.65 (ref. map. Intell: Map No. 2. RUE DU BOIS). Enemy garrison was annihilated + one light machine gun captured. Casualties suffered by the party were light, 1 man being killed, and Lieut. H. D. Vaughan (slightly) + 3 O.R. wounded.	BWV
			Congratulatory messages were received from the ~~[illegible]~~ Corps + Divisional Commanders.	Appendix 1.
	7.6.18		Battn. relieved by 1/6th South Staffordshire Regt. and moved into Divl. Reserve (Billets in VERQUIN + bivouacs in VAUDRICOURT PARK).	BWV
	8.6.18.		2/Lieut. H. G SHENTON wounded in Action.	BWV
VERQUIN.	10.6.18		Lieut. Col. B.W VANN, M.C. rejoined from Rest Station + took over Command of Battalion.	BWV
VERQUIN	11.6.18		Battn. relieved 1/4 Leicestershire Regt. in Brigade Reserve of ESSARS Sector.	BWV

A6945 Wt. W11422/M1160 350,000 12/16 D. D. & L. Forms/C./2118/14.

41S

Instructions regarding War Diaries and Intelligence Summaries are contained in F. S. Regs., Part II. and the Staff Manual respectively. Title pages will be prepared in manuscript.

WAR DIARY
or
INTELLIGENCE SUMMARY.
(Erase heading not required.)

Army Form C. 2118.

Place	Date	Hour	Summary of Events and Information	Remarks and references to Appendices
LONDON GAZETTE	14.6.18		2/Lieut J.F. DENNIS, M.C. to be Lieutenant, 25/4/18	B.W.V.
ESSARS	15.6.18		Battn relieved 8th Sherwood Foresters in the LEFT Subsector of ESSARS Sector	B.W.V.
	18.6.18		2/Lieut W MEAKIN, 2/Lieut H.A. PAINE + 2/Lieut C.R. FREARS joined Battn	B.W.V.
TRENCHES	19.6.18		Battn relieved by 5 South Staffordshire Regt and moved into Divisional Reserve in VAUDRICOURT PARK.	B.W.V.
	19.6.18		Corps Commander awarded Bar to Military Medal to 240138 Sgt. T.W. SPENCER M.M., and 240244 Cpl E.H. WHITE, M.M., for gallantry + devotion to duty during Raid of 6/7th inst.	B.W.V.
	19.6.18		Surg. Major A.W. SHEA, D.S.O. rejoined Battn from Rest Station.	B.W.V.
VAUDRICOURT PK	23.6.18		Battn relieved 1/5th Leicestershire Regt in RIGHT Subsector of GORRE Sector.	B.W.V.
	26.6.18		Lieut. J.W. POTTER + 2/Lieut BADCOCK joined Battn	B.W.V.
TRENCHES	27.6.18		Battn relieved by 1/5 Sherwood Foresters + moved into Brigade Reserve in LE QUESNOY	B.W.V.
	28.6.18		2/Lieut. W. MEAKIN wounded in action	B.W.V.

B.W. Vann Lieut. Col.
Cdg 1/6 Sherwood Foresters

SECRET.

Operation Order No. 43, by Major J. O. Robinson, M.C., Commanding 1/6 Battalion Sherwood Foresters.

COPY No. 6

2nd. June. 1918.

1. Front line Coys. will be relieved on night 3/4th. June as under:- "A" Coy. will be relieved by "C" Coy. on Left.
"B" " " " " " "D" " " " Right.

2. On relief, "A" Coy. will take over positions vacated by "C" Coy in Bn. Support, & "B" Coy. will take over positions vacated by "D" in Bn. Reserve.

3. "C" Coy. will commence their relief at 10.30 p.m.; D Coy. at 10.45 p.m. Movement will be by platoons at 200 yards interval.

4. All details with regard to guides &c. will be arranged between O.C. Coys. direct.

5. Lewis Guns & Ammunition, Officers' Mess Kit &c. will be carried under Coy. arrangements.

6. O.C. Coys. & at least 1 N.C.O. per platoon will reconnoitre their new positions this evening.

7. Defence Schemes, Aeroplane photos. Trench Stores &c. to be taken over on relief.

8. Relief complete of Front line Coys. to be reported to Bn. H.Qrs. by code word "DRC".

9. "A" & "B" Coys to report to Bn. H.Qrs. as soon as they have taken over their new positions by code word "SALLY".

10. ACKNOWLEDGE.

T Evans

Capt. & A/Adjt.
1/6th Bn. Sherwood Foresters.

Issued at 9.30 p.m. by runner:-
Copies to:-

Copies nos.	1–5.	O.C. Coys.
Copy no.	6.	Adjt. for C.O.
" "	7.	Quartermaster Transport Officer.
" "	8.	Medical Officer.
" "	9.	Intelligence Officer.
" "	10.	O.C. Reserve Personnel
" "	11.	File.
" "	12.	War Diary.

SECRET. Operation Order No. 44, Copy No. 9

by Major H.O. Robinson, M.C.

Commanding 1/6 Sherwood Foresters.

Ref. MAP: Intell. Map. No. 2, RUE DU BOIS. 4 June, 1918.

1. A Raid will be carried out at on 5/6th June, Lieut. Vaughan in Command.

2. Objective: Area enclosed by X.23.c.97.80 — X.23.c.85.60 — X.23.d.00.50 — X.23.d.10.65.

3. Enemy dispositions as on attached sketch.

4. Artillery will co-operate with barrage shown on attached map.

5. At Zero, the raiding party, 2 Officers, 53 Other Ranks, will be lined up along Main Drain from X.23.c.75.70 to X.23.c.78.60.

At Zero — 30, 1 N.C.O. & 5 O.R. will occupy Post P.9 at X.23.c.85.60 & report to Lieut. Vaughan that they have done so.

6. At Zero, parties will move as follows:

PARTY "A": Lieut. Vaughan, 25 other ranks.

1 N.C.O. & 5 O.R. will establish post at X.23.d.00.50 to watch Right flank.

2 N.C.O's & 8 men will rush trench at X.23.d.05.65 from direction of P.9.

1 N.C.O. & 8 O.R. remain in Reserve under Lieut. Vaughan at P.9.

PARTY "B": 2/Lieut. Couch, 23 Other Ranks.

To cross MAIN DRAIN at X.23.c.78.68.

2 N.C.O's. 12 O.R. to proceed N. of ditch running E. of MAIN DRAIN to bridge at X.23.d.05.68, and take trench X.23.d.05.65 in rear. This party will carry two 8 ft. floorboards, & will leave 1 N.C.O. & 3 men to guard approach to bridge from N.

N.C.O., 10 O.R. to proceed S. of same ditch, & rush post at X.23.c.97.70.

PARTY. Left flanking Party, 4 N.C.O's, 4 men, 3 L.G's at X.23.c.80.80 to cover enemy post at 23.a.90.00.

COPY. No. 12.

SECRET. Operation Order No 45 by Major V. O. Robinson, MC,
Commanding 1/6 Battn. Sherwood Foresters.

Ref. Map. GORRE. 1/20,000. 6 June, 1918.

1. The Battn. will be relieved by the 1/6 South Staffordshire Regt. in the LEFT SUBSECTOR of the GORRE SECTOR on the night 7/8th June, 1918.

2. Companies will be relieved as under:-

"C" Coy. 1/6 S. F. will be relieved by "C" Coy. 1/6 S. Staffs on the left.
"D" Coy ------------- "B" ------------- right.
"A" Coy. ------------- "A" ------------- in Support.
"B" Coy. ------------- "D" ------------- in Reserve.

3. 5 guides from A, B & D Coys. to be at MIDLAND BRIDGE about F. 2. d. [illegible], at 10.15 pm. Cpl. VANES will be in charge of guides, who will report to him at Bn. HQrs. at 9.30 P.M. Guides from D Coy. will report to Bn. HQrs. before "Stand down" on morning of 7th.

4. Lewis Guns & ammunition, & Officers Mess kit of C & D Coys. to be handed to Sgt. Bellamy at LEVEL CROSSING, F. 7. b. 1. 7, & carried from here by limbers. Officers mess kit of A & B Coys & H.Qrs. & spare Lewis Gun magazines, medical kit & other stores, to be dumped at Battn. Dump (opposite Bn. HQrs) by 9.45 P.M.

5. All Secret Disposition Maps, aeroplane photos, Programmes of Work & trench stores, will be handed over on relief.

6. All trenches, Coy. HQrs. &c. will be handed over in a perfectly clean & sanitary condition.

7. Relief complete to be reported to Bn. HQ. by code word "JILL".

8. On relief, Platoons will march out independently via MIDLAND BRIDGE, F. 7. b. 1. 7, along railway to E. 17. d. 6. 4 & E. 23. a. 7. 9 & along track to VERQUIN, and take over billets at VERQUIN & bivouacs at VAUDRICOURT WOOD, vacated by 6 North Staffs. Guides found by Details at BRUAY will be at E. 29. c. 2. 7.

9. In the event of an enemy operation interfering with relief after Bn. has left sector, & before arrival at VERQUIN, messages will be sent to Temporary Bn. HQrs. at F. 18. b. 99. 80.

10. Companies to report arrival in billets or bivouacs by runner.

11. ACKNOWLEDGE.

[signature]
Capt. & A/Adjutant,
1/6 Bn. Sherwood Foresters.

Issued at 11.35 pm. by runner.

Copies to Nos. 1 – 5. OC Coys.
" 6. Adjt. for C.O.
" 7. M.O.
" 8. T.O. & Q.M.
" 9. O.C. 1/6 S. Staffs.
" 10. O.C. Reserve Personnel.
" 11. File
" 12. War Diary.

7. The order to withdraw will be given by Officer i/c of parties.

8. Enemy opposition from W. of LOUVANNE River will be met by 3 Lewis guns posted by O.C. "D" Coy. about X.23.c. 50.60, previous to Zero.

9. Dress:- Box respirator, rifle, bayonet, 20 rounds S.A.A. Officers & N.C.O's will carry wire-cutters and knobkerries, & in addition, Officers will carry compasses & revolvers.

10. Preparation:- (a). N.C.O's. i/c Covering Lewis Guns will prepare their positions night 4/5th. placing sticks to show direction of fire.

(b) O.C. "D" Coy. will arrange to collect two 8 ft. floorboards and six 6 ft. floorb[illegible] to on the night 4/5th. at Coy. H.Qrs.

11. The password will be "SHENTALL", & watches will be synchronised at Right Coy. H.Qrs. at Zero - 2 hours

Capt. & A/Adjt.
1/6 Bn. Sherwood Foresters.

Issued at p.m. by runner.

Copies to:-

Copy. No. 1. Lieut. Vaughan.
" " 2. 2/Lieut. Touch, D.C.M.
" " 3.
" " 4.
" " 5. O.C. Coys.
" " 6.
" " 7.
" " 8. File
" " 9. War Diary
" " 10. Adjt. for C.O.
" " 11.
" " 12. 139th Inf Brigade.

I Corps No.287 (G.O).
46th Division G.70/5.

46th Division.

The Corps Commander has made the following remarks on the report of the minor enterprise carried out by the 1/6th Bn, Sherwood Foresters, on the night 6/7th June, forwarded under your No.G.70/4 of 7/6/18 :-

"A most excellently planned and carried out enterprise. I wish to congratulate all concerned on their work. It is enterprises of this nature which give us moral superiority over the enemy."

(sgd) G.V. Hordern, B.G.,
G.S., I Corps......

10/6/18.

(2)

139th Infantry Brigade.

Forwarded for your information and communication to those concerned. The G.O.C desires me to say that he considers great credit is due to the battalion and congratulates all concerned in the operation. He wishes the urgency of obtaining identifications to be again impressed on all ranks.

Lieut-Colonel,
General Staff, 46th Division.

11/6/18.

I Corps No.287 (C.O).
46th Division G.70/5.

46th Division.

The Corps Commander has made the following remarks on the report of the minor enterprise carried out by the 1/6th Bn, Sherwood Foresters, on the night 6/7th June, forwarded under your No.G.70/4 of 7/6/18 :-

"A most excellently planned and carried out enterprise. I wish to congratulate all concerned on their work. It is enterprises of this nature which give us moral superiority over the enemy."

(sgd) G.V. Hordern, B.G.,
G.S., I Corps......

10/6/18.

(2)

139th Infantry Brigade.

Forwarded for your information and communication to those concerned. The G.O.C desires me to say that he considers great credit is due to the battalion and congratulates all concerned in the operation. He wishes the urgency of obtaining identifications to be again impressed on all ranks.

[signature]

Lieut-Colonel,
General Staff, 46th Division.

11/6/18.

46th DIVISION. No. 70/4

Date 7.6.18

G.O.C. Signed D.

G.S.O. 1

G.S.O. 2

G.S.O. 3 seen

Int. Offr.

Att. Offr.

Q. A.

C.R.A. C.R.E.

A.D.M.S. M.G. Batt.

Signals

RETURN TO "G" OFFICE.

Printed in France by A.P. & S.S. Press B. 2008. 5000. 4-18.

S E C R E T
* * * * * *

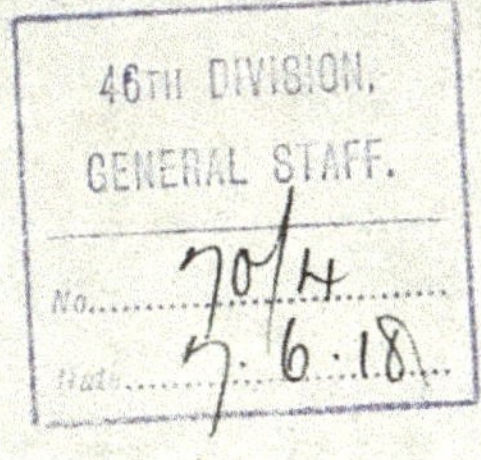

Headquarters,

46th Division.

Herewith report of O.C.Battalion on minor operation carried out against enemy post at X.23.d.0.7., on the night 6th/7th June, 1918 :-

"At the time of the raid, the enemy had a wiring "party out of from 20 to 30 men, on the front of attack. "On our barrage opening, this party ran back to trench at "X.23.d.0.7.

"Our parties moving forward all met thin wire, which "they cut through. The enemy threw a few bombs from his "post and opened fire to our right flank, from his light "machine gun in the Post (at the time of capture this gun "had fired some 60 rounds). Our parties rushed the Post "and bayonetted the German who was still firing his gun. "Several other Germans were killed in the Post.

"One German was seized by one of our men and hauled "out of the Post. He refused to move and was apparently "consequently killed. The remainder of the Post and "wiring party ran away and attempted to cross the dyke at "X.23.d.1.7. There they met Sergt. WAGG's party (less six "men who had joined in the fight at the Post). "Sergt.WAGG and three men shot several of the fleeing enemy "and charged the remainder who turned back and were lost "apparently running into the barrage about X.23.d.3.6.

"At this time Lieut.TOUCH gave the recall signal, it "having been reported to him that a prisoner had been "secured.

"The enemy attempted to fire a Gun at ZERO plus 2' "from X.23.a.95.00. This was silenced and completely "controlled by our three flanking Lewis Guns.

"The enemy fired red lights from Cse.du RAUX and "X.23.a.95.20., at 1.12 am., and the first shell fell at "1.15 am., behind our front line.

"The device of throwing up Verey lights from 200 yards "to the right flank of raid for illuminating the dark night "was particularly successful, the effect being one of "bright moonlight.

"Owing to the fact that it was believed a prisoner "had been secured, sufficient care was not taken to obtain further "identification. On return, an hour after the raid, a "further patrol was sent out for this purpose but was unable "to enter the post as there were 4 Germans there and a party "of 20 were advancing over the open towards the Post. Fire "was brought to bear on this party"

"Our casualties were :-

1 Officer accidentally wounded
1 man slightly wounded.

"The enemy received a number of casualties, apart from "the fact that they ran away into our barrage.

"The light Machinegun was brought back to our lines"

/sd/V.O.ROBINSON Major.
Commanding 1/6th Bn.S.Foresters".

I Corps. Forwarded. I am exceedingly annoyed at no identification being obtained. (sgd) [illegible]

7/6/18

J. Wood
Brig-General.
Commanding 139th Inf.Brigade.

46th Division.

No. 284 (G.O.) 10th June, 1918.

46TH DIVISION.
GENERAL STAFF.
No. 70/5
10.6.18

The Corps Commander has made the following remarks on the report of the minor enterprise carried out by the 1/6th Bn. Sherwood Foresters, on the night 6th/7th June, forwarded under your No.G.70/4 of 7/6/18:-

"A most excellently planned and carried out enterprise. I wish to congratulate all concerned on their work. It is enterprises of this nature which give us moral superiority over the enemy.".

G.V. Hordern.

Brigadier General,
General Staff, I Corps.

“A” Form

Army Form C. 2121
(In pads of 100.)

MESSAGES AND SIGNALS.

No. of Message............

Prefix.............Code..............m.	Words	Charge.	This message is on a/c of:	Recd. at......m.
Office of Origin and Service Instructions	Sent		............................Service.	Date..............
	At ....m.			From ....
	To		....	
	By		(Signature of "Franking Officer")	By..............

TO { I Corps   3rd 55th Division

Sender's Number.	Day of Month.	In reply to Number.	AAA
G 70/3	6		

Pole Brigade are carrying out minor operation at 1 am 7/6/18 against aaa X 23 c 97 50 and X 23 a 10 85 aaa Acknowledge

From 6th Division
Place
Time 5 0 Am

The above may be forwarded as now corrected. (Z)

.... Censor.

Signature of Addressor or person authorised to telegraph in his name

* This line should be erased if not required.

Order No. 1625. Wt. W3253/ P 511 27/2 H. & K. Ltd. (E. 2634).

46th DIVISION. No. 70/2

D[illegible] 6-6-18

G.O.C. [illegible]

G.S.O. 1 [illegible]

G.S.O. 2

G.S.O. 3 [illegible]

Int. Offr. [illegible]

Att. Offr. [illegible] [illegible]

Q. A.

C.R.A. C.R.E.

A.D.M.S. M.G. Batt.

Signals

RETURN TO "G" OFFICE.

Printed in France by A.P. & S.S. Press B. 2008. 5000. 4-18.

SECRET.

I CORPS COUNTER-BATTERY ORDER NO 79.

1. In support of an Operation to be carried out by the 46th Division, on the night of 6th/7th June 1918, in X25, Hostile Batteries will be neutralized as under:-

Brigade.	Calibre.	Hostile Batteries.
7th.	1-9.2" how on each 2-60 p'drs ,, ,,	R28c40.40. R28d20.40 SD21. SD28.
44th.	1-8" how on each 2-6" hows on 1-6" ,, ,,	XB12. RD81. RD75(N pits), RD75(S pits), X4d70.10. X12a95.67. XB60.
46th.	2-6" hows on each 1-6" ,, ,, 2-60 p'drs on each	S8a70.90, S8a63.45, X5a65.85. X4d50.10. S1b77.12 to 80.04. SA10, SA51. RD91.
99th.	2-6" hows on	S7d80.70.

2. RATES OF FIRE:-

Zero to Zero plus 7 mins. = RAPID.

Zero plus 7 mins. to Zero plus 20 mins. = SLOW.

,, ,, 20 ,, ,, ,, ,, 25 ,, = RAPID.

,, ,, 25 ,, ,, ,, ,, 35 ,, = SLOW.

3. ZERO HOUR will be notified.

4. ~~PLEASE ACKNOWLEDGE BY WIRE.~~ Done

O C Du Port
Lt Col. R.A.,

June 6th.1918.

C. B. S. O. I Corps.

Copies to:-

H.Q.	R.A. I Corps.	(1)	H.Q. 7th. B'de.R.G.A.	(4)
,,	H.A. do.	(1)	,, 44th. ,, ,,	(4)
"G"	46th. Division.	(1)	,, 46th. ,, ,,	(6)
H.Q.	46th. Div Art'y.	(1)	,, 99th. ,, ,,	(3)
O.C.	No 8 Group.F.S.Co.	(1)	File.	(2)

S E C R E T
****

No. G.1510/1.

46th Division

To all recipients of G.1510.

ZERO HOUR will be 1 am 7th instant.

ACKNOWLEDGE.

Captain.

June 6th, 1918.

Brigade Major, 139th Inf.Brigade.

46th DIVISION. No. 70 + 70/1

Date 6.6.18

G.O.C.

G.S.O. 1 D

G.S.O. 2

G.S.O. 3

Int. Offr.

Att. Offr.

Q. A.

C.R.A. C.R.E.

A.D.M.S. M.G. Batt.

Signals

RETURN TO "G" OFFICE.

Printed in France by A.P. & S.S. Press B. 2008. 5000. 4-18.

SECRET
******

No. G.1510.

46th Division

Ref Map :- Intelligence Map No. 2. RUE DU BOIS.

1. The 1/6th Battalion Sherwood Foresters will carry out a minor operation on night 6th/7th June, against the area enclosed by X.23.c.97.80 - X.23.c.85.60 - X.23.d.00.50 - X.23.d.10.85.

ZERO hour will be notified later.

2. The GORRE and ESSARS GROUPS R.A., and No. 1 Group 46 M.G.Battalion, are co-operating. Artillery arrangements have been issued to all concerned.

Machine Guns will fire as under :-

GUNS	TASK	TIME	RATE OF FIRE
5 & 6.	Neutralizing hos-tile M.Guns in area around Cse.du RAUX.	ZERO plus 2' to ZERO " 6'.	RAPID
9 & 10. 11 & 15		ZERO plus 6' to ZERO " 32'	SLOW

3. Watches will be synchronised with GORRE GROUP R.A. and No. 1 Group 46 Bn.M.G.C., at Brigade Headquarters at 8 pm., 6th instant. A watch will be sent to Officer Commanding 1/6th Battalion Sherwood Foresters at 8.30 pm., 6th instant.

4. ACKNOWLEDGE. Done

[signature]
Captain.
Brigade Major, 139th Infantry Brigade.

June 6th, 1918.

Issued to :-

46th Division.
164th Inf. Brigade.
No.1 Group 46 Bn.M.G.C.
5th Bn.S.Foresters.
8th Bn.S.Foresters.
139 T.M.Battery.
Bde.Signal Officer.
138th Inf. Brigade.
GORRE GROUP R.A.
Staff Captain.
6th Bn.S.Foresters.
8th Bn.S.Foresters.
465 Field Coy.R.E.

SECRET. Operation Order No. 47. Copy No 14.

by Lieut. Colonel B. W. Vann M.C. Cmdg. 1/6th Bn. Sherwood Foresters.

14th June 1918.

1. The Battalion will relieve the 8th Bn. Sherwood Foresters in the left sub-sector of the Brigade Sector tomorrow night.

2. Battalion will be distributed as follows:-

Battalion Headquarters X. 19. b. 95.40.

"B" Coy. will relieve "A" Coy. 8th S.F. on the RIGHT.

"A" Coy. will relieve "D" Coy. 8th S.F. on the LEFT.

"D" Coy. will relieve "C" Coy. 8th S.F. in SUPPORT.

"C" Coy. will relieve "B" Coy. 8th S.F. in RESERVE.

Battalion Aid Post X. 20. d. 50. 80.

3. Guides for "A", "C", "D" and H.Qrs. will be at the CRUCIFIX. X. 20. c. 6. 4. at 10.45 p.m., for "B" Coy. at cross roads X. 20. b. 85. 15. at 10.45 p.m.

There will be no movement from present position before 10.15 p.m.

4. Lewis Guns & Ammunition and all Coy. Stores will be carried in under Company arrangements.

5. Relief complete to be reported to Battalion H.Qrs. by code word "SALVAGE".

6. ACKNOWLEDGE.

[signature]
Captain & Adjutant.
1/6th Battn. Sherwood Foresters....

Issued at 10.30 p.m. by runner.

Copies to:-

Copy no. 1. O.C. "A" Coy.
" " 2. O.C. "B" Coy.
" " 3. O.C. "C" Coy.
" " 4. O.C. "D" Coy.
" " 5. O.C. "H.Q." Coy.
" " 6. Adjutant for C.O.
" " 7. Medical Officer.
" " 8. Quartermaster.
" " 9. Transport Officer.
" " 10. O.C. 1/8th Sherwood Foresters.
" " 11. O.C. 1/5th Sherwood Foresters.
" " 12. O.C. Reserve Personnel.
" " 13. File.
" " 14. War Diary. ✓

7. The order to withdraw will be given by Officer i/c of parties.

8. Enemy opposition from W. of LOUANNE River will be met by 2 Lewis guns posted by O.C. "D" Coy. about X.23.c. 50.60, previous to Zero.

9. Dress:- Box respirator, rifle, bayonet, 20 rounds S.A.A. Officers & N.C.O's. will carry wire-cutters and knobkerries, & in addition, Officers will carry compasses & revolvers.

10. Preparation:- (a). N.C.O's. i/c Covering Lewis Guns will prepare their positions night 4/5th. placing sticks to show direction of fire.

(b). O.C. "D" Coy. will arrange to collect two 8 ft. floorboards and six 6 ft. floorbds. do on the night 4/5th. at Coy. H.Qrs.

11. The password will be "SHENTALL", & watches will be synchronised at Right Coy. H.Qrs. at Zero - 2 hours.

Capt. & A/Adjt.
1/6 Bn. Sherwood Foresters.

Issued at p.m. by runner.

Copies to:-

Copy. No. 1. Lieut. Vaughan.
" " 2. 2/Lieut. Louch, D.C.M.
" " 3.
" " 4.
" " 5. O.C. Coys.
" " 6.
" " 7.
" " 8. File
" " 9. War Diary
" " 10. Adjt. for C.O.
" " 11.
" " 12. 139th Inf Brigade.

1/6th BN THE SHERWOOD FORESTERS

Instructions regarding War Diaries and Intelligence Summaries are contained in F. S. Regs., Part II, and the Staff Manual respectively. Title pages will be prepared in manuscript.

WAR DIARY
or
INTELLIGENCE SUMMARY.
(*Erase heading not required.*)

Army Form C. 2118.

Vol 42

Place	Date	Hour	Summary of Events and Information	Remarks and references to Appendices
LE QUESNOY.	1-7-18		Capt. T. GREAVES wounded in action & died of wounds. 2/Lieut W. BLOOD wounded in action	BWT
"	1-7-18		Battalion relieved by 1/6th N. STAFFORDSHIRE REGT & moved into Divisional Reserve in VAUDRICOURT PARK.	BWT
VAUDRICOURT PARK	2-7-18		Lieut. N H G. LAWLESS proceeded to England to report to War Office.	BWT
"	4-7-18		Major V.O ROBINSON, M.C. proceeded to Senior Officers' School, ALDERSHOT, and struck off strength.	BWT
"	5-7-18		Bn. relieved 1/5th Bn LINCOLNSHIRE REGT. in the LEFT Subsector of the ESSARS SECTOR.	BWT
TRENCHES	—		Major W. G HUTCHENCE, 1st Bn. D.L.I. cross-posted from 1/6th S. STAFFORDSHIRE REGT & joined Battalion.	BWT
"			2/Lieut. B.M. BADCOCK killed in action.	BWT
"	13-7-18		2/Lieut. J NEWELL and 2/Lieut C.B. NEWELL joined Battalion.	BWT
"	15-7-18		Battalion relieved by 1/6th Bn. S. STAFFORDSHIRE REGT, and moved into Divl. Reserve. Two Companies & H.Qrs in VERQUIN, ~~two~~ Companies in VAUDRICOURT PARK.	BWT
VERQUIN.	16-7-18		2/Lieut. A. MACKINTOSH and 2/Lieut. W. BAVIN joined Battalion.	BWT
"	17-7-18		The Battalion found a Working party of 545 O.R. for work on a	BWT

1/6th BN THE SHERWOOD FORESTERS

Instructions regarding War Diaries and Intelligence Summaries are contained in F. S. Regs., Part II. and the Staff Manual respectively. Title pages will be prepared in manuscript.

WAR DIARY
or
INTELLIGENCE SUMMARY.
(Erase heading not required.)

Army Form C. 2118.

Place	Date	Hour	Summary of Events and Information	Remarks and references to Appendices
			Cable trench in BETHUNE and vicinity.	BWV.
			The Battalion was congratulated by the G.O.C. Division ~~on~~ the work done.	
VERQUIN.	21-7-18.		Battalion relieved 1/6th S. STAFFORDSHIRE REGT. in Brigade Support of the ESSARS SECTOR	BWV
TRENCHES.	24-7-18.		2/Lieut. R.E.H. STOTT and 2/Lieut. D.J. CLARKSON joined Battalion.	BWV
"	25-7-18		2/Lieut. L.A.B. BECHER joined Battalion.	BWV
"	25-7-18		2/Lieut. S.N. DEVRANCE proceeded to England to report to War Office.	
"	25-7-18		Battn relieved 1/5th SHERWOOD FORESTERS in the LEFT SUBSECTOR of the ESSARS SECTOR.	BWV.
"	26-7-18.		2/Lieut. C.E. BRODBECK killed whilst on daylight patrol.	BWV.
"	27-7-18		2/Lieut. J. NEWELL proceeded to 39th Bn. M.G. CORPS for 1 month's attachment as Company Transport Officer, & struck off strength.	BWV.

3/8/18.

B.W. Vann Lieut.-Col.,
Cdg. 1/6 Sherwood Foresters

A6945 Wt. W11422/M1160 350,000 12/16 D. D. & L. Forms/C./2118/14.

Instructions regarding War Diaries and Intelligence Summaries are contained in F. S. Regs., Part II. and the Staff Manual respectively. Title pages will be prepared in manuscript.

WAR DIARY
or
INTELLIGENCE SUMMARY.
(*Erase heading not required.*)

Army Form C. 2118.

1/6 Notts + Derby

43

Place	Date 1918 August	Hour	Summary of Events and Information	Remarks and references to Appendices
ESSARS.	2nd		Battalion relieved by the 1/6th Bn. North Staffs in the Left Subsector of the ESSARS SECTOR and moved into Divisional Reserve in VAUDRICOURT PARK.	JAS
VAUDRICOURT PARK	4th		Major W G HUTCHENCE proceeded to 5th Army School as Instructor.	
"	"		2/Lieut. W.H. HOPCRAFT joined the Battalion from 5th Sherwood Foresters.	JAS
"	5th		Major J. R. SHEDDEN, M.C., Scottish Rifles joined the Battalion as 2nd in Command.	
"	night 5th/6th		Battalion provided a working party of 500 Other Ranks on cable trench in forward area (ESSARS). 2/Lieut. F. TOUCH D.C.M., "Wounded in Action"	JAS
"	8th		Battalion relieved the 1/5th Lincolnshire Regt in Left Subsector of the GORRE SECTOR.	JAS
GORRE	9th		2/Lieut. D. J. CLARKSON "Killed in Action" when on patrol.	
"	13th		2/Lieut. T. A. LAKE reported "missing" off patrol. This Officer led a fighting patrol against an enemy post which he had previously reconnoitred by day.	
"	14th		240391 L/Cpl. J. HOLMES awarded M.M. for gallantry in action on a daylight patrol.	JAS
"	"		Battalion relieved in Left Subsector of the GORRE SECTOR by the 1/5th Lincolnshire Regt. and took over the Left Subsector of the ESSARS SECTOR from the 5th South Staffs Regt.	JAS
ESSARS	16th		Battalion relieved in Left Subsector of the ESSARS SECTOR by 5th Bn. Sherwood Foresters and moved into Brigade Reserve.	JAS
FOUQUIERES	20th		2/Lieut. C.E. WARDLE and 2/Lieut. J. C. CAIRD joined the Battalion.	
ESSARS.	20th		Battalion relieved by the 1/5th Bn South Staffs and moved into Divisional Reserve in VAUDRICOURT PARK	JAS
VAUDRICOURT PARK	21st.		240244 Cpl E.H WHITE, MM, awarded the D.C.M. for gallantry in action on a daylight patrol	JAS
"	22nd.		Battalion provided a working party of 500 Other Ranks for work on trenches in vicinity of NEWCASTLE LINE, GORRE SECTOR	JAS
"	24th		The following awarded the M.M 240526 Cpl. J. VANES 240286 Pte F. WRIGHT for gallantry in action on a fighting patrol led by 2/Lieut. T. A. LAKE. 306187 Pte C. SWIFT for gallantry in action under fire.	JAS
"	25th		Battalion was inspected by G.O.C. Division on the Training Ground at HESDIGNEUL. Report stated "Satisfactory" "Great pains had been taken with the turnout"	JAS
"	26th		Battalion relieved the 5th Bn. Lincolnshire Regt. in the Left Subsector of the Main Line of Resistance, GORRE SECTOR.	
"	30th.		Battalion relieved 5th Bn. Sherwood Foresters in the Front Line, GORRE SECTOR, 'A' Coy on Left, 'B' Centre, 'D' Right.	

Instructions regarding War Diaries and Intelligence Summaries are contained in F. S. Regs., Part II, and the Staff Manual respectively. Title pages will be prepared in manuscript.

WAR DIARY
or
INTELLIGENCE SUMMARY.
(Erase heading not required.)

Army Form C. 2118.

Place	Date	Hour	Summary of Events and Information	Remarks and references to Appendices
	1918 August			
GORRE SECTOR	31st		"D" Company captured EPINETTE E. KEEP and pushed forward to posts in front.	[illegible]
			"B" Company established posts 200 yards in advance.	[illegible]
			"A" Company straightened line along RUE des CHAVATTES and formed defensive flanks along KING GEORGES ROAD	
			James A Sladden [illegible] Major.	
			Commanding 1/6th Bn. Sherwood Foresters.	

APPENDIX A

Report on Operations 29th September 18

At Zero - 30 the Battalion was in its appointed Assembly position.

At 9.30 AM an order was received for the Battalion to move up to positions vacated by the 8th S.F. These orders were received to follow up closely keeping touch with the 8th S.F. The Companies however had already begun to move forward - and as there was a very thick fog it was impossible to keep any communication.

However all Companies got to the second assembly position and were ordered to push on over Canal.

The Canal was crossed between 11.0 and 11.15 am and the Battalion moved.

Two Companies on the right found the 8th S.F. about the BROWN LINE and advanced with them helping them to take the YELLOW LINE - clearing out Dug outs on the way.

In the centre and on the left the

M.G fire was very heavy, particularly on forward slopes of the hills. Most of the fire was coming from the S. of the CANAL at about 800 yards range and one battery of Field Guns was firing at us at point blank range

As no other troops were in front of us and no tanks had appeared I sent back asking for a smoke screen to be put across ridge S of CANAL. The right companies managed to work forward along CANAL meeting with fairly strong M.G fire, but as soon as the left companies pushed over crest of hill G. 35 d   with few casualties considering the M.G. fire, the Boche surrendered in large parties

One gun team kept firing at tanks who came up about 500 yards behind us. This team was shot down and two wounded prisoners taken. The Field Guns from S of CANAL and the battery in M   in ELBE ALLEY had by about 1-0 P.M knocked out 5 tanks.

We took the YELLOW LINE about 1.15 P.M. and the DOTTED BLUE LINE.

The enemy made one or two feeble attempts to counter attack from the right flank S of CANAL and twice were driven off by our L.G. fire.

The third time an Officer on horse back was trying to rally his men who rushed up the hill, our L.G's killed him and his horse.

The left Company and two platoons of the right Company pushed on to LIHAUCOURT and established three posts in village by 1.30 P.M. Working round to the left we met the 5th S.F. who came up on the left, and withdrawing my left Company I left two platoons to hand over the EASTERN and S.E. side of the village to their boys who came up some time later. We had a few casualties in LIHAUCOURT but took many prisoners and 2 guns there

Our casualties were

2/Lieut	H. A. PAINE	Killed
2/Lieut	W. BAVIN	"
2/Lieut	W. MEAKIN	Wounded
2/Lieut	A. MACKINTOSH	"
5	Other Ranks	Killed
8	—	Missing
42	—	Wounded

Captures

8 Field Guns
10 K 15 M G's
1 Tank Gun
400 Prisoners

46th Division. G.114/33. 29th September, 1918.

I cannot express in words my feelings of intense admiration and pride in the magnificent ~~xxxxx~~ effort of the DIVISION today.

Well have the troops answered my call, and what appeared well nigh impossible has been carried righ t through to a great victory.

The story of the storming of the ST. QUENTIN CANAL, the capture of BELLENGLISE and the subsequent advance will make one of the most glorious stories in the History of the War.

I heartily congratulate and thank all Commanders and their Troops, Infantry, Heavy and Field Artillery, Machine Gunners, Engineers and Pioneers who have one and all contributed to our success.

(sd) G.F. BOYD, Major Gener
Commanding 46th Division.

SPECIAL ORDER OF THE DAY
BY
LIEUT. GENERAL SIR WALTER BRAITHWAITE, K.C.B.,
COMMANDING IX CORPS.

30th September, 1918.

Yesterday the 46th (North Midland) Division stormed and captured the CANAL Defences on a front of 3,500 yards, took BELLENGLISE, MAGNY LA FOSSE, and LEHAUCOURT and attained all its objectives. In executing this feat of arms the Division captured about 4,200 prisoners. In addition to these prisoners some 40 - 50 guns were taken, and many hundred machine guns and trench mortars.

In congratulating Major General G.F. BOYD, C.M.G., D.S.O., D.C.M., I desire to place on record my admiration of his skilful leadership, and my appreciation of the completeness of his preparations.

To the troops under his Command, and especially to Brigadier General J.V. CAMPBELL, V.C., C.M.G., D.S.O., and the 137th Brigade, I record my unstinted admiration for their splendid gallantry and dash. The whole Division has proved itself a fighting force of the first rank, and it was due to their efficiency that the casualties they suffered were comparatively slight. Each Battalion has added laurels to the Battle Honours of its Regiment which can never fade.

I desire to congratulate the 1st and 6th Divisions without whose less spectacular but fine dogged fighting during the past fortnight the task of the 46th Division would have been rendered more difficult of achievement. They have indeed well prepared the way.

The 32nd Division, having passed through the 46th Division, is now exploiting the success already gained with determination and confidence.

In regard to the Artillery now under my Command, I desire to place on record my great appreciation of their accurate shooting and their unwearied efforts to prepare the way for, and to support, the Infantry and thus render success complete. Their action during the whole period has been worthy of the highest traditions of the Royal Regiment.

A congratulatory telegram from the Army Commander, 4th Army, and my reply thereto, is attached.

It is with feelings of pride at being at the Head of such fine troops that I have the honour to sign my name as Commander of the IX Army Corps.

(sd) WALTER BRAITHWAITE,
Lieutenant General.

Instructions regarding War Diaries and Intelligence Summaries are contained in F. S. Regs., Part II. and the Staff Manual respectively. Title pages will be prepared in manuscript.

WAR DIARY
or
INTELLIGENCE SUMMARY.
(*Erase heading not required.*)

Army Form C. 2118.

Place	Date	Hour	Summary of Events and Information	Remarks and references to Appendices
LEVERGIES	10/10/18		Battn moved to MERICOURT.	GHC
MERICOURT	12/10/18		Battn left MERICOURT, + bivouacked in vicinity of Railway near BOHAIN	
			Lieut A.F. BRIGGS joined Battn	GHC.
	14/10/18		Bn moved into billets in FRESNOY LE GRAND.	GHC
FRESNOY	16/10/18		Battn moved into Brigade Reserve for Operations of the 17th inst. Battn was not called on during the attack, but took over the line at night. Before morning, French + 138th Inf. Bde had linked up in front of Bn.	GHC
	18/10/18		Battn moved to FRESNOY + remained in billets for 12 days. Great interest was taken in training, + inter-platoon football league.	GHC
	20/10/18		Corps Commander awarded follg decorations for gallantry + devotion to duty during operations of 29th Septr:-	
			BAR TO MILITARY MEDAL. 240197 Cpl. J. Chatterton.	
			MILITARY MEDAL. 23097 Pte. J Bateman. 269354 L/Cpl. W. Thorpe	
			240349 Cpl. F Huckerby 242546 Pte. F. Twinn.	
			240499 L/Cpl. F. Clough. 240136 Sgt. G. Davenport.	
			93877 Pte. G. Johnson. 241535 L/Cpl. C. Tanner	
			266053 Pte. A.W. Brown.	GHC

GHChapman ? Lt Col

Army Form C. 2118.

Instructions regarding War Diaries and Intelligence Summaries are contained in F. S. Regs., Part II. and the Staff Manual respectively. Title pages will be prepared in manuscript.

WAR DIARY
or
INTELLIGENCE SUMMARY.
(*Erase heading not required.*)

Place	Date	Hour	Summary of Events and Information	Remarks and references to Appendices
	28/10/18		Corps Commander awarded the MILITARY MEDAL to the undermentioned for gallantry & devotion to duty during the Operations of 3rd October:—	
			98212 L/Cpl Wilsea B. — 74123 Pte W. Grainger	
			242278 Cpl H. West. — 242568 Cpl T. Selby.	
			241104 Pte J. Purseglove — 240409 Pte R. Smith.	
			240522 Sgt G.P. Bagshaw — 92039 Cpl F. Broom.	
			240839 Pte E. Large — 201505 Cpl T.W.S. Badder.	
			240805 L/Cpl J.E. Gratton — 240358 Pte F. Hollinshead.	
			241130 Pte R. Richardson. — 241115 Pte C. Redshaw.	
			200057 L/Cpl J.W. Cook.	[initials]
FRESNOY	30/10/18		Bn moved to billets in BOHAIN.	[initials]
			NOTE:- Ref. map for Operations referred to, ETAVES, 1/40,000.	

[signature]
Lieut/Col.
Cdg 1/6 Sherwood Foresters.

Appendix I.

Special Order of the Day
by
Major-General G.F. BOYD, C.M.G., D.S.O.,D.C.M.,
Commanding 46th Division.

3rd.October. 1918.

I called on the Division for another effort today, and right well they have responded. The enemy's last organised line for miles has been broken, and our success has enabled other troops to come up on our flanks. Although we could not hold all the ground by ourselves alone, we have done enough to make the name of the Division doubly famous. We have taken over 2,000 prisoners from 28 different battalions and five different divisions, in itself a splendid feat of arms.

Again I thank every one of you.

(sd) G.F. BOYD, Major-General,
Commanding 46th Division.

War Diary

I wish to express my unbounded admiration for the magnificent fighting qualities shown by the Officers, N.C.Os. & men of the Battalions and the Trench Mortar Battery in the Brigade during the recent operations.

They have had two operations to carry out - both of them difficult and one at short notice.
In each case the Battalions have reached all their objectives and made almost record captures of prisoners - Machine guns and guns.
In the second operation the fighting was very severe and a difficult situation was overcome by the very fine leadership of the Regimental Officers and the splendid spirit of the men.
I feel it a very great honour to have been placed in Command of a Brigade comprised of such fine fighting Battalions as the 5th, 6th & 8th Battalions, Sherwood Foresters.

4th October 1918. John Harington

Brig. General.
Commanding, 139th Infantry Brigade.

To,

Battalion H.Qrs (2)
Company Commnders (1 each)
Platoon " (1 ")
139 T.M.Battery. (6)
Brigade Signal Section. (3)
Brigade H.Qrs. (2)

7

Translation of an Article in "LE JOURNAL" dated 4/10/1918.

PRODIGIOUS EXPLOIT BY THE HEROES OF THE 46th DIVISION.

Whilst to the South and North of the LA BASSEE CANAL the Army of VON QUAST is retiring by forced marches thus freeing for us the Mining districts from LENS to ARMENTIERES, a magnificent episode of the War has just occurred on the HINDENBURG LINE at BELLENGLISE:-

Here the trench systems of the Field Marshal - "he of the nails" - consists of three lines,- one on the west covered by barbed wire, then the CANAL of ST QUENTIN which is full of water, then again on the other bank of the Canal a further labyrinth of communication trenches and saps extending to a depth of one kilometre. A wonderful system, you will agree, from which the enemy machine gunners naturally thought they could never be evicted.

But the masterpiece of this gigantic mining work is the secret tunnel twenty feet high which passes under the Canal, joining the two trench systems and which I have just come back from inspecting. This tunnel is two kilometres long and is lit up like the passages of an underground railway by three powerful dynamos from the workshops of LEIPSIG. A tramway runs along it in both directions and can be used in case of attack to bring up reinforcing troops in a few seconds under the cover of its concrete vaults. Never has anyone seen a better example of ingenuity combined with defensive art. It amounts to this - that there were two trenches - the Canal - and the Tunnel which had to be carried on the morning of the 29th before General RAWLINSON'S Army could break through on the North of ST QUENTIN, and so enable General DEBENEY to free the captive City.

The honour of overcoming all these difficulties fell to the 46th Division composed of soldiers from the Midland Counties.

The General Commanding one of these Brigade is already known to you. Two years ago at the time of the first British Armies on the French front, I told you about the almost epic adventure of this young General of tiger like red moustache, who in former days was a Colonel in the guards and who, like ROLAND at RONCEVREAUX, led the charge at LESBOEUFS sounding on his silver horn the hunting calls of old SCOTLAND. His name is General X -, a brave man and a gallant hero. Two days before the attack, being in the line on the edge of the SOMME CANAL he put his brigade through a general rehearsal for the crossing. The brave lads of the Midland Counties, furnished with the same lifebelts which they wear when crossing the Channel, threw themselves into the water,- swimmers and non-swimmers alike, and all with the same courage. The rehearsal took place on a bitterly cold afternoon.

Then came dawn of Sunday the 29th, and on the whistle being sounded by their young leader, part of the division, under cover of the half light of daybreak, threw themselves into the Canal under the direct fire of Boche machine guns, touched bottom, and hauling themselves onto the bank, engaged and overcame the outposts in a bombing duel. Then, having completed this mopping up, they threw out steel cable on to which clung the men who were coming to grief in the water.

It is true there is a bridge at BELLENGLISE, but was it still standing? A corporal and four men, slipping into the trenches on the further bank, went off on a reconnaissance. On the approach to the bridge, still intact, they surprised three sentries. One was despatched to a better world, and another went to keep him company; the third, kept quiet by the revolver of the corporal, never budged. Willing or not, he was obliged to point out the mine chambers hidden in the sides of the bridge. A soldier then cut the leads. A flare was the signal for the success of this mission, and the whole division swarmed over.

There remained the tunnel; a company manhandled up a medium calibre gun and two mortars, and then at the very entrance to the subterranean passage, opened a point blank fire. Then came grenades, thick as a hailstorm, followed by shrieks of horror and every sign of panic. Out of the smoke, there emerged, one by one, two regiments of panic stricken Huns: a thousand men, livid with fear, were picked up here without any further trouble than that of disarming them.

Then the Division, having overcome the fortifications, pushed forward. A strong patrol, surpirsing two batteries in the open, bayonetted the men serving the guns, and seized the guns and munitions.

By midday, the Division has pushed forward to a depth of six kilometres and captured seventy guns and four thousand prisoners; one prisoner went off struggling,- a record in these days.

The following day, our cavalry, bursting through the gap, the Boche retreated and the French entered ST QUENTIN.

--- *** ---

46th Division H.Q.
5th October, 1918.

SPECIAL ORDER OF THE DAY
BY
LIEUTENANT GENERAL SIR WALTER BRAITHWAITE, K.C.B.
COMMANDING IX CORPS.

5th October, 1918.

The following telegram from the Field Marshal Commanding-in-Chief referring to the operations carried out by the IX Corps on the 29th September which was delayed in transmission, is published for the information of all ranks, together with the reply forwarded by the Corps Commander.

J.C. HARDING NEWMAN, Brig-Genl,
D.A. & Q.M.G., IX Corps.

FROM FIELD MARSHAL SIR D. HAIG, TO FOURTH ARMY dated 30th Sept.

Please convey to General BRAITHWAITE, Commanding IX Corps, and all Officers and men under his Command my warm congratulations upon the success of their operations yesterday North of ST QUENTIN.
The brilliant achievement of the 46th Division in forcing the passage of the ST QUENTIN CANAL and mastering the defences of a large Sector of the famous HINDENBURG Line is worthy of the highest credit.

To FOURTH ARMY FLO. GENERAL BRAITHWAITE.
4th October,

Please convey to Field Marshal SIR D. HAIG the deep appreciation of the IX Corps for his congratulatory telegram of 30th ult., which has been published for information of all ranks.

7

Special Order of the Day
by
Major-General G.F.BOYD, C.M.G., D.S.O., D.C.M.
Commanding 46th Division.

Message received from The MAYOR of BUXTON.

2000 Boys and Girls from BUXTON SCHOOLS, DERBYSHIRE, assembled in the Market Place to-day saluted the Union Jack in honour of the glorious deeds of the 46th Division They thank you for all you have done for them send their love and pray God to bless you all.

To The Mayor of Buxton, from Major-General G.F.BOYD.

Your touching message on behalf of the Boys and Girls of BUXTON Schools will inspire us all to greater efforts to bring the war to a victorious end. No thanks are due to me but to the splendid soldiers I have the honour to command, in including the SHERWOOD FORESTERS BRIGADE, who have more than upheld the traditions of the Country. Please give the Boys and Girls my love.

Message received from The MAYOR OF WALSALL.

On behalf of people of WALSALL congratulate you and your Division upon brilliant success of recent attack. We are proud to remember it is a Midland Division and includes our own 5th South Staffordshire Batt.

To The MAYOR of WALSALL from Major-General G.F.BOYD.

Your telegram received and more than appreciated by all ranks of my Division. It will urge us on to even greater efforts to obtain a victorious peace. The STAFFORDSHIRE BRIGADE played a leading part in our success.

R. Duckworth
Lieut-Colonel.
A.A. & Q.M.G. 46th Division....

5/10/1918.

7

Special Order of the Day
by
Major General G.F. BOYD, C.M.G., D.S.O.,D.C.M.
Commanding 46th Division.

=

The following letters are published for the information of all ranks :-

From the Secretary,
Derbyshire Imperial Veterans' Association.

The Members of the above Association wish me to express their admiration, and to congratulate you and the gallant men under your Command, on the recent brilliant achievement in penetrating the defence of the HINDENBURG LINE.

From General BOYD to the Secretary,
Derbyshire Imperial Veterans' Association.

Please thank the Members of the Derbyshire Imperial Veterans' Association most sincerely for their kind letter of congratulation which is much appreciated by all ranks of my Division.
The successes of my Division are largely due to the gallant part played by the Sherwood Foresters Brigade commanded by Brigadier General J. HARINGTON, D.S.O., The Rifle Brigade.

From Major General Sir E. MONTAGU STUART-WORTLEY, late Commanding 46th. Division.

I have read with great pride and admiration the accounts of the magnificient attack made by the Division near ST. QUENTIN - the results of which have been unsurpassed during the War. Would you kindly convey to the Division my heartfelt congratulations. The same splendid spirit prevails in the Division as displayed on every occasion since January, 1915, when I had the honour to take them to France. I cannot express in adequate terms my profound admiration for their gallantry and dash.

R.M. Rawcroft

Lieutenant-Colonel,
A.A. & Q.M.G., 46th. (N.M.) Division...

Issued down to Platoon and Battery Commanders.

13th. October, 1918.

Special Order of the Day
by
Major General G.F. BOYD, C.M.G.,D.S.O.,D.C.M.
Commanding 46th. Division.
=

The following telegrams are published for the information of all ranks :-

From the Mayor of ILKESTON.

Citizens of ILKESTON heartily congratulate 46th. Division on the great gallantry displayed by them in the recent attack on the HINDENBURG LINE.

Henshaw.

To the Mayor of ILKESTON.

Your telegram much appreciated by all ranks of my Division. The fine work of the Sherwood Foresters Brigade largely contributed to the success of the operations.

General Boyd,
Commanding 46th. Division.

R. Dun Kerson (?)

Lieutenant-Colonel,
A.A. & Q.M.G., 46th. Division...

Issued down to Platoon and Battery Commanders.

15th. October, 1918.

7

Special Order of the Day

: - by - :

BRIGADIER GENERAL J.HARINGTON. D.S.O.
Commanding, 139th Infantry Brigade.

=

The following letter is published for the information of all ranks :-

From the Secretary,
Notts Territorial Force Association.

I beg to forward the following copy of Resolution passed by the Notts Territorial Force Association at a Meeting held on Thursday the 10th inst. :-

It was resolved to convey to the G.O.C. 46th Division and to the Brigadier of the 1/1st Sherwood Foresters Brigade the very best congratulations of the Association on the magnificent results achieved by the Division in the recent fighting in France and that the Secretary be also asked to convey personally the feelings of the Association to any of the Commanding Officers he may have the opportunity of meeting.

A message of thanks has been sent to the Notts Territorial Force Association for their kind congratulations.

E.J.GRINLING. Captain.
15.10.18. Brigade Major, 139th Infantry Brigade.

Issued down to Platoon Commanders.

7

Special Order of the Day
by
Major General G.F. Boyd, C.M.G., D.S.O., D.C.M.
Commanding 46th. Division.
=

The following letters and telegrams are published for the information of all ranks.

From the Notts Territorial Force Association.

I beg to forward the following copy of a Resolution passed by the Notts Territorial Force Association at a Meeting held on Thursday the 10th. instant :-

" It was resolved to convey to the G.O.C., 46th. Division
"and to the Brigadier of the 1/1st. Sherwood Foresters
"Brigade the very best congratulations of the Association
"on the magnificient results achieved by the Division in
"the recent fighting in France and that the Secretary be
"also asked to convey personally the feelings of the Asso-
"iation to any of the Commanding Officers he may have the
"opportunity of meeting."

Yours very truly,

(sd) E.T. Baines, Major.

Secretary.

From General Boyd to the Secretary,
Notts Territorial Force Association.

Please convey to the Members of the Notts Territorial Force Association the thanks of Major General G.F. Boyd, C.M.G., D.S.O, D.C.M., Commanding 46th. North Midland Division and Brigadier General J. Harington, D.S.O., Commanding the Sherwood Foresters Brigade for the message of congratulation on the successful achievements of the 46th. North Midland Division in the recent operations.

Yours faithfully,

(sd) R. Duckworth, Lt-Col.,
A.A. & Q.M.G., 46th. (N.M.) Division.

From The Postmen's Federation,
Burton-on-Trent.

Please accept our heartiest congratulations on your recent victory.

Postmen's Federation, Burton-on-Trent.

To The Postmen's Federation,
Burton-on-Trent.

Your telegram of congratulation much appreciated by all ranks of my Division, especially by the Staffordshire Brigade.

General Boyd,
Commanding 46th. Division.

R. Duckworth

17th. October, 1918.

Lieutenant-Colonel,
A.A. & Q.M.G., 46th. Division.

Instructions regarding War Diaries and Intelligence Summaries are contained in F. S. Regs., Part II. and the Staff Manual respectively. Title pages will be prepared in manuscript.

WAR DIARY
or
~~INTELLIGENCE~~ SUMMARY.
(Erase heading not required.)

1/6 Bn Sherwood Foresters

Army Form C. 2118.

VS 46

Place	Date	Hour	Summary of Events and Information	Remarks and references to Appendices
BOHAIN	2/11/18		2/Lieutenants J.H. DRURY + A.T. AULT joined from England.	GtC
BOHAIN	1-3/11/18		Battn in Training. Great interest taken in Inter-platoon Football competition	GtC
BOHAIN	3/11/18		Battn moved into bivouacs near LA HAIE-MENNERESSE.	GtC
	4/11/18		Battn fell in at 06.00hrs, moved up to L'ARBRE DE GUISE and formed part of a General Reserve to the 1st + 32nd Divisions' attack on the OISE — SAMBRE CANAL. Orders received to move again, + in the afternoon, Battn. moved up to vicinity of LA LOUVIERE. Night 4/5th at CATILLON	GtC
CATILLON	5/11/18.		Battn moved in early morning (03.00hrs) to N. outskirts of LA GROISE, + later, passing through the LINCOLN + LEICESTER Brigade, followed up the enemy to the outskirts of PRISCHES. (Appendix 1). This village, being held in strength by M.G. rearguards, it was decided to stay during night 5/6th in the positions reached. Casualties: 1 OR KILLED, 1 OR MISSING, 12 OR WOUNDED.	GtC
	6/11/18.		The enemy having retired during the night, the Battn. entered PRISCHES, amidst the great excitement + enthusiasm of the civilian inhabitants (Vide Appendix 2). Battn billeted in PRISCHES.	GtC
PRISCHES	9/11/18		Battn moved into billets in the vicinity of BOULOGNE (NORD).	GtC
BOULOGNE	11/11/18		Armistice signed. Hostilities ceased at 11.00 hrs.	GtC
	13/11/18		The following decorations were awarded by the C-in-C for gallantry + devotion to duty during the attack on BELLENGLISE + LEHAUCOURT, 29th Sept. 1918:– MILITARY CROSS. Lieut (A/Capt) H.S. PINK; 2/Lieut F. TOUCH, D.C.M.; " R.A. FRITH.; Lieut J.N. WIGHTMAN; 2/Lieut C. BIMROSE; " A. MACKINTOSH. DISTINGUISHED CONDUCT MEDAL 265035 C.S.M. Greenwood C. 240819 Pte. Howe A.L.	GtC
	14/11/18		Battn moved to billets in LANDRECIES. 46 Dvn. left IX Corps, + joined XIII Corps. Divn not detailed to form part of Army of occupation. (Appendix 3)	GtC
LANDRECIES	14-30/11/18.		Bn engaged in Salvage work. Battalion, Brigade + Corps Football competitions. (For results to end of month, see Appendix 4)	GtC

465

Army Form C. 2118.

Instructions regarding War Diaries and Intelligence Summaries are contained in F. S. Regs., Part II. and the Staff Manual respectively. Title pages will be prepared in manuscript.

WAR DIARY
or
INTELLIGENCE SUMMARY.
(Erase heading not required.)

Place	Date	Hour	Summary of Events and Information	Remarks and references to Appendices
LANDRECIES.	23/11/18		Lieut V.T.G. HORE proceeded to England for tour of duty	Gtc
	25/11/18		Follg. decorations awarded for gallantry & devotion to duty near RAMICOURT on 3rd Oct. 1918.	Gtc
			DISTINGUISHED SERVICE ORDER. Lieut (A/Capt) J.W. POTTER	
			MILITARY CROSS. Lieut V.T.G. HORE.	
	29/11/18.		2/Lieuts. A.J. BRISTOW, C.E. FINCH, W. HAXELL, S. PFOB, M.M., joined from England.	Gtc
	29/11/18.		33 Coal miners sent to England for work under Class W. of the Army Reserve.	Gtc
	30/11/18.		Follg. decorations awarded for gallantry & devotion to duty near RAMICOURT on 3rd. Oct. 1918	
			DISTINGUISHED SERVICE ORDER. Lieut (A/Major) J.A. SHEDDEN, M.C.	Gtc
			BAR TO MILITARY CROSS. Lieut (A/Capt). E KERSHAW, M.C.	
			MILITARY CROSS. Capt (A/Major) E.F. WINSER. 2/Lieut. C.B. NEWELL.	
	30/11/18.		2/Lieuts. R.H. TAYLOR, H. CRAVEN, & E.N. SMITH joined from England	Gtc

[signature]
Lieut. Col.
Cdg 1/6 Sherwood Foresters.

Appendix 1

Copy No. 18...

OPERATION ORDER NO 80
-: by :-
LIEUT COLONEL G.S. CLAYTON.,D.S.O.
COMMANDING 1/8TH BATTALION THE SHERWOOD FORESTERS.

5th November 1918.

Ref Maps WASSIGNY) 1/40,000.
51 a)

1. INFORMATION:- As part of a Major Operation the 1st and 32nd Divisions captured the RED LINE yesterday. Vide Map "A" - issued to all concerned.

2. INTENTION:- The 139th Brigade with Brigades working on the flanks will attack and capture the following:-
1st OBJECTIVE. High ground in N.8, 15, and 21.
2nd OBJECTIVE. N.5, 12 and 18.
3rd OBJECTIVE. GREEN LINE (Vide Map "A")
Brigade Boundaries are as follows:-
NORTHERN:- M.11.a.9.6. - N.9.b.0.7. - N.5.d.9.9. - I.13.c.00.00 - ?31
I.32.c.0.3. - I.34.b.0.3. - I.36.b.2.3.
SOUTHERN:- M.23.a.00.70. - N.20.a.00.30 - N.21.c.90.30 - N.22.a.9.4.
N.23.a.9.7.- N.18.b.9.8. - O.13.a.1.9. - O.10.b.7.4. -
O.11.a.9.6. - O.12.b.3.3.
The main direction of the attack will be along CATILLON - PRISCHE RD - thence through PRISCHE - PT FAYT - O.5.a.3.2. - O.5.d.5.6.

3. INSTRUCTIONS:- The Battalion will be the leading Battalion of the Brigade. In case of serious opposition the Battalion will deploy as follows:-
"A" Company RIGHT.
"B" Company CENTRE.
"C" Company LEFT.
"D" Company will be in SUPPORT.
In the event of only minor opposition the Battalion will form the Advance Guard and move along the main CATILLON - PRISCHE RD.

4. The following units are attached to the Battalion:-
1 section 139 T.M.Battery.
2 sections 46th M.G.Battn ("A" Coy)
1 section Field Artillery.
2 sections R.E.
Lieut Colonel G.S.CLAYTON.,D.S.O. will be in command of the Advance Guard.
Special instructions will be issued to O's.C.above units at the starting point

5. The Battalion will move through the 14th Brigade, 32nd Division.
Battalion Headquarters will move along main direction of attack.
All reports will be sent to Battalion H.Qrs.

6. R.A.P. will move with Battalion H.Qrs. Casualties will be evacuated along PRISCHE - CATILLON RD.

7. ACKNOWLEDGE.

[signature]
Captain & Adjutant.
1/6th Battalion The Sherwood Foresters . . .

Issued at 03.45 hours by runner.
Copies to:-
Nos 1 to 5 O's.C.Companies.
6 Adjutant for C.O.
7 Medical Officer.
8 Transport Officer.
9 Quartermaster.
10 Intelligence Officer.
11 Signalling Officer.
12 Headquarters 139th Brigade.
13 O.C. 5th Sherwood Foresters.
14 O.C. 8th Sherwood Foresters.
15 G.O.C. 14th Brigade.
16 G.O.C. 138th Brigade.
17 War Diary.
18✓ File.

appendix 2

COPY.

Au Divin Messee

Aux Braves soldats Allies, de passage a PRISCHES (Nord) 7 Nov 1918.

Refrain.

Venez, Chers Defenseurs,
Sauvez la FRANCE infortunee,
Bien aimes de nos cœurs,
VENEZ, VENEZ, VENEZ.

Couplet.

Vite, accourez, hutez vos pas,
Sauvez la FRANCE du trepas,
Secourez-nous, re tardez pas;

(sd) F.CLAISE.
Cure.

L'ABBE
F.CLAISE.

Appendix 3. 7

Special Order of the Day
by
Major General G.F. Boyd, C.M.G.,D.S.O.,D.C.M.
Commanding 46th. Division.

=

The Divisional Commander is proud to be able to publish the following letter which he has received from Lieutenant General Sir W.P. BRAITHWAITE, K.C.B., Commanding IX Army Corps, on the Division being withdrawn from its position on the right of the British Army.

He is confident that the great name won by the North Midland Division will be fully uphold by every Officer, Non-Commissioned Officer and Man during the days of comparative peace which are ahead.

From :- Lieutenant General Sir. W.P. BRAITHWAITE, K.C.B.,

" Headquarters, IX Corps.
13th. Nov. 1918.

My dear General,

I tried to tell you to day with what regret I am losing your splendid Division. I would have liked so very much to have taken with me to GERMANY the Divisions which fought so splendidly at BELLENGLISE and in the subsequent advance.

However, it has been ordered otherwise and there is no more to be said.

But, as you have to leave the Corps, I cannot let you go without expressing my most grateful thanks to the 46th. Division, and my unstinted admiration for their gallant fighting.

You must be - indeed, I know you are - a proud man to command men such as you have under your Command, and I too share your pride in having had the honour to have them in my Corps.

I wish you and them every good fortune and, once more expressing my very real regret at parting with your gallant Division,

Believe me,

Yours very sincerely,

Walter P. Braithwaite.

Major General G.F. Boyd, C.M.G., D.S.O., D.C.M.,
Commanding 46th. Division. "

P.T.O.

=2=

From :- Major General G.F. BOYD, C.M.G., D.S.O., D.C.M.,
Commanding 46th. Division.

"

Headquarters, 46th. Division.
13th, November, 1918.

My dear General,

Thank you most heartily in the name of the whole Division for your letter.

It has been not only an honour, but a pleasure to have served in the IX Corps under your Command, and we are more than proud to have earned your admiration.

We have done our best and only regret that it will not be our good fortune to march with you to the RHINE.

The sentiments expressed in you letter will always be cherished with pride by all ranks of the North Midland Division and all ranks join with me in wishing you, your Staff, and your Corps the best of luck during your march into the enemy's country.

Believe me,

Yours very sincerely,

Gerald Boyd.

Lieutenant General Sir W.P. Braithwaite, K.C.B.,
Commanding IX Army Corps. "

Lieutenant-Colonel,
A.A. & Q.M.G., 46th. Division......

13th. November, 1918.

Issued down to Battery and Platoon Commanders

appendix 4.

1/6TH BATTALION THE SHERWOOD FORESTERS.

:-:-:-:-:-:-:-:-:-:-:-:-:-:-:-:

BATTALION INTER COMPANY LEAGUE TABLE UP TO 30TH NOVEMBER 1918.

Company.	Played.	Won.	Drawn.	Lost.	Goals for.	Goals against.	POINTS.
"C"	4	3	1	0	14	2	7.
"D"	4	3	0	1	12	8	6.
"A"	2	0	1	1	2	6	1.
"B"	4	0	0	4	3	15	0.

@@

appendix 5

SPECIAL ORDER OF THE DAY
by
MAJOR GENERAL G.F.BOYD., C.M.G., D.S.O., D.C.M.
COMMANDING 46th DIVISION.

29th November 1918.

The Divisional Commander has received the following letter dated 23rd November 1918 from General Sir H.S.Rawlinson, Bart G.C.V.O.,K.C.B. K.C.M.G., Commanding the Fourth Army, which he publishes with pride to all ranks of the Division.

" It is a matter of very deep regret to me that the 46th Division is not accompanying the Fourth Army to the frontier. I desire, however, to place on record my appreciation of the splendid performances of the Division during the recent operations, and to congratulate all ranks on the conspicuous part they have played in the battles of the 100 days. The forcing of the main HINDENBURG LINE on the Canal and the capture of BELLENGLISE ranks as one of the finest and most dashing exploits of the war. The attacks of October 3rd., and the subsequent operations about BOHAIN, together with the latest advance beyond the SAMBRE Canal, constitute a record of which all ranks of the Division may justly feel proud.

I offer to all ranks my warmest thanks for their great gallantry, and to the leaders and staffs my admiration of their skilful direction and staff work throughout these battles.

To every Officer, N.C.O., and man of the Division I offer my warm thanks and hearty congratulations, and trust that at some future time they may again form part of the Fourth Army."

The above letter is being printed and copies will be sent out for distribution to each Officer/Non-commissioned Officer and Man.

(sd) R.DUCKWORTH
Lieutenant Colonel.
A.A. & Q.M.G., 46th Division.

Instructions regarding War Diaries and Intelligence Summaries are contained in F. S. Regs., Part II, and the Staff Manual respectively. Title pages will be prepared in manuscript.

WAR DIARY
or
~~INTELLIGENCE SUMMARY.~~
(Erase heading not required.)

V82 47

Army Form C. 2118.

1/6th Bn Sherwood Foresters

Place	Date	Hour	Summary of Events and Information	Remarks and references to Appendices
LANDRECIES	1/12/18		The following decorations were awarded for gallantry and devotion to duty during the operations ~~in front of PRISCHES 4/11/18~~ around RAMICOURT 3/10/18 DISTINGUISHED CONDUCT MEDAL. 240804 Sgt GREATOREX. C. 241116 L/Cpl POYSER T. 241535 L/Cpl TANNER E.C. M.M 241182 Pte THOMAS. A	JAS
LANDRECIES	2/12/18		Battalion Inter Company Football League. A Coy. 0 B Coy. 0 Colour Party under SURGEON MAJOR. A.N. SHEA. D.S.O left for England	JAS
LANDRECIES	3/12/18		Corps Inter Coy Football Competition C Coy 6th S.F. 0. D Coy 8th S.F. 1	JAS
LANDRECIES	4/12/18		Corps Inter Coy Football Competition D Coy 6th S.F. 3 A Coy 5th S.F. Nil Cross Country Run	JAS
LANDRECIES	5/12/18		Lieut G GLOSSOP joined the Battalion from the Base	JAS
LANDRECIES	6/12/18		The following decorations were awarded by C in C for gallantry and devotion to duty during the operations in front of PRISCHES 4/11/18. MILITARY MEDAL. 267156 L/Cpl JOHNCOCK. P.E. 266576 Pte JENNINGS. F	JAS
			Battalion Inter Company Football League. A Coy. 1. B Coy. 1	JAS
LANDRECIES	9/12/18		Whist Drive and Dancing in the Barracks.	JAS
LANDRECIES	10/12/18		36 Coal Miners were sent to England for work under Class W. of the Army Reserve.	JAS
CHESTERFIELD	11/12/18		The Regimental Colours were withdrawn from CHESTERFIELD PARISH CHURCH by the Regimental Escort VIDE. Appendix (1) (attached)	JAS
LANDRECIES	11/12/18		Cross Country Run.	JAS
LANDRECIES	14/12/18		40 Coal Miners were sent to England for work under Class W. of the Army Reserve.	JAS
LANDRECIES	15/12/18		Football. D Coy 6th S.F. 2 Div H.Qrs. 3.	JAS
LANDRECIES	17/12/18		Football C Coy. 2 A Coy. 0.	JAS
LANDRECIES	18/12/18		Colour Party rejoin Battalion	JAS

James A Shedden
Major
Cmdg 1/6th Bn Sherwood Foresters

(A9175) Wt W2358/P160 600,000 12/17 D. D. & L. Sch. 52a. Forms/C2118/15.

475

Instructions regarding War Diaries and Intelligence Summaries are contained in F. S. Regs., Part II. and the Staff Manual respectively. Title pages will be prepared in manuscript.

WAR DIARY
or
~~INTELLIGENCE SUMMARY~~.
(Erase heading not required.)

Army Form C. 2118.

1/6th Bn Sherwood Foresters

Place	Date	Hour	Summary of Events and Information	Remarks and references to Appendices
LANDRECIES	19/12/18		Lieut. Col. B. W. VANN. M.C. awarded VICTORIA CROSS for most conspicuous bravery, devotion to duty and fine leadership during the attack at BELLENGLISE and LEHAUCOURT on Sept 29th 1918. 2/Lieut. W. BLOOD joined the Battalion from the Base. 70 Coal miners were sent to England for work under Class W. of the Army Reserve.	JAS
LANDRECIES	20/12/18		Football A Coy 1. Bn H.Qrs 1.	JAS
LANDRECIES	21/12/18		Football B Coy 6th S.F. 3 D Coy 8th S.F. 2.	JAS
LANDRECIES	22/12/18		86 Coal Miners were sent to England for work under Class W of the Army Reserve.	JAS
LANDRECIES	23/12/18		Football 1/6th Bn S.F. 6 1/5th Bn S.F. 2.	JAS
LANDRECIES	24/12/18		22 Coal Miners were sent to England for work under Class W of the Army Reserve.	JAS
LANDRECIES	25/12/18		Six-a-side Football Competition	JAS
LANDRECIES	26/12/18		Christmas Dinners	JAS
LANDRECIES	27/12/18		2/Lieut L.K. BEARD joined Battalion. 7 Quarrymen were sent to England for work under Class W of the Army Reserve.	JAS
LANDRECIES	30/12/18		2/Lieut ? PARKINSON joined Battalion. 2 Quarrymen were sent to England for work under Class W. of the Army Reserve.	JAS

James A. Hedder
Major.
Cmdg. 1/6th Bn Sherwood Foresters

(A9175) Wt W2358/P360 600,000 12/17 D. D. & L. Sch. 52a. Forms/C2118/15.

4[6]

Instructions regarding War Diaries and Intelligence Summaries are contained in F. S. Regs., Part II. and the Staff Manual respectively. Title pages will be prepared in manuscript.

WAR DIARY
or
~~INTELLIGENCE SUMMARY.~~
(Erase heading not required.)

1/6 N & Derby

Army Form C. 2118.

9/8 48

Place	Date	Hour	Summary of Events and Information	Remarks and references to Appendices
LANDRECIES	1/1/19		2/Lieut L K BEARD proceeded on leave.	WR Maj.
do.	2/1/19		2/Lieut. S PFOB rejoined from Hospital.	
do	3/1/19		Captain E.S. RIVINGTON proceeded to Trinity College, Oxford	WR Maj.
			2/Lieut. F TOUCH, M.C. D.C.M. rejoined from leave	
			"C" Company Football Team beat Brigade H.Qrs. 1 - 0.	WR Maj
do.	5/1/19		The following awards were announced in the London Gazette:-	
			MILITARY CROSS. — Date of Gazette	WR Maj.
			Captain F.W. HIPKINS. — 1 - 1 - 19.	
			MENTIONED IN DESPATCHES.	
			Lieut Colonel B.W. VANN, V.C, M.C — 27 - 12 - 18	
			Captain E. KERSHAW. M.C. — do.	
			240304 Sgt F. POTT. — do.	
			DISTINGUISHED CONDUCT MEDAL.	
			240424 Sgt. J. ATTERBURY. — 1 - 1 - 19.	
			MERITORIOUS SERVICE MEDAL.	
			240421 Sgt. H.G. BENSTEAD. — 18 - 1 - 19	
			240203 " H. HODGKINSON — do.	
do	7/1/19		Audit Board assembled at Battalion H.Qrs.	WR Maj.
do	11/1/19		The Battalion moved to billets in CARTIGNIES.	WR Maj
CARTIGNIES	13/1/19		2/Lieut E.M. DAVIDSON rejoined from leave.	WR Maj
do.	"		2/Lieut H. CRAVEN proceeded to England for demobilization	WR Maj.
do.	14/1/19		Battalion Football Team beat 230 Bde R.F.A. Team 1 - 0.	WR Maj.
do	16/1/19		240999 Pte. F WEBSTER awarded the DECORATION MILITAIRE.	WR Maj.
do	17/1/19		Lecture on Demobilization by 2/Lieut R.A. FRITH, M.C.	WR Maj.
			D Coy Football Team v Royal Horse Guards Team. Result Draw 1 goal each	WR Maj.
do	18/1/19		B Coy Football Team beat B Coy 8th S.F. Team 3 - 1.	WR Maj.
do	19/1/19		2/Lieut J.C. CAIRD proceeded to England for demobilization	WR Maj.
			Captain E. KERSHAW, M.C. rejoined from leave.	
do	20/1/19		Captain T.F. DENNIS, M.C. proceeded to England for demobilization	WR Maj.
do	21/1/19		Commanding Officer's Team beat "C" Coy Football Team 3 - 2.	WR Maj.
do	22/1/19		Bn Football Team v D.A.C. Result Bn NIL D.A.C. 2.	WR Maj.

(A9475) Wt W2358/P360 600,000 12/17 D. D. & L. Sch. 52a. Forms/C2118/15.

58

Instructions regarding War Diaries and Intelligence Summaries are contained in F. S. Regs., Part II. and the Staff Manual respectively. Title pages will be prepared in manuscript.

WAR DIARY
or
~~INTELLIGENCE SUMMARY.~~
(Erase heading not required.)

Army Form C. 2118.

Place	Date	Hour	Summary of Events and Information	Remarks and references to Appendices
CARTIGNIES.	26/1/19.		2/Lieut. A.J. BRISTOW proceeded to England for demobilization	WR Maj.
"	27/1/19.		Surgeon Major A.W. SHEA, D.S.O. proceeded on leave	WR Maj.
"	28/1/19.		'D' Coy Football team beat 'A' Coy team 2-1.	WR Maj.
"	31/1/19.		2/Lieut R.H. TAYLOR proceeded to England for demobilization	WR Maj.
			121 N.C.O's and men were demobilized during the month.	WR Maj.

W Robinson. Major
Cmdg. 1/6th Sherwood Foresters

(A9475) Wt W2358/P560 600,000 12/17 D. D. & L. Sch. 52a. Forms/C2118/15.

Army Form C. 2118.

Instructions regarding War Diaries and Intelligence Summaries are contained in F. S. Regs., Part II. and the Staff Manual respectively. Title pages will be prepared in manuscript.

WAR DIARY
or
~~INTELLIGENCE SUMMARY.~~
(Erase heading not required.)

1/6th Battalion The Sherwood Foresters.

Vol 49

Place	Date	Hour	Summary of Events and Information	Remarks and references to Appendices
CATILLON	1/2/19		Major W.H. Shedden proceeded to England for Demobilization	
"	5/2/19		Concert by "D" Company.	
"	6/2/19		Inspection by G.O.C. Division	
"	"		Lieut H.J. Wood proceeded to England for Demobilization.	
"	7/2/19		Lecture on "South Africa" by Pte Jones of the South African Brigade	
"	12/2/19		Football Match:- "C" Company 6th S.F. 4 goals "D" Company 6th S.F. 2 goals.	
"	13/2/19		Football Match:- 1/1 N.M. Field Ambulance 6 goals "C" Company 6th S.F. 1 goal	
"	18/2/19		Rev. W.A. Blackwall proceeded to England for Demobilization.	
"	19/2/19		Battalion moved to billets at CATILLON.	
	20/2/19		Battalion moved to billets at BETHENCOURT.	
BETHENCOURT	27/2/19		Captain H.J. Pink proceeded to England for Demobilization.	
			Number of O.R.'s proceeding for Demobilization during the month of February - 206	
			Average number of O.R.'s attending Educational Classes during month of February - 50	
			Average number of O.R.'s attending Dancing Classes from 1/2/19 to 18/2/19 - 150	

W. Robinson
Major.
Cmdg 1/6th Battalion The Sherwood Foresters.

495

(A9175) Wt W2358/P360 600,000 12/17 D. D. & L. Sch. 52a. Forms/C2118/15.

Instructions regarding War Diaries and Intelligence Summaries are contained in F. S. Regs., Part II, and the Staff Manual respectively. Title pages will be prepared in manuscript.

WAR DIARY
or
~~INTELLIGENCE SUMMARY.~~
(Erase heading not required.)

Army Form C. 2118.

1/6th Battn The Sherwood Foresters

Vol 50

Place	Date	Hour	Summary of Events and Information	Remarks and references to Appendices
BETHENCOURT	5.3.19		2/Lieut L.E.A. Stott proceeded to join his own Regiment.	
	6.3.19		2/Lieut C.E. Finch proceeded for duty with 379 P.o.W. Coy.	
	11.3.19		Result of 6-a-side Football Match (46 Divn Compt^n) 6th Sherwood Foresters 9 points, 454 Coy. R.A.S.C. 3 points	
	13.3.19		Result of Draughts Competition 6th Sherwood Foresters 26 points, 454 Coy. R.A.S.C. 10 points	
	15.3.19		Capt J.W. Potter & 2/Lt. S. Pyott proceeded to England for demobilization.	
	"		Result of Brigade Final of 6 a-side Football Competition. 1/6th Sherwood Foresters 16 points, 1/5th Sherwood Foresters Nil.	
	18.3.19		Trip by Lorry to Le Cateau to see "Foresters" Concert Party at Siege Park Theatre.	
	19.3.19		Result of Semi-Final of 6-a-side Football Competition 1/6th Sherwood Foresters 11 points, C.231 Battery R.F.A. 6 points	
	20.3.19		Result of Final of 6-a-side Football Competition 230 Bde Ammn Column 3 points 1/6th Sherwood Foresters 2 points	
	22.3.19		240048 A/R.S.M. Dakin G.W. awarded Rumanian Medaille Barbatie Si Credinta, 1st Class.	
	25.3.19		Lt. E.H. Smith, Lt A.G. Tyrrell & 2/Lt L.W. Haxell proceeded to England for demobilization	
	28.3.19		The Commanding Officer inspected the Cadre Establishment of the Battalion.	
			During the month several trips were made by lorry to VALENCIENNES to see 1st Army Concert Party, "Les Rouges et les Noirs".	
			Total number of Other Ranks demobilized during month 66.	

3/4/19

(A9475) Wt W2358/P360 600,000 12/17 D. D. & L. Sch. 52a. Forms/C2118/15.

V.O. Robinson Major.
Cmdg 1/6th Battalion The Sherwood Foresters.

Instructions regarding War Diaries and Intelligence Summaries are contained in F. S. Regs., Part II. and the Staff Manual respectively. Title pages will be prepared in manuscript.

WAR DIARY
or
INTELLIGENCE SUMMARY.
(Erase heading not required.)

Army Form C. 2118.

1/6 N & Derby

Ⅵ 82 51

Place	Date	Hour	Summary of Events and Information	Remarks and references to Appendices
BETHENCOURT	1/4/19		Captain F.S. ROWLAND, Lieut L. PARKINSON, 2/Lieut A.T. AULT and 63 Other Ranks proceeded to join 120 P of W Company.	Ham. Lt.
			Captain G. GLOSSOP, Lieut W.A. GRUNDY + 2/Lieut R.A. FRITH and 51 Other Ranks proceeded to join 182 P of W Company	Ham. Lt.
			Battalion reduced to cadre strength.	Ham. Lt.
do	11/4/19		Officers entertained the men to Dinner.	
do	12/4/19		Officers entertained the Sergeants to Dinner	Ham. Lt.
do	15/4/19		Captain W.T. STEPHENS and Lieut W.H. HOPCRAFT proceeded to join 82 P of W Company.	Ham. Lt.
do	21/4/19		Lieut W.A. LYTLE, M.C. proceeded to St Quentin Sub Area.	Ham. Lt.
do	25/4/19		6th Bn Cadre beat 5th Bn Cadre at Football 5 - NIL.	Ham. Lt.
do	28/4/19		2/Lieut C.R. FREARS proceeded to England for demobilization.	Ham. Lt.

H.A. Mycock Captain
1/6th Bn Sherwood Foresters

51S

A7092 Wt. W128 9/M1293 750,000. 1/17. D. D & L. Ltd. Forms/C2118/14.

Instructions regarding War Diaries and Intelligence Summaries are contained in F. S. Regs., Part II. and the Staff Manual respectively. Title pages will be prepared in manuscript.

WAR DIARY

or

~~INTELLIGENCE SUMMARY.~~

(Erase heading not required.)

Army Form C. 2118.

1/6 N + Derby

9 R 5 B

Place	Date	Hour	Summary of Events and Information	Remarks and references to Appendices
BETHENCOURT	3/6/19		Lt Col V.O. ROBINSON M.C. proceeded on leave to England.	VOR
-do-	4/6/19		Captain E. KERSHAW, M.C. proceeded on leave to England.	VOR
-do-	14/6/19		2/Lieut E.M. DAVIDSON proceeded on leave to England	VOR
-do-	22/6/19		Lt Col V.O. ROBINSON, M.C. rejoined from leave.	VOR
-do-	29/6/19		Captain S.B. BOULTON proceeded on leave to England.	VOR
-do-	29/6/19		2/Lieut E.M. DAVIDSON rejoined from leave.	VOR
			Captain E. KERSHAW, M.C. was demobilized whilst on leave	VOR
			3 Other Ranks were demobilized during the month	VOR

V O Robinson Lieut Colonel
Cmdg. 1/6th Bn. Sherwood Foresters

52S

(A9475) Wt W2358/P360 600,000 12/17 D. D. & L. Sch. 52a. Forms/C2118/15.

www.ingramcontent.com/pod-product-compliance
Lightning Source LLC
Chambersburg PA
CBHW080832010526
44112CB00015B/2496
9781474525732